THE END OF
APARTHEID
IN SOUTH AFRICA

**Other Titles in the Greenwood Press Guides
to Historic Events of the Twentieth Century**
Randall M. Miller, Series Editor

The Persian Gulf Crisis
Steve A. Yetiv

World War I
Neil M. Heyman

The Civil Rights Movement
Peter B. Levy

The Holocaust
Jack R. Fischel

The Breakup of Yugoslavia and the War in Bosnia
Carole Rogel

Islamic Fundamentalism
Lawrence Davidson

Frontiers of Space Exploration
Roger D. Launius

The Collapse of Communism in the Soviet Union
William E. Watson

Origins and Development of the Arab-Israeli Conflict
Ann M. Lesch and Dan Tschirgi

The Rise of Fascism in Europe
George P. Blum

The Cold War
Katherine A. S. Sibley

The War in Vietnam
Anthony O. Edmonds

World War II
Loyd E. Lee

The Unification of Germany, 1989–1990
Richard A. Leiby

The Environmental Crisis
Miguel A. Santos

Castro and the Cuban Revolution
Thomas M. Leonard

THE END OF APARTHEID IN SOUTH AFRICA

Lindsay Michie Eades

Greenwood Press Guides to
Historic Events of the Twentieth Century
Randall M. Miller, Series Editor

Greenwood Press
Westport, Connecticut • London

Library of Congress Cataloging-in-Publication Data

Eades, Lindsay Michie, 1962–
    The end of apartheid in South Africa / Lindsay Michie Eades.
      p. cm.—(Greenwood Press guides to historic events of the
twentieth century, ISSN 1092–177X)
    Includes bibliographical references and index.
    ISBN 0–313–29938–2 (alk. paper)
    1. Apartheid—South Africa.   2. South Africa—Politics and
government.   3. South Africa—Race relations.   I. Title.
II. Series.
DT1757.E33   1999
305.8′00968—dc21   98–45032

British Library Cataloguing in Publication Data is available.

Library of Congress Catalog Card Number: 98–45032
ISBN: 0–313–29938–2
ISSN: 1092–177X

First published in 1999

Greenwood Press, 88 Post Road West, Westport, CT 06881
An imprint of Greenwood Publishing Group, Inc.
www.greenwood.com

Printed in the United States of America

∞™

The paper used in this book complies with the
Permanent Paper Standard issued by the National
Information Standards Organization (Z39.48–1984).

10 9 8 7 6 5 4 3 2 1

Front cover photo: Nelson and Winnie Mandela salute well-wishers as he leaves prison after 27 years of imprisonment. Courtesy of CORBIS/REUTERS.

Back cover photo: Riot police arrest Soweto demonstrator. Courtesy of Amnesty International.

To Jenny and Chris McConnachie
and to "Prof" Gamede

Contents

A photo essay follows page 100

Series Foreword

As the twenty-first century approaches, it is time to take stock of the political, social, economic, intellectual, and cultural forces and factors that have made the twentieth century the most dramatic period of change in history. To that end, the Greenwood Press Guides to Historic Events of the Twentieth Century presents interpretive histories of the most significant events of the century. Each book in the series combines narrative history and analysis with primary documents and biographical sketches, with an eye to providing both a reference guide to the principal persons, ideas, and experiences defining each historic event, and a reliable, readable overview of that event. Each book further provides analyses and discussions, grounded in both primary and secondary sources, of the causes and consequences, in thought and action, that give meaning to the historic event under review. By assuming a historical perspective, drawing on the latest and best writing on each subject, and offering fresh insights, each book promises to explain how and why a particular event defined the twentieth century. No consensus about the meaning of the twentieth century emerges from the series, but, collectively, the books identify the most salient concerns of the century. In so doing, the series reminds us of the many ways those historic events continue to affect our lives.

Each book follows a similar format designed to encourage readers to consult it both as a reference and a history in its own right. Each volume opens with a chronology of the historic event, followed by a narrative overview, which also serves to introduce and examine briefly the main themes and issues related to that event. The next set of chapters is composed of topical essays, each analyzing closely an issue or problem of interpretation introduced in the opening chapter. A concluding chapter suggesting the long-term implications and meanings of the historic event brings the strands of the preceding chapters together while placing the event in the larger historical context. Each book also includes a section of short biographies of the principal persons related to the event, followed by a section introducing and reprinting key historical documents illustrative of and pertinent to the event. A glossary of selected terms adds to the utility of each book. An annotated bibliography—of significant books, films, and CD-ROMs—and an index conclude each volume.

The editors made no attempt to impose any theoretical model or historical perspective on the individual authors. Rather, in developing the series, an advisory board of noted historians and informed high school history teachers and public and school librarians identified the topics needful of exploration and the scholars eminently qualified to examine those events with intelligence and sensitivity. The common commitment throughout the series is to provide accurate, informative, and readable books, free of jargon and up to date in evidence and analysis.

Each book stands as a complete historical analysis and reference guide to a particular historic event. Each book also has many uses, from understanding contemporary perspectives on critical historical issues, to providing biographical treatments of key figures related to each event, to offering excerpts and complete texts of essential documents about the event, to suggesting and describing books and media materials for further study and presentation of the event, and more. The combination of historical narrative and individual topical chapters addressing significant issues and problems encourages students and teachers to approach each historic event from multiple perspectives and with a critical eye. The arrangement and content of each book thus invite students and teachers, through classroom discussions and position papers, to debate the character and significance of great historic events and to discover for themselves how and why history matters.

The series emphasizes the main currents that have shaped the modern world. Much of that focus necessarily looks at the West, especially Europe and the United States. The political, commercial, and cultural expansion of the West wrought largely, though not wholly, the most fundamental changes of the century. Taken together, however, books in the series reveal the interactions between Western and non-Western peoples and society, and also the tensions between modern and traditional cultures. They also point to the ways in which non-Western peoples have adapted Western ideas and technology and, in turn, influenced Western life and thought. Several books examine such increasingly powerful global forces as the rise of Islamic fundamentalism, the emergence of modern Japan, the Communist revolution in China, and the collapse of communism in eastern Europe and the former Soviet Union. American interests and experiences receive special attention in the series, not only in deference to the primary readership of the books but also in recognition that the United States emerged as the dominant political, economic, social, and cultural force during the twentieth century. By looking at the century through the lens of American events and experiences, it is possible to see why the age has come to be known as "The American Century."

Assessing the history of the twentieth century is a formidable prospect. It has been a period of remarkable transformation. The world broadened and narrowed at the same time. Frontiers shifted from the interiors of Africa and Latin America to the moon and beyond; communication spread from mass circulation newspapers and magazines to radio, television, and now the Internet; skyscrapers reached upward and suburbs stretched outward; energy switched from steam, to electric, to atomic power. Many changes did not lead to a complete abandonment of established patterns and practices so much as a synthesis of old and new, as, for example, the increased use of (even reliance on) the telephone in the age of the computer. The automobile and the truck, the airplane, and telecommunications closed distances, and people in unprecedented numbers migrated from rural to urban, industrial, and ever more ethnically diverse areas. Tractors and chemical fertilizers made it possible for fewer people to grow more, but the environmental and demographic costs of an exploding global population threatened to outstrip natural resources and human innovation. Disparities in wealth increased, with developed nations prospering and underdeveloped nations starving. Amid the crumbling of former European colonial empires, Western technology, goods, and culture increasingly enveloped the globe, seeping into, and undermining, non-Western cultures—a process that contributed to a surge of religious fundamentalism and ethno-nationalism in the Middle East, Asia, and Africa. As people became more alike, they also became more aware of their differences. Ethnic and religious rivalries grew in intensity everywhere as the century closed.

The political changes during the twentieth century have been no less profound than the social, economic, and cultural ones. Many of the books in the series focus on political events, broadly defined, but no books are confined to politics alone. Political ideas and events have social effects, just as they spring from a complex interplay of non-political forces in culture, society, and economy. Thus, for example, the modern civil rights and woman's rights

movements were at once social and political events in cause and consequence. Likewise, the Cold War created the geopolitical framework for dealing with competing ideologies and nations abroad and served as the
touchstone for political and cultural identities at home. The books treating
political events do so within their social, cultural, and economic contexts.

Several books in the series examine particular wars in depth. Wars are defining moments for people and eras. During the twentieth century war became more widespread and terrible than ever before, encouraging new
efforts to end war through strategies and organizations of international cooperation and disarmament while also fueling new ideologies and instruments
of mass persuasion that fostered distrust and festered old national rivalries.
Two world wars during the century redrew the political map, slaughtered or
uprooted two generations of people, and introduced and hastened the development of new technologies and weapons of mass destruction. The First
World War spelled the end of the old European order and spurred communist
revolution in Russia and fascism in Italy, Germany, and elsewhere. The Second World War killed fascism and inspired the final push for freedom from
European colonial rule in Asia and Africa. It also led to the Cold War that
suffocated much of the world for almost half a century. Large wars begat
small ones, and brutal totalitarian regimes cropped up across the globe. After (and in some ways because of) the fall of communism in eastern Europe
and the former Soviet Union, wars of competing cultures, national interests,
and political systems persisted in the struggle to make a new world order.
Continuing, too, has been the belief that military technology can achieve political ends, whether in the superior American firepower that failed to "win"
in Vietnam or in the American "smart bombs" and other military wizardry
that "won" in the Persian Gulf.

Another theme evident in the series is that throughout the century nationalism has continued to drive events. Whether in the Balkans in 1914 trigger-
ing World War I or in the Balkans in the 1990s threatening the post–Cold
War peace—or in many other places—nationalist ambitions and forces
would not die. The persistence of nationalism is yet another reminder of the
many ways that the past becomes prologue.

We thus offer the series as a modern guide to and interpretation of the historic events of the twentieth century and as an invitation to consider how and
why those events have defined not only the past and present but also charted
the political, social, intellectual, cultural, and economic routes into the next
century.

Randall M. Miller
Saint Joseph's University, Philadelphia

Preface

Every facet of South Africa is complex: its people, politics, economy, and even geography. To get some sense of the country's recent history and momentous change, an examination of South Africa's background, divisions, and the internal and external pressures on the South African government is necessary. Through this approach, this book attempts to give a broad picture of the political and social factors that influenced the end of apartheid. It also explores as much as possible the actual events that signified the change from government by racial division to government through unity and political and social liberty.

The history of the South African state provides understanding of the source of racial divisions that became part of government legislation in 1948. Explanation of the separation of groups—and groups within groups—shows how the apartheid system developed and operated. By the same token, examination of group separation shows the increasing pressure these divisions put on the apartheid system and the rise of resistance to apartheid. A discussion of the political parties that arose before and during apartheid further highlights the divisions within South Africa. Pressure and resistance were matched by growing international pressure on the South African government in the 1970s and 1980s, which contributed to the system's collapse. An overview of recent events since the 1994 free election reveals the achievements and problems of South Africa's post-apartheid government.

The documents selected for this book are intended to give a direct sense of legislative and political changes that occured in South Africa during and after the years of apartheid. There are, for example, very obvious and significant differences between the early legislation of apartheid and the South African Constitution of 1996, and between Nelson Mandela's position in South Africa in 1961 and in 1990. The book is written as both a reference work and a supplement or textbook for courses on South African and southern African history; as well as a source of information for those interested in South Africa and the ending of apartheid.

There is, of course, no simple answer as to why apartheid ended in South Africa. But, as argued throughout this book, one large factor was the determination among the majority of groups not only to end apartheid but to create a new system based on greater unity. It is the extent of this determination and its consistency that will largely determine the future of the new South Africa.

Acknowledgments

I would like to thank my former colleagues at the University of Transkei who first influenced the work that went into this book, especially Vangeli Gamede, Vuyani Mtunxcgwana, Jeff Peires, Vincent Mahali, Wilna Venter, Pule Phoofolo, Meshach Mputo, and Pumzile Mfazwe. I would also like to thank my friends in South Africa, especially Kogi Thangavelu for all her valuable insight, and the McConnachies for their constant encouragement and help; and the *East London Daily Dispatch* for supporting the freelance work I did in the Eastern Cape. Thanks also go to Thembeka Nobanda for information on her friendship with Stephen Biko; to Ellen Moore and Cassandra Volpé of Amnesty International; and to the reference staff at the libraries of the University of North Carolina and the University of Colorado at Boulder. Finally, very special thanks to my series editor Randall Miller for his painstaking editorial efforts, sound advice, and constant encouragement; to Barbara Rader for her infinite patience; and to Dan for his continuous support, humor, and kindness.

Chronology of Events

Millennia B.C.	Khoikhoi and San ancestors living in Southern Africa.
1652	Dutch East India Company sets up post on Cape of Good Hope.
1806	Britain takes control of Cape Colony.
1816–1828	Shaka's Zulu kingdom launches *Mfecane* in southeastern Africa.
1834–1835	British conquer Xhosa.
1835–1840	The Great Trek.
1879	British defeat Zulus at Battle of Isandhlwana.
1899–1902	South African War.
1910	Formation of Union of South Africa.
1912	Formation of South African Native National Congress (SANNC); later becomes ANC.
1913	Natives Land Act; Segregation laws begin.
1914–1915	National Party (NP) founded.
1948	NP elected to power under D. F. Malan.
1950	Population Restriction Act; Group Areas Act.
1951	Separate Registration of Voters Act; Bantu Authorities Act; Bantu Education introduced.

1952	ANC launches defiance campaign.
1955	Freedom Charter drafted.
1959	Founding of Pan-Africanist Congress (PAC).
1960	Sharpeville massacre; formation of Umkhonto we Sizwe (MK).
1961	South Africa leaves British Commonwealth and becomes a republic.
1964	Nelson Mandela, Walter Sisulu, and seven other ANC activists sentenced to life imprisoment.
1966	H. F. Verwoerd assassinated; J. B. Vorster made Prime Minister.
1976	Soweto uprisings; Transkei becomes "independent" homeland.
1977	Death of Stephen Biko.
1978	P. W. Botha elected prime minister.
1982	Conservative party breaks from NP.
1983	United Democratic Front (UDF) formed; tricameral parliament established.
1984–1986	Botha becomes president; uprisings in townships and State of Emergency.
1985	Congress of South African trade unions formed.
1986	Repeal of pass laws.
1987	250,000 African mine-workers go on three-week strike.
1988	South African government agrees to withdraw from Angola and cooperate in Namibia's transition to independence under the auspices of the UN.
1989	F. W. deKlerk elected president.
1990	
February	Nelson Mandela released; ANC and other protest parties unbanned.
March	Namibia becomes independent.
July	Inkatha Freedom Party (IFP) formed.
August	ANC formally suspends armed struggle.

1991

April	Repeal of Land Acts, Group Areas Act, Population Registration Act, and Separate Amenities Act.
September	National Peace Accord.
December	Formation of Convention for a Democratic South Africa (CODESA).

1992

March	DeKlerk holds white referendum.
June	Boipatong massacre; ANC breaks off talks with NP government and launches campaign of mass action.
September	Bisho massacre; ANC and NP draw up Record of Understanding.

1993 Mandela and deKlerk share Nobel Peace Prize.

March	CODESA II formed.
April	South African Communist Party Secretary-General Chris Hani assassinated by white extremists.
June	White right-wing extremists storm World Trade Center in Johannesburg.
July	IFP leader Mangosuthu Buthelezi walks out of talks.
October	Freedom Alliance (FA) formed.

1994

March	DeKlerk and Transitional Executive Council declare state of emergency in Kwa/Zulu/Natal; white paramilitary groups launch failed invasion to protect Bophutatswana leader Chief Lucas Mangope; disentegration of FA.
April	Buthelezi calls off boycott of elections and includes IFP on the ballot; bombing campaign across South Africa by right-wing extremists; first free and democratic election in South Africa; Nelson Mandela elected president.
May	Mandela launches Reconstruction and Development Plan (RDP).
1996	Hearings of Truth and Reconciliation Commission begin; South African constitution signed into law.
1997	Truth and Reconciliation Commission hearings end; Nelson Mandela resigns as ANC president and is succeeded by Thabo Mbeki.

THE END OF APARTHEID
IN SOUTH AFRICA
EXPLAINED

OLD SOUTH AFRICA

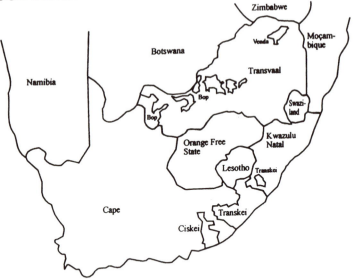

NEW SOUTH AFRICA

Courtesy of the South African Embassy, Washington, D.C.

I

Historical Background

On February 11, 1990, the political landscape of South Africa shook as Nelson Mandela walked out of prison after twenty-seven years of political confinement. The release of the African National Congress leader and ultimate political symbol of opposition to the policy of apartheid unleashed a torrent of emotion. People from all sections of the South African population demonstrated, and black South Africans "toi-toied" (performed political dancing in the street). People crowded around radios and televisions to witness the event. The atmosphere combined feelings of hope, excitement, and fear: hope for continued progressive action on the part of the government, excitement over the event itself, and fear over the varied responses to this new beginning and over Mandela's long hidden persona and ability. The release of Mandela marked a boldness on the part of the South African government and increased desire on the part of Africans, coloreds, Indians, and many whites for a continued pattern of change away from a system of almost complete white domination and racial segregation known as apartheid that had violently disrupted their country internally and increasingly isolated them externally. Such a momentous decision on the part of South Africa's president F. W. deKlerk was a statement concerning the country's past, as well as a message for the future of South Africa.

The system of apartheid—"apartness" between the races—began in 1948 and within one generation wove itself into every aspect of South African life. Apartheid was a radical and extreme extension of a system of segregation originating with colonial conquest and gradually evolving into complex and sometimes uncoordinated institutions in the late nineteenth and early twentieth centuries. To understand the magnitude of the reversal of such a policy in South Africa's history, some examination has to be made of how such a determinedly repressive system came to be.

South African historians writing during the years of apartheid traditionally pinpointed the year 1652 as the "beginning of South Africa" when the Dutch East India Company established a fort at Table Bay. Although inaccurate in terms of the history of the Africans, this year does arguably symbolize the beginning of modern South African history. That history, from the initial clash of European settler and native African, marks a period characterized by continuous violence and war. Before colonial conquest, the very southern regions of the African continent had developed complex societies and markedly diverse economies. The pastoral people of the Cape region were the first group to be affected by the Dutch settlers and, from the 1670s, lost their independence. Clashes continued as the settlers expanded into the interior of the region. Control was established over the conquered Africans through a system of forced pass-carrying, which restricted them to certain areas at certain times, and use of captured prisoners by the colonists as indentured servants. By the late eighteenth century, the colony stretched across the Cape to the area largely occupied by the Xhosa people in the eastern region.

Rival control over the Cape came from the British in the eighteenth century. A major rebellion against the Dutch settlers by Khoi and San servants who joined forces with resisting Xhosa chiefs in 1799–1806 gave British forces the opportunity to intervene decisively and to establish permanent control over the Cape in 1806. As Britain increasingly gained the upper hand in colonial administration in the Cape, the descendants of the Dutch settlers, Cape farmers known as "Boers," expressed their opposition to British encroachment and policies in a mass migration out of the colony known as "The Great Trek." The Boer settlers moved north and west, with some going beyond the great plains, or "vaal." Economic poverty was a partial factor in this exodus as the Trekkers had found themselves closely regulated and excluded from land ownership under British rule, but their objections also represented a clash of policy between the British and Boer settlers.[1] The Trekkers left particularly in opposition to the ending of slavery, the British refusal to extend to them representative government, and the fact that freed slaves and Khoi servants were put on an equal footing with Christians, a policy the Trekkers regarded as "contrary to the laws of God and the natural distinction of race and color."[2] After the Trekkers settled in the interior, they formed two republics, the Transvaal and the Orange Free State.

The opposition of the Boer settlers led to an ideological divide between the Cape liberalism of the British colonists and the conservatism of the Boer republics. The Boer attitude toward Africans developed out of the traditions of their early settlement. They had fought hardship in a hostile world to survive and had maintained a hold on their land through toughness and force, which lent a harsh conservatism to their character. In the words of one historian, the Boers had developed "a hard and sometimes violent masculinity as well as strong patriarchalism which were later available as cultural reference points."[3] The Boer republics set up in the interior reflected their rigid stance on human hierarchy. This was illustrated in the 1858 constitution of Transvaal, which stated that "the people desire to permit no equality between colored people and the white inhabitants of the country, either in church or state."[4] No Indians were allowed in the Orange Free State, and both it and the Transvaal republic required Africans to carry passes and prohibited them from carrying guns and registering land ownership.

During the second half of the nineteenth century, a major change in colonial domination throughout the world shaped Europeans' interest in and perceptions of Africa. Through a combination of missionary zeal, economic expansion, and political competition—all influenced in various ways by the sentiment of social Darwinism that justified the supremacy of one race over another—the so-called scramble for Africa rapidly divided the continent into European domains. South Africa became a treasured and controversial piece of the African pie. Africa itself was to be opened up, according to the adventurous English missionary David Livingstone, by the three *C's*: commerce, Christianity, and civilization. But there was a fourth *C* that directly affected the Africans, and that was conquest.[5] Already begun in previous centuries, conquest took on a more determined nature in the late nineteenth century. Rivalries among European countries became fierce, and imperialism became a primary outcome of the industrial revolution.

Imperialism in terms of conquest was no stranger to many African groups who relied on conquest to expand themselves, as illustrated in the leadership of the powerful Zulu in South Africa. For this and many other reasons, Africans offered strong resistance to colonial encroachment. Violence and warfare therefore intensified in the final decades of the nineteenth century and involved not only brutal defeat of Africans by Europeans, but also bloody battles between the Boer settlers (the "white tribe") and the British, with Africans enlisted on both sides. This tension between the Boer and British colonies reached its climax in the South African War at the turn of the century.

With the discovery of diamonds in South Africa in 1867 and the great rush to the Kimberly diamond fields that followed, Britain's policy of control in that region became more direct and invasive. Aggressive imperialism now overtook Cape liberalism, motivated by the need to gain labor for the mines and plantations spreading throughout South Africa and by the overall desire to reap the political and economic benefits from this area, seemingly rich in resources. This change of policy also led the British to see the native Africans less as potential allies or consumers of British goods and more as obstacles to "progress" and objects of manipulation. Internal conflict among Africans was exploited, direct intervention increased, land was seized, taxes were imposed, and the Africans found themselves pushed into European society, influenced unwittingly by its economics, religion, politics, and warfare. Africans fought back in several ways throughout these decades, including war. At the historic battle at Isandhlwana, the Zulu momentarily crippled British forces in 1879. But the Zulus' spears and defiance were no match for the British guns and the determined sweep of imperial conquest. Britain took control of Zululand in 1887, and the Natal region was drawn into the British colony in 1897. The Zulu soon became part of the migrant labor system. The majority of the Xhosa in what was known as British Kaffraria and those Africans in the Cape Colony already had come under British rule in the 1860s.

Britain's steady acquisition of territory in South Africa aroused resentment and increased nationalism in the Boer republics. In 1877 the British had annexed the Transvaal after it suffered economic hardship and near-collapse. The Boers, however, resisted annexation. After a rebellion in 1881 (sometimes called the First Boer War) in which the Boers twice defeated British forces, Boer independence was restored in the Transvaal, with the British keeping the right to intervene, particularly in foreign relations. By the end of the century, the British regretted their concessions to Boer autonomy in the Transvaal. The region's diamond mines and location on a strategic trade route had made it, to British eyes, the most valuable region in South Africa. In the last two decades of the nineteenth century, the president of the Transvaal, Paul Kruger, meanwhile, strengthened his republic and asserted greater control over the Africans. Kruger's increased challenge to British power, together with pressure within the British government to create a united South Africa under the British flag, led to the South African War, or Second Boer War, in 1899. The war lasted three years and resulted mainly from a combination of personal ambition, conflict over a sea route to India, and most importantly, competition for control of the gold-mining developing in Witwatersrand.

The South African War caused great destruction and loss of life, not least among the Africans sucked into it, and solidified the animosity between the British and Boers that lasted well into the twentieth century. Through scorched-earth tactics and the internment of Boer prisoners and civilian refugees in concentration camps, Britain eventually achieved victory but only after severe devastation. The Africans played a significant role in the British military effort by relaying messages, acting as lookouts, and assisting in transportation, but such assistance did not ensure a secure place for Africans in a united British South Africa. After a brief period of relative freedom for the Africans when the war ended, the British redoubled efforts to control African land and labor in 1905.

The South African War and developments in the early twentieth century ended the old pattern of colonial rule in South Africa and the hope on the part of the Africans for recovering their own land, while also leading to a new assertion of racial hierarchy. The Union of South Africa was formally declared in 1910 with Louis Botha as president of the British commonwealth. Evident throughout the new political construction was the affirmation of white dominance. A nonracial franchise was only maintained in the Cape province, but even this was thwarted by property qualifications. In order to preserve white unity after the severe conflict between Afrikaner and Briton, the British government had conceded to Boer strength in Transvaal and the Orange Free State, and the African population paid the price in terms of political rights, land tenancy, and ownership. South Africa's boundaries were officially established, and after the invasion of German Southwest Africa during World War I, South Africa acquired a mandate over Namibia (as German Southwest Africa was called) through the League of Nations. Racial dominance secured white unity in the South African state of the twentieth century.

European conquest of land had meanwhile laid the foundations for the political and economic development of twentieth-century South Africa. A single state had been created but not a single nation. One clear sign of this was the tradition of African chiefdoms and the demography of South Africa, which remained as residue from the previous centuries and greatly influenced future developments in that country. What emerged in the first half of the twentieth century was a pattern of racial dominance complicated by the rise of a capitalist economy with its sometimes conflicting connection between the mining industry and the agricultural community of South Africa, and developments within the racially dominated communities—Indians, coloreds, and Africans—in response to increased segregation and labor control.

The system of segregation that began to arise in the twentieth century was not strictly a new development. Its roots go back to the immediate division of races caused by the institution of slavery. The process of racially discriminatory laws easily followed, and the discovery of gold and diamonds in South Africa in the nineteenth century introduced a pattern of industry that upheld segregation. This, in turn, led to apartheid. By the end of the nineteenth century, the policy toward "natives," which followed a Victorian liberal tradition of viewing them as moral beings open to missionary appeals and the products of Western civilization, was being replaced by a more repressive approach, based in part on belief in the innate inferiority and savagery of non-Western "colored" peoples. In 1894 the Glen Gray Act was passed in the Eastern Cape. This act placed a restriction on African production and introduced a tax for non-wage earners (mostly farmers). The motivating element behind this act was the fact that African agricultural prosperity was of no benefit to the government because it removed potential labor from the towns. Regulations were also imposed at the turn of the century increasing the separation between races. These became part of a general political program of segregation that included pass laws (laws that restricted black population of white areas), a differentiation in wage levels, mission-based schools, and a white franchise (except in the Cape).

One of the earliest forms of segregation was the "sanitation syndrome" of the early 1900s that accounted for residential segregation in the towns not overtaken by mining, such as Cape Town and Port Elizabeth. In response to an outbreak of bubonic plague, Africans were expelled in these towns, and with no other housing provided, they ended up squatting on land outside the city. In Durban, the plague led to enforced segregation in "native locations," which the city financed by exercising a monopoly over the brewing of sorghum beer produced for African consumption.[6]

Over the next half century, whites added to the restrictions on black Africans and developed, by law, a culture of racial separation and white privilege. In 1913 the Natives Land Act was passed, which prohibited African purchase or lease of land outside certain areas known as "reserves." These reserves were set far apart from more-lucrative areas and the white farming community. The act removed African resistance to being absorbed into the migrant labor system advantageous to the mines, and to the wage labor setup of the white farms—two aspects of the alliance of "gold and maize" (farmers and industrialists) established by the Act of Union. The Natives (Urban Areas) Act of 1923 carried urban segregation a step further: Africans were denied freehold property rights and were only allowed in South African cities "For so long as their presence is demanded by the wants of the white population."[7] Through the Native Trust and Land Act and the Native Representation Act of 1936, Africans in the Cape were finally legally denied the vote, politics was separated, and a Native Representative council was set up, which operated as little more than a "toy telephone" body.[8] Meanwhile, in the rural areas, whites increased the distance between themselves and their black workers and lessened their humanity by giving them names of coins, kitchen utensils, and animals.

Under the leadership of Prime Minister Jan Smuts (1919–1924), the underlying principles of segregation became entrenched. The Pact government of J. B. Hertzog carried out similar policies even more enthusiastically. Hertzog had formed a separate National Party in 1914, allied with the White Labour Party in 1924, and won the election of that year. His election speeches of 1929 marked the "Black Peril" as a constant theme, and a special Native Economic Commission he appointed in 1930 reported that Africans had a different mentality from Europeans because of their race and historical background. It claimed that Africans' natural tendencies toward violence had been encouraged by colonial peace.[9]

This increased movement toward legal separation in almost all aspects of society and politics left the oppressed populations to develop their own cultures in their segregated spaces and, thereby, resist the debasement segregation implied. The rise of industry in the 1930s and 1940s, which brought a greater number of Africans into towns, meant a rise in crude housing in the backyard spaces of the slums. These were "cleared" through the Slums Act of 1934, but large shantytowns continued to grow around Cape Town and Durban. A popular culture known as "Marabi" also arose out of the Witwatersrand shebeens (unlicensed liquor houses). Marked by a distinctive style of music influenced by ragtime and American jazz, Marabi grew into a society closed to outsiders and in many ways functioned as a means of dealing with poverty and low levels of subsistence—one example, among many in South Africa, of the use of creativity to combat hardship.[10]

African national identity and increasingly organized resistance also arose in the twentieth century. Ironically, the sense of identity that marked resistance after the turn of the century found its roots in the growth of African churches. The rise of these independent churches revealed the capacity of Africans to fend for themselves and begin to call more confidently for "Africa for the Africans" while at the same time spreading the influence of Christianity. A key figure in late-nineteenth-century politics was J. T. Jabavu, editor of the African newspaper *Imvo Zabantsunda* ("Voice of the People"). The newspaper voiced strong protest against increased franchise qualifications of the Cape at that time and expressed other African grievances. Jabavu was conciliatory in his approach, however, and reluctant to form an energetic national African organization that might alienate the white population. In 1902 more-assertive nationalists formed an alternative news-

paper, *Izwi Labantu* ("Voice of the Black People"), which criticized capital-
ism and segregation and spawned the South African Native Congress
(SANC) based in East London and led by Walter Rubusana and Allan Soga.
The Congress became the center of African political expression in the
Cape, and in 1910 Rubusana became the only African to gain a seat in the
Cape when he was elected to the Provincial Council in Thembuland. (He lost
in 1914.)

Another nationalist movement arose in Transkei in the late 1920s. Known
as the "Wellington Movement" for its founder Wellington Butelezi, and influenced by the Jamaican-born pan-Africanist Marcus Garvey, this movement called for no assimilation with whites and upheld the principle of
"Africa for the Africans." It believed that American blacks would come and
liberate black South Africans from their white oppressors. Branches of Garvey's United Negro Improvement Association were set up in Cape Town and
Durban, and a "rural Africanists" philosophy emerged combining traditional rural ideas and leadership with missionary-educated Africans. Although salvation from America never came, support for the "Wellington
Movement" continued in the Transkei throughout the 1930s.[11]

The early African nationalists such as those who formed the SANC were
not necessarily anti-imperial. They shared a liberal belief in a multiracial environment, and in their proposals for reorganization of the South African nation, they included citizenship in South Africa for whites. English became
their language of expression and was later pronounced the language of liberation (as opposed to Afrikaans, the Boer language of oppression). One of
the earliest of the SANC representatives, John Dube, was a U.S.-educated
minister who was influenced by and echoed Booker T. Washington's philosophy of self-improvement. He founded the Ohlange Institute, similar to
Tuskegee Institute in Alabama, and emphasized an industrial and academic
education, feeling less confidence in the intentions of whites and more in African ambition.

A flurry of organizing political parties occurred in the 1920s as various
African interests and peoples struggled for definitions of "African" identity.
But as segregation began to be asserted increasingly in the policies of the
South African governments, a desire grew among African leaders for a
stronger definition of their identity. Out of their concern came the South African Native National Congress (SANNC), formed in Bloemfontain in 1912,
which later became the African National Congress (ANC). John Dube was
its president and Solomon Plaatjie its secretary. It focused first on land issues
and then took up the issue of urban rights and passes. As the early ANC leaders found difficulty in creating unity among different African factions, frus-

trated African labor formed the Industrial and Commercial Workers Union of South Africa (ICU) and began overtaking the ANC in reach and initial success. In the 1920s the original version of the Zulu party, Inkatha, also formed and by this time involved John Dube, who had left the ANC.

All African movements of the early 1900s were influenced by the homelands of South Africa, but they also incorporated the political ideal of a nonracial and nonviolent policy, asserting their identity in a state dominated by whites. These hit a snag in the early 1930s, when the ANC was still relatively small, the ICU dissolved, and the Communist Party of South Africa (SACP), another opposition group founded in 1921, weakened through internal problems. Revival occurred in 1935 with the establishment of the All Africa Convention (AAC), which jolted the ANC and Communist party leaders into calling their own conference. Unions also revived and organized more along racial lines.

The policies of segregation carried out in the 1930s were justified both ideologically and morally in terms of protecting Africans from land expropriation, urban corruption, and foreign ideology (meaning communism). One method of counteracting African protest against political exclusion, as well as the dangers of communism, was to promote African communalism, which meant diverting African populations back to their rural traditions and local rule. Supporters of communalism claimed that their program would shield the Africans from corruption and exploitation and safeguard their customs, an approach influenced by the tradition of British colonialism in Africa. As part of this process, in 1939 the "Betterment" proclamation was issued, which included the establishment of village societies, the separation of arable land from grazing, and the culling of livestock. It met with great rural resistance in the 1940s, mainly because cattle were seen by the rural Africans as a staple to their whole economy and a measure of status.

The 1940s also marked a general rise in the cost of living. This sparked more collective action on the part of squatters and an increase in the number of black trade unions. In 1946 mine workers led a general strike that involved close to 70,000 workers around the rand. The strike was brutally squashed by the Jan Smuts government, but the incident increased fear and paranoia among the white population and became a major factor in the outcome of the apartheid election of 1948. Smuts, who had become head of the United Party (UP) in 1943, found his government facing increased criticism of policies that—however suppressive they could be viewed externally—were seen within the country as too liberal, particularly among the growing number of right-wing groups that paralleled European fascism. Smuts, for example, had given limited concessions, including some representation and rights, to the Indian population, which much of the white population regarded as too generous. As blacks increasingly challenged the status quo under wartime pressure, whites moved ideologically to the right. The harsh conditions in the postwar period only served to increase this division. Afrikaner paramilitary groups began looking to the party D. F. Malan formed in 1934, which called itself the *Gesuiwerde* (purified) National Party. The party's base of support included whites from all sections of South African society: civil servants, teachers, farmers, as well as the Afrikaner educated classes of the Western Cape. It received approval from the Dutch Reformed churches and extended the interpretation of *volk* to mean not only common history and culture but a complete mind-set and approach to life, a concept picked up by the younger generation, many of whom had been educated in German universities. During World War II these elements had opposed fighting on the side of Britain and against Germany.

In the election of 1948, Smuts's United Party lost support from the cities as whites made clear their fears of the black working class. Sections of the Transvaal and the Orange Free State began consolidating their support behind Malan's Nationalists and particularly expressed the sentiments of farmers who had begun to doubt that the United Party was truly sympathetic to their problems. Most attractive to these sections of South African society was the "apartness" slogan of the Nationalists. The UP, in comparison with Malan's party, appeared loosely connected and not as organized. Although it maintained some support from Afrikaans-speakers, it lost narrowly in some suburban and rural constituencies, and suffered a protest vote of a certain number of English-speakers.

Thus Malan replaced Smuts in the election of 1948, and the system of apartheid became rooted in South Africa until 1994. The politics and policies of apartheid separated South Africa from the rest of the world through systematic and legal segregation upheld and defined by a small but powerful white bureaucracy. White racism was, of course, not limited to South Africa, but in no other country after World War II did it become a basic element of society and definition of public order. In the rest of Africa, especially after 1945, a pattern of energetic decolonization and majority rule emerged as part of the revulsion against a century or more of European colonialism and, more recently, the European fascist regimes and their racial policies of the 1930s and 1940s. Racial separation in South Africa, however, became almost more important to the ruling class than even nationalism, as nationalism was in many ways a tricky concept in a country with its own history of divided whites from Dutch and British backgrounds. The white elite did its best to consolidate its power and force through its policies. It did so with a ruthlessness that created terrible bitterness and strife over the next forty years. Outside protest was meanwhile strenuously resisted and had little effect until the late 1960s.

The basis of the new government strategy of apartheid was to separate all South Africans by race, and in the years following the election of 1948, legislation was passed to complete this separation. People were officially classified into four distinct groups through the Population Registration Act: white, colored (mixed race), Asiatic (Indian), and Native (later Bantu, or African); and the Group Areas Act laid the foundations for comprehensive separation of the races into distinct residential areas. "Mixed Marriages" were prohibited. In 1950 the Immorality Act denied all sexual contact between races. In 1951 the Bantu Authorities Act replaced the Natives Representative Council created in 1936 with chiefs in reserves (sanctioned by the government), and African representation in towns and white rural areas was eradicated. The only nonwhite representation remaining in Parliament was that of the Cape coloreds, and even they were largely circumscribed when, in 1956, coloreds were made to register on a separate roll and permitted to elect only four white representatives to Parliament. In 1960 all nonwhite representation was abolished.

Apartheid affected all institutions of life. The Bantu Education Act of 1953 removed funding and administration from the missions, and provincial authorities came under the central control of the Secretary of Native Affairs. The Nationalists thought that too much emphasis had been placed on English and liberal ideas, which had encouraged protest among the African elite, so they moved to limit Africans' access to Western thought. Vernacular language was imposed on education up through high school, with emphasis shifting to technical skills and syllabi that came under central jurisdiction. As opposed to white education, African schooling was not free or compulsory, and the educational institutions—schools, polytechnics, and universities—were systematically separated throughout the 1950s. H. F. Verwoerd, then Minister of Native Affairs, justified apartheid education by claiming that previous policies had misled Africans "by showing them the green pastures of European society in which they are not allowed to graze."[12] Social segregation was also officially imposed through the separate Amenities Act of 1953. All public aspects of social life—including transportation, movies, restaurants, and sports—were separated according to race.

In 1954 Malan died and was replaced by J. G. Strydom. Supported by white workers and farmers in the Transvaal, Strydom was even more publicly adamant on the subject of racial separation and nationalist ideology than his predecessor. In the election of 1958, the NP won nearly double the number of seats of their opposition. This outcome was partly the result of the political changes imposed by the government (such as removal of the colored franchise), but it also reflected general support for apartheid among white South Africans. The Afrikaners were particularly drawn to the government's break from British influence as well as the greater expression of their identity. English-speaking whites felt the appeal of restriction of Africans residing in the cities and increased control over African resistance. Probably the strongest factor in white support, however, was this group's continued economic prosperity and rise in living standards.

As has been noted, the rise of Malan's party and its success in the 1948 election was part of a reaction to increased African organized protest. From the 1940s the ANC had been revived under the leadership of Dr. Alfred B. Xuma. After the mine workers' strike of 1946, younger members of the organization formed a radical group within the Congress Youth League. They included two former students at the University of Fort Hare: Nelson Mandela and Oliver Tambo. The organization had been greatly influenced by several external developments: the world war against racism and for democracy, the movement for India's independence from British colonial rule, and the rise of nationalism in other African countries. By the late 1940s, at the same time that white nationalism was gaining support, mass black protest had moved toward consolidation and planning and had received attention and some sympathy from Smuts's government. The success of Malan's movement represented a severe blow to African protest, and in 1949 Dr. Xuma was voted out of the ANC presidency mainly for taking an approach that was too cautious. The Congress Youth League promoted a "Program of Action" that placed greater emphasis on confrontation: demonstrations, boycotts, and passive resistance along the lines of Gandhi's *satyagraha*. Connections between the ANC, the Natal Indian Congress, white radicals in the Congress of Democrats, and the now banned Communist party were strengthened, and a call went up for "National Freedom," political independence, and denunciation of segregation.

In 1955 the Congress movement came together and drafted the Freedom Charter, which affirmed its commitment to a nonracial democracy, equal opportunity for all people, and some redistribution of wealth. The charter was endorsed by all member organizations and established as a pillar of opposition to apartheid for the next thirty-five years. It also served as the basis of ANC ideology. Clauses within the charter stressed that "South Africa belongs to all who live in it, black and white, and no government can justly claim authority unless it is based on the will of the people . . . [and] the rights of the people shall be the same regardless of race, color, or sex." The charter demanded equal access to health, education, and legal rights and envisioned a future democratic and multiracial South Africa.[13] The movement also set up its own Congress of Trade Unions (SACTU).

Opposition to the Freedom Charter arose among the Africanists who viewed charterism as a rejection of the vision of South Africa for Africans. This ideology was taken up by younger members of the ANC who also objected to an alliance with the Indian Congress and the Communist party. Internal dissension gave way to the formation of the Pan-Africanist Congress (PAC) in 1959 under Robert Sobukwe and reflected the impatience of younger Africans and the sense of frustration felt in the townships. The PAC often attempted to upstage the ANC with stronger rhetoric and mass mobilization.

The 1950s marked a difficult period for the ANC. The South African government stepped up banning and imprisonment to restrict action and protest. In a long, drawn-out trial set up by the government, many Congress leaders were charged with treason. Although the trial ended with acquittals for all who had been charged, it used up many of the resources of the Congress in terms of money and lawyers, and diverted the Congress from its principal mission. In December 1959 the ANC announced a series of one-day demonstrations against the pass laws. The PAC called for expansion of this campaign against passes and demonstrations at police stations, and activity centered on a peaceful march to the police station at Sharpeville in March 1960. As the demonstrators converged on the police, the latter panicked at the size of the crowd and opened fire from behind armored cars. Sixty-nine demonstrators were killed and 180 wounded.

The Sharpeville shootings had a great effect on black and white communities and marked a watershed in South African history. Strikes and stayaways were called, and the South African government declared a state of emergency. ANC and PAC leaders were detained, and both organizations were banned. The event awakened national interest and international protest. Economic sanctions against South Africa were proposed at the United Nations but vetoed by Britain and the United States. In 1960, at the Commonwealth Conference, rising criticism of the NP's policies led South Africa to withdraw from the British Commonwealth. South Africa declared itself a republic and set a pattern of increased isolation from other countries for the next two decades.

Apartheid intensified during the 1960s. H. G. Verwoerd, prime minister from 1958, turned his back on international criticism of the Sharpeville shootings and increased the size of his police force, consisting mostly of Afrikaners. Through the General Law Amendment Act of 1963, the police gained the power to detain people without charge and the use of solitary confinement. The repressive system of the 1960s was in many ways personified by Verwoerd and J. B. Vorster, who rose to power as Minister of Justice. Vorster had been interned during World War II for sabotage as a member of the *Ossewabrandwag* (OB) or ox-wagon guard, a right-wing paramilitary group, originating in the Orange Free State, which adopted terrorist tactics against Smuts's government and celebrated Afrikaner culture. He would later become prime minister when Verwoerd was assassinated in 1966. Under Verwoerd's and Vorster's leadership, the number of individuals detained and banned rose with the outlawing of the ANC and PAC, and detention and banning as a whole (which allowed for avoidance of judicial procedure) laid the foundations of repression for the next thirty years. Verwoerd's philosophy stressed a social Darwinist approach, playing on white fears and notions of purity—especially with regard to protection of white women. Under his leadership the "pillars" of apartheid were established. These included race definition, control over African migration, white control of politics, separation of labor, separate institutions, and separate amenities.

The 1960s therefore marked a period of much greater separation. The creation of homelands, passes, and group areas, combined with the ideology dominating white rule, kept black South Africans almost out of sight from whites. Whites rested on the assumption that they understood their own Africans better than the outside world, which meant that they could close their ears to overseas influence and criticism and exist in a kind of segregated vacuum. This process was encouraged by Verwoerd's method of separate development that created reserves known as "homelands" that allowed for economic as well as political division. In 1959 eight (and later ten) "Bantu Homelands" were established, each with limited self-government. Ethnic identity was stressed over nationalist sentiment, the underlying approach being that of ancient Rome's "divide and rule" strategy. The South African government conducted large-scale forced relocation of Africans, which combined with the Group Areas Act that focused on urban removal to dispossess and move great populations of Africans literally out of sight. Under this legislation 3.5 million people were moved between 1960 and 1983.[14] Such a dramatic separation created severe hardships for many Africans in terms of lack of employment and general deprivation in the areas to which they were moved. Protest against increased separation and repression in the 1960s was relatively muted. This was due, in part, to the vigor with which the government carried out suppression, and to great separation, which diffused opposition. But, to a large measure, a rise in economic prosperity during this decade explains the lack of protest. The white population quite obviously reaped the fruits of this development, but black unemployment levels dropped also. Economic stability and state suppression joined to create a successful apartheid system in the 1960s.

Protest, however, never died. It was particularly evident in the rural areas in reaction to the Bantu Authorities Act. The most long-term protest occurred in the Eastern Pondoland but ended in a massacre by the police and army of people at a mass meeting in Lusikisiki. The ANC and PAC, meanwhile, had gone underground and in 1961 developed a new strategy proposed by Mandela and Sisulu together with other former Youth League members. The strategy called for direct action and the formation of an underground guerrilla army known as Umkhonto we Sizwe (Spear of the Nation—MK). The tactics employed would be sabotage of power stations and government buildings for the next three years. The idea of an armed struggle gained currency because ANC members argued that the efforts of their nonviolent approach had been exhausted and that the government itself used violence to maintain control. The ANC also sent representatives abroad, but resistance from a position of exile proved to be much more difficult than within South Africa. Even though bases were established in neighboring countries such as Zambia, Lesotho, and Tanzania, the ANC and PAC both found themselves cut off from developments within South Africa. Only with the breakdown of white rule in Angola, Mozambique, and Zimbabwe in the late 1970s did greater advantages arise. For the most part, however, in the 1960s and early 1970s, these resistance groups suffered from a lack of resources and an abundance of internal division. One blow to the movement was the arrest and imprisonment of Mandela in 1964.

In many ways Nelson Mandela's own dramatic life outlines the progress of black nationalist politics as a whole from the 1950s to the 1960s. Mandela was born in Thembuland the son of a less powerful chief who died when Mandela was young. He was raised first by his Christian mother and then taken into a Thembu chief's homestead where he was educated. Influenced by the emphasis on schooling by the Transkeian Christian elite, Mandela attended Fort Hare, which was the main institution of higher education for blacks. Like many of his peers, Mandela became greatly influenced by politics and resistance at Fort Hare and as a consequence of his actions was expelled.

In 1941 Mandela trained as a lawyer in Johannesburg, becoming increasingly involved in a multiracial political environment, and he contributed to the radicalization of the ANC. He became secretary-general of the Youth League of the ANC in 1948 and was central to its organization for the next ten years. As part of Oliver Tambo's legal practice, which acted as a network for the Congress's political connections, Nelson Mandela played a major role in the transition of the ANC from a national opposition group to a national liberation movement after the Sharpeville massacre. Tambo stated, "Of all that group of young men, Mandela and his close friend and co-leader Walter Sisulu were perhaps the fastest to get to grips with the harsh realities of the African struggle against the most powerful adversary in Africa."[15]

Throughout the 1950s Mandela was banned at different times by the government and was one of the leaders put on trial in 1956. In 1963 he was again put on trial at first for incitement to strike and leaving the country without a valid permit. He was convicted and had served nine months of his five-year sentence when in 1964 he was charged, along with several members of the ANC and PAC, with sabotage. It was under these circumstances, at the celebrated Rivonia trial, that Mandela issued a stirring speech on his decision to choose death if necessary in the struggle against apartheid. The speech lasted over four hours, and the case itself attracted international attention. This attention, Mandela believed, spared him the death penalty, but pressure from the South African government and the judge's own people caused the sentence for all the accused to be the next harshest: life imprisonment.[16] Mandela was held for seventeen years on Robben Island until he was removed to Pollsmoor Prison in 1981, and then Victor Verster Prison in 1988, where he remained until his release in 1990. Increasingly, during his twenty-seven years of internment, he became a personal representation of the struggle against apartheid, to such a degree that his release was probably the most symbolic statement of the end of apartheid.

With the diffusion of organized resistance to apartheid in the 1960s, what emerged instead within South Africa was a less politically centered but more ideological movement known as Black Consciousness. The philosophy of this movement originated in the universities as part of a reaction to white dominance in the National Union of South African Students (NUSAS). In 1969, black students led by Steve Biko separated themselves from NUSAS to form the South African Students Organization (SASO). Influenced by U.S. "black power" and student protest movements in the 1960s, SASO set up self-help programs in black communities. Arguing that the long tradition of oppression had kept blacks from achieving effective organization and realizing their own identity, Biko contended that blacks' failure to organize was in part due to their own fear from which they needed liberation by establishing a strong sense of themselves: "What Black Consciousness seeks to do is to produce real black people who do not regard themselves as appendages to white society."[17]

In contrast to the platforms of the ANC and PAC, Black Consciousness's message tended to be broad and vague. It stressed a community of blacks, incorporating the principle of shared wealth, criticizing the cooperation of the African elite, and using the word "black" to challenge the language of apartheid (which tended to use terms such as "non-white" or "non-European"). The use of the word "black," which included coloreds and Indians, was part of the process of proclaiming an actual identity. The tradition of Africanism played a part in Black Consciousness as did aspects of the ANC and PAC, the influence of the American civil rights and black power movements, international liberation theology of the 1960s, and liberation struggles as expressed in works by the revolutionaries Frantz Fanon and Ernesto Che Guevara. While including Indians and coloreds, Black Consciousness separated itself from antiapartheid white liberals. Biko argued that these whites tended to imply that they had greater intelligence and moral judgment than blacks, and should therefore set "the pattern and pace for the realization of the black man's aspirations."[18] Those whites who opposed apartheid, according to Biko, should concentrate their efforts on their "racist brethren."[19]

Initially, the South African government tolerated and to a certain degree approved of Biko's movement because it seemed to support the idea of separate development. Biko, however, strongly criticized the Bantustans and their collaborators, and Black Consciousness increasingly became a threat to apartheid's status quo. While the philosophy of Black Consciousness was espoused from churches and universities, and by writers, political action on behalf of the movement was most effectively carried out by school students who, given the circumstances of apartheid education and resistance, represented a mixture of deprivation and expectation. In the highly politicized area of Orlando in Soweto, the South African Students Movement (SASM) was strongest. SASM set up an Action Committee and organized a demonstration for June 16, 1976, where protesters met to march to Orlando stadium. The South African police overreacted, killing several students, whereupon SASM carried out counterattacks against the police, administration buildings, and beer halls. These in turn led to further attacks and raids by the police. Migrant workers in Soweto were encouraged to challenge students who tried to get the beer halls closed, which gave rise to more conflict. By the end of 1976, official figures (which were probably far less than the real numbers) reported 575 dead and 2,389 wounded.[20] Protest spread to colored schools on the Western Cape, and attacks on shebeens (private houses that sold beer) and liquor stores were prominent. Many of the students fought particularly against the aspects of apartheid that they saw as encouraging their parents to waste money on alcohol, declaring, "We can no longer tolerate seeing our fathers' pay-packet emptied into shebeens."[21]

The South African government reacted to the increased challenge of Black Consciousness and the resulting conflicts by harassing its leaders in the 1970s. Vorster's response to the events of 1976 became more repressive. His government banned the South African Council of Churches, Black Consciousness organizations, and many individuals. In 1977 Biko himself was detained and died under torture, while many young members of his group fled the country. But Black Consciousness had revived resistance. The raised fist and freedom cry "amandla awethu" (power to us, the people) remained as strong symbols of the belief that "the system" would collapse.

Much of this resistance stemmed not only from the pattern of black opposition and white suppression that marked the development of South Africa in the twentieth century, but from growing protest grounded in the religious and writing establishments of that country. Christianity had become deeply rooted in South African society in the early part of the century and remained the dominant religion of both South African blacks and whites. Increasingly, the growing number of independent African churches (Methodist, "Ethiopian," fundamentalist-apostolic, and Zionist) strongly illustrated the capacity of Africans to fend for themselves and claim "Africa for the Africans." By the early 1970s about 3,000 independent African churches had established themselves in South Africa, of which about 900 were in Soweto. Maintained within an African context, these churches encouraged social cohesion, faith, and routine among people facing urban insecurity and social uncertainty. Although disparaged by uncomfortable middle-class blacks as "escapist," the churches provided a forum for release of distress and contributed some material advantages to the lives of their followers.[22] Later, in the mid-1980s, antiapartheid voices within the black churches came to prominence as many of the other leaders of opposition went into exile, were in prison, or were banned. The most prominent of these religious voices were Anglican Archbishop Desmond Tutu of Cape Town (winner of the Nobel Peace Prize in 1984), President of the World Alliance of Reformed Churches Allan Boesak, and Boesak's successor Frank Chikane.

White churches also had gone through a significant process of development. From the mid-nineteenth century, the Dutch Reformed Church had sanctioned separation of "colored" and white congregations and the establishment of mission churches for the subordinate population. In 1948 the Dutch Reformed Church stayed quiet on the new policy of apartheid, but leaders of other white South African churches criticized apartheid, setting a pattern of increased conflict between clergy and the South African government.

In 1968, for example, the South African Council of Churches proclaimed apartheid to be a pseudogospel that contradicted Christian principles.[23]

Originally most of the Afrikaner clergy had upheld apartheid. In 1962, however, C. F. Beyers Nande, former moderator of the primary Dutch Reformed Church in the Transvaal, broke from established doctrine and founded the Christian Institute. The Institute brought black and white Christians of different denominations together and began the Study Project on Christianity in Apartheid Society (SPROCAS), which encouraged challenges of the official church view. The South African government banned Nande and his institution in 1977, but this development among the Afrikaner Christians revealed controversy within the Dutch Reformed Church, and a group of Afrikaner clergy followed the banning of Nande with a radical critique of apartheid in 1978.[24]

Prominent writers in South Africa also turned their talent in the direction of opposition and exposure of injustice and deprivation under the apartheid system. E. Hellman's *Rooiyard* (1948), Alan Paton's *Cry the Beloved Country* (1948), and Peter Abrahams's *Mine Boy* (1989) all provided vivid descriptions of black urban life, as did *Marabi Dance* (1973) by Modikwe Dikobe, one of the first black working-class novelists in South Africa. Nadine Gordimer's novels (many of which were banned) portrayed the profound guilt and self-criticism of white society struggling with its own immoral basis. Writers and novelists of the *Sestiger* (sixties) movement such as André Brink probed the threatening themes of interracial relationships, Afrikaner insecurity, and the tradition of violence and exploitation within South African society. Alan Paton strongly criticized apartheid in his writings throughout the 1950s and 1960s, issuing powerful statements in his essays and through the messages of his novels. By the 1970s, many of these authors were collectively and strongly illustrating the debilitating effect of South African racism through their plays and novels.

Many of the political resistance leaders who fled South Africa in the late 1970s joined the exiled ANC and PAC in neighboring African countries. Meanwhile, the end of white government in Mozambique and Angola served as further inspiration to resistance. In 1979, after a lengthy conflict, Rhodesia also gave way to African rule, renaming itself Zimbabwe with Robert Mugabe as president. South Africa was being surrounded by independent African states. In Southwest Africa, government control was being challenged by SWAPO from bases in Angola, the ANC was establishing bases closer to South Africa, and the socialist government of Mozambique loomed to the north. The South African government responded by sponsoring RENAMO rebels to challenge the authority of Mozambique's Frelimo government. A political scandal had meanwhile scarred the government of Vorster in 1978 when his security and information chief was charged with misusing public funds in order to campaign for world recognition. The timing of the scandal was bad, coming in the midst of the struggle to quell Black Consciousness resistance, and it especially hurt the "moral" image of the Afrikaner government. Pieter Willem Botha emerged to take over the leadership, holding on to it throughout the 1980s. Botha had a reputation as a consummate politician, domineering and dedicated to the National Party. He had operated as party organizer in his twenties, directly contributed to the original racial policy of the party as a member of the Sauer Commission in 1946, and as minister of defense from 1966, had organized a large, powerful, and intimidating South African army.

On assuming power, Botha began adopting a government policy more favorable to business. That move led to division within the National Party as the traditional base of support—white workers and farmers—quickly grew disillusioned with the new government policy. The division resulted in a formal split in 1982 when the disaffected broke to form the Conservative party under the leadership of Andries Treurnicht. This was a blow to Botha's government as even before the official divide the Prime Minister had begun searching for a strategy to reassert power under the increasing threats of black resistance and conservative reaction. What emerged was a policy referred to as "total strategy" that combined stricter security measures with government attempts at reform to undermine the basis of protests. Facing regional and internal challenges, Botha, in arguing for the political necessity of reform, warned the white population to "adapt or die," but the security crackdown that accompanied reform measures moved power from the police to the army, a move that heightened conflict and tragedy in the 1980s.

Reform was a response not only to black protest but also to the changing economic climate. The 1980s introduced British Prime Minister Margaret Thatcher's and U.S. President Ronald Reagan's free market approach to economics, and this philosophy began infiltrating South African politics. Government reformers began adapting to the idea of matching liberal economics with conservative social policies, while at the same time joining in the chorus against communism. Under pressure from industry and with the recommendation of the Wiehahn Report of 1979, the Industrial Conciliation Amendment Act of 1981 increased the rights of Africans who qualified to stay in the cities, granted more mobility between urban areas, and established more control over government in townships. Expenditure on African education was also increased, and the de Lange report on education of 1981 led to permission of multiracial private schools. This latter move was part of the "total strategy" idea of replacing racial division with class differentiation.[25]

The South African government also made an attempt to reform political representation; for example, it established a partly elected Colored Persons' Representative Council in 1968. In 1983 the South African government made another gesture toward political reform when a white referendum approved a tricameral parliament that included two new parliaments for coloreds and Indians. The two were to sit separately from the whites but take part in the president's council. The plan did not satisfy antiapartheid forces as they viewed it as a means by which the government could share power without losing control. The presidency of South Africa was at the same time changed from a ceremonial to an executive position, and Botha's title changed from prime minister to president, with the white parliament and National Party still under control of his council.

"Total strategy" reforms further included abolition of the Immorality and Mixed Marriages Acts—an indication of a change from the strict racial control of the 1950s. The government desegregated public amenities, but these changes seemed cosmetic with no real attempt to change the political or social system of apartheid. Some basic changes were carried out through the formation of the Urban Foundation, privately founded but financially backed by the government, which aided programs to improve living conditions in the townships. The government also made a crude attempt to create a class of willing collaborators through the Black Local Authorities Act of 1982, which granted Community Councils in the townships greater administrative powers, but this move failed in popular appeal.

The army, meanwhile, fulfilled its role as the focus of heightened security, and the State Security Council, which had been established in 1972, gained increased powers under the leadership of the new Minister of Defense Magnus Malan. A campaign of destabilization against the new governments of the bordering African states was another component of "total strategy." South Africa stepped up military support for RENAMO in Mozambique and for UNITA in Angola, and South African forces raided suspected ANC headquarters in Lesotho, Swaziland, Zimbabwe, and Botswana, while continuing the bitter guerrilla war against SWAPO in Namibia. This aspect of government strategy met with some success. In 1984 South Africa made the Nkomati nonaggression accord with Mozambique under which the Maputo government agreed to expel ANC guerrilla camps in return for South Africa withdrawing support from RENAMO.

There is some question as to whether "total strategy" heralded real reform in the early 1980s or whether it merely served to bolster continued white dominance. Segregation still existed, as did homeland independence; Africans were still denied political rights; and the increased involvement of the army in government policy meant still further suppression. Those reforms carried out, however, were arguably radical enough to threaten the conservative white tradition, especially that of Afrikaners. That threat was a factor in the conservative split and the later emergence of right-wing extremist groups.

The truly paradoxical outcome of Botha's policies was, in fact, the rise and intensification of opposition and resistance. The late 1970s and early 1980s witnessed a drop in gold prices, a balance-of-payments crisis, greater dependence on loans from the International Monetary Fund and foreign banks, and an overall sluggish economy. Inflation and unemployment rose, which meant increased deprivation for the black population and anxiety for the white population. The relaxation of pass controls under the umbrella of reform brought a larger number of Africans to the cities, especially Cape Town, and larger squatter camps arose, most noticeably that of Crossroads. The mass migration caused a failure in differentiation between permanent and temporary residents. From 1979 to 1980, a fresh wave of protest swept across South Africa and found its greatest outlet in educational establishments. Boycotts and burnings were prominent throughout the country, and demands for real reform became ever louder. The boycotts, meanwhile, hurt white business as increased popular resistance and mobilization became a hallmark of the 1980s. Stronger trade unions formed and began leading political resistance. It became evident to many within South Africa that Botha's government was not eradicating apartheid but merely changing it to maintain power. Reform only served to heighten the possibility of strong opposition. As historian William Beinart argues, reform from a position of power under pressure is a problematic exercise "which often raised the expectations of the oppressed and unleashed further powerful forces for change."[26]

In August 1983 the United Democratic Front (UDF) came together at a mass rally in Mitchell's Plain. Its platform was broad and populist, and it adopted a Chartist approach to opposition, rejecting apartheid, boycotting the tricameral system, and accepting the principles of the Freedom Charter. Winnie Mandela, the outspoken wife of Nelson Mandela and international symbol of survival of the Congress tradition, identified with the UDF, propelled as much by her convictions as by her experience of frequent harassment and banishment by the South Africa government since her husband's imprisonment. Albertina Sisulu, a major figure in the ANC Women's League and the wife of imprisoned ANC activist Walter Sisulu, became joint president of the UDF. The movement was determinedly multiracial and influenced by the philosophy of the ANC. In the same year, the National Forum (NF) was set up, whose base of support included Black Consciousness members of the Azanian People's Organization (AZAPO) and the Cape Unity Movement. The NF rejected the broad approach of the UDF. It called for no cooperation with the ruling class parties and for a workers' republic of "Azania" that was nonracial and democratic. The basic difference between the two was one of class—the NF being more worker-based and critical of the UDF for its middle-class approach.

Government crackdowns on resistance only served to heighten opposition. The pattern of protest rooted in schools, universities, factories, and townships in 1976 reached a dramatic climax in 1984–1986, when resistance to rent increases and service charges in the townships led to widespread rebellion. In August and September 1984, protest exploded into battles between Africans and police. Councillors were killed in Sebokeng, and the mayor of Sharpeville was slain in front of his house after shooting two demonstrators. On Sharpeville Day in 1985 police fired on a political funeral procession in the Eastern Cape, killing twenty people. Conflict intensified between youths and the police. School boycotts were reported in reaction all over South Africa. Police stations and stores were burned, "people's courts" were set up against "collaborators," and in extreme and highly publicized instances the accused were "necklaced" with burning tires. Many students began adopting the slogan "liberation before education."

The conflicts of 1984–1985 in many ways led to great unity among opposition movements. Workers coalesced with students, and broad philosophies provided resistance with a new sense of purpose. ANC banners began to appear at the funerals of political victims; "Nkosi Sikel' iAfrika" (God Bless Africa) was sung; Nelson Mandela and Oliver Tambo were hailed as heroes; "Viva!," the cry of the ANC, was shouted; and general support for the ANC increased. The Congress began to take on the role of a legitimate government in exile, as Umkhonto we Sizwe stepped up attacks on power stations and the military headquarters of the Defense Force in Pretoria.

The state reacted forcefully to resistance and conflict in the 1980s. The government moved large numbers of troops into the townships to align with the police. Township war escalated, with troops facing street barricades and Molotov cocktails. In July 1985 Botha declared a state of emergency in many parts of the country and extended the detention powers of the police, which remained in effect until 1990. In the first eight months of the 1985 state of emergency, 8,000 people were detained and 22,000 charged with political crimes. The UDF and AZAPO were banned. In 1986 Malan set up a network of local administrative councils headed by the police and military known as "security controls." In June 1986 the government declared a new emergency, and 26,000 more people were detained.[27] The government further placed reporting—and especially filming—under tight control just as disturbing reports of police assassination began to emerge. Hit squads with black and white members were formed and consolidated in 1988 under the Civil Corporation Bureau. Throughout the 1980s, political and social divisions deepened under the promotion of the Security Services, especially in tense and complicated areas such as Natal where conflict arose between Mangosuthu Buthelezi's Inkatha party (later the Inkatha Freedom Party–IFP) and the UDF. In such cases as Natal, the state could fuel division in secret and then publicly distance itself from the resulting excesses of violence, portraying itself as a stable force in a dangerously crumbling society.

Rejection of Botha's "total strategy" meanwhile arose in the business community. In 1985 Foreign Minister Pik Botha raised the hope of concrete change only to be angrily contradicted by the president, who made clear there was no chance of majority rule under his government. The economic result of this speech was the calling in of loans of 1982 from foreign banks, the collapse of the rand, and the temporary shutdown of the Johannesburg Stock Exchange. The economic crisis led prominent business leaders to meet with the ANC in Lusaka to discuss legitimate change. International denunciation of South Africa increased; so, too, did the policies of "disinvestment" carried out by the United States, along with British Commonwealth and European Community states.

In May 1986 a group of Commonwealth representatives traveled to South Africa, but government raids on suspected ANC bases in Harare, Lusaka, and Gaborone destroyed the atmosphere of the visit. World criticism rose further. By this time, however, Botha had recovered some control of the country. Although his government had lost the initiative with the failure of "total strategy," the burgeoning groups of resistance were still not sufficiently organized to take over. The state's problem—and eventual undoing—was that control was based on force and the aid of unpopular black allies, while the economic crisis and outside sanctions began to bite into South African society. Right-wing resistance was growing, especially among the white workers and farmers hit hardest by financial crisis.

International events were also subverting government tradition, especially its role as a bulwark against communism. In 1988 tension between the United States and the Soviet Union eased after President Mikhail Gorbachev offered to withdraw Soviet involvement in Cuba. In return, he called on the United States to demand democratic elections in Namibia. South Africa

.ı to this request. In 1989 SWAPO won 57 percent of the vote, taking ـe and announcing Namibian independence the following year.

Further developments occurred within the government itself. Botha's ɩnovement away from the British parliamentary system and the constitutional reforms he imposed diminished the power of the National Party. Corruption and violence infiltrated the now loosely controlled agencies, and Botha himself became increasingly irascible and dictatorial. A stalemate arose between the president and those progressive nationalists who wanted to carry further the pattern of reform. In 1989 Botha suffered a stroke. That same year the NP reorganized party and governmental leadership by separating the office of president of South Africa from party leader and naming Minister of National Education F. W. deKlerk head of the party. In August 1989 Botha was forced by his cabinet to resign, and deKlerk replaced him as president. The white election of 1989 gave deKlerk the confidence to launch a startlingly fast-paced program of reform. Since the UDF and Congress of South African Trade Unions (COSATU) had merged in the Mass Democratic Movement (MDM) during the final stages of Botha's presidency, challenging the government with a national campaign of civil disobedience to bring down segregation, deKlerk took one of his initial steps in preparation for change by diminishing police attacks against protesters. In September and October several peaceful marches of blacks and whites together occurred with no governmental interference.

Partly through inspiration, partly through intent to seize the initiative from the opposition, deKlerk, in his opening address to Parliament on February 2, 1990, announced the unbanning of the ANC, PAC, and SACP, as well as the planned release of a list of political prisoners, including Nelson Mandela. Throughout the next few years, many aspects of apartheid legislation were revoked, including the Group Areas Act, the Land Act, and the Population Registration Act. The ANC held its first full conference after unbanning in July 1991, and Mandela struggled together with Sisulu to reassert the moral leadership of the ANC. The personality of Mandela played a key role in the reestablishment of the legitimacy of the ANC. The dignity and capability of his character combined with his personal history to lend credence to the Congress's appeal to the masses. With Mandela's cooperation, the ANC meanwhile sidelined the role of Winnie Mandela after her involvement in a criminal trial concerning the murder of a fourteen-year-old boy by members of her personal "football team," or bodyguards. The ANC viewed the trial as a threat to the moral authority of the movement, and the case illustrated the dangers of "the struggle" becoming exploited or overtaken by petty rivalries. Later in 1991 the Convention for a Democratic South Africa

(CODESA) was held to begin the process toward a new constitution in a post-apartheid era. Commitment to democratic rights and a democratic nation was asserted as the South African state finally realized that political reform was the only practical method for achieving economic revival and stability.

Political settlement did not immediately ensue. Delay occurred amid the government jockeying for a more favorable bargaining position, increased division within opposition groups, and periodic eruptions of violence due to the deadly combination of expectation and frustration. From 1990 conflict centered on the Rand region where disguised assassins indiscriminately attacked trains. Tension and conflict also increased in Natal. In both areas separation widened between Inkatha and the ANC, complicated by underlying social conditions. With reports of government secret assistance to Inkatha and other revelations coming from the press, mutual suspicion arose between the government and the ANC.

At CODESA, differences were expressed in terms of the type and time of constitutional changes. Negotiations broke down in 1992. Following the massacre of residents in Boipatong (an ANC stronghold), ANC leaders withdrew from the convention, calling for a full-fledged investigation into the sources of conflict and tighter control over the police and army. DeKlerk appointed an investigative commission to address the problem of violence, and the security forces were revealed to be highly involved, thus fueling internal and international pressure for a complete constitutional reordering of South Africa.

The latter half of 1992 was marked by increased tension as the ANC began to warn of mass action. The complexity of the whole process of change was illustrated in an ANC march to the homeland Ciskei, which was fired on by Ciskei forces. The Zulu political leader Mangosuthu Buthelezi added to the strain by threatening to withdraw IFP participation from a unified constitutional system due to a feeling of being shunted aside. The Conservative party and extreme right-wing groups refused to participate in any form of negotiation that involved a loss of white political control and instead called for segregation based on territories within a federated state. The most extreme of these, the Afrikaner Resistance Movement (AWB) led by Eugene Terre'Blanche, threatened to wage war if CODESA decided upon majority rule. The economy meanwhile continued to falter, affected by the worldwide recession of the early 1990s. Policing became less tight, and a wave of crime swept through black and white communities. Attacks against whites became more common, and it appeared to many that the country was on the verge of disintegration. ANC support had decreased to below 50 percent of the black population as compared to the two-thirds majority support it had enjoyed in 1990.[28]

During the political turmoil of the early 1990s, "mavericks" within the ANC movement arose, the most prominent of these being Winnie Mandela. A left-wing space emerged, which she and others filled to exploit the growing sense of frustration over the slow rate of negotiation and the expanding view that the ANC was giving too much away. In 1992 she denounced the idea of power-sharing as a devil's pact between the "elite of the oppressed and the oppressor," a statement that served to arouse bitterness against the ANC leadership among the more militant sections of resistance. In stepping into this arena, Winnie Mandela achieved a startling comeback to South African politics, going on to regain her office as president of the ANC Women's League in December 1993 and successfully establishing a base of support among the squatter camps of areas such as the ravaged East Rand.

In 1993 the major parties began negotiating again on the basis of a transitional government. The differences over the timing of the election had much to do with a struggle between the parties to maintain an advantageous position. But as the country appeared to be slipping into potential chaos, major party leaders soon realized that setting the date of the election was crucial to the transition of power itself. The feeling that time was running out for a peaceful election and positive transition of power was amplified when Chris Hani, leader of Umkhonto we Sizwe and the ANC Youth, was shot by an AWB assassin. Renewed protest, particularly among black youths, erupted all over the country. The murder and the ensuing protest highlighted an important crossroads in the constitutional process, as the government and the ANC attempted to maintain a responsible position between right-wing violence and the alienated black youth of South Africa.

By the end of April 1993 the ANC was demanding that an election date be announced before any further issues were decided. The government agreed. Democratic elections for a Constituent Assembly were to be held in April 1994, and the major parties of South Africa were to share power for a fixed period. Agreement on these aspects of the transition and negotiations for the election process were carried out mainly through Roelf Meyer of the NP and Cyril Ramaphosa of the ANC, who agreed in principle on an elected constituent assembly with defined time limits and regulation of any deadlock that might occur.

An important aspect of the election was that representation was to be proportional rather than based on constituencies, with parties running a list of candidates (200 national candidates, 200 from nine regions, and nine separate lists for each provincial legislature). By this process, voters would be selecting a party as opposed to one particular candidate. The system most favored the ANC and was least advantageous to the small parties. A multi-party rule would be created to select the interim parliament made up of all parties that won at least 3 percent of the vote. The Parliament would elect the president, who would choose a proportional Cabinet from all parties having 5–10 percent of the vote to rule five years under the interim constitution. The Assembly also would write the final constitution based on a two-thirds majority rule formula but limited to those principles decided on by the multi-party negotiations.

This basic agreement changed in response to the political dynamics within South Africa. After a brief flirtation with Buthelezi's party, the NP decided to abandon that potential alliance, and in October 1993 the IFP joined with the governments of Ciskei and Bophuthatswana, and with the right-wing *Afrikaner Volksfront*, to form the Freedom Alliance (FA). Their main source of unity was opposition to the constitutional process. The ANC and the NP maintained the middle ground, however, and the FA began to fall apart as concessions on the part of the negotiators attracted support away from this loose alliance. These concessions included greater provincial power, a double ballot, and a general but not closely defined form of self-determination. The FA disintegrated, and Buthelezi got his party back into the election in the last week of campaigning. Because it also was weakened by political changes in 1994, the NP made further important concessions in the final draft of the agreement: It abandoned its demand of power-sharing as a constitutional principle, it agreed to limit the deputy president's role in cabinet policy to consultation with no veto power, it accepted the supremacy of the central government by conceding to it the power to override provincial action, and it accepted the proposal granting the president authority to appoint the majority of the constitutional court.

From April 26 to 28, 1994, South Africa held its first general election for citizens of all races. Despite threats to boycott the election from the Zulu nation and Inkatha and in the face of preelection violence, South Africans turned out in massive numbers, sometimes walking miles to vote. Foreign observers monitored the election and reported little evidence of fraud or intimidation. The international press covered the election closely. On May 6, 1994, the results were read out. The ANC received a national percentage of 62.6 votes, and Nelson Mandela became president. The percentage meant that under the two-thirds rule of the constitution no one party in the new government could fundamentally change the agreed constitution without the involvement of other parties in the parliament. But the ANC had come out 42 percent ahead of its nearest rival, the NP—a unique election outcome when one considers that in Western democracies governments rarely win competitive elections by such a large margin. Mandela and his party could, with some confidence, claim a mandate from the majority of South Africa as it moved into a post-apartheid era. The large majority also raised expectations that Mandela and the ANC would bring significant, and immediate, social and economic progress.

That the deKlerk government accepted the results of the election and transferred power peacefully boded well for the new South Africa. That some disaffected whites, especially Afrikaners in the countryside, stepped up militia training and warned of an impending Armageddon did not. Balancing the interests of South Africa, while meeting the expectations of the black majority without completely alienating the white, colored, and black political and ethnic minorities, formed the program of the man and the movement that had changed from outlaw status to democratically elected leadership in less than a decade.

NOTES

1. J. B. Peires, "The British and the Cape, 1814–1834," in R. Elphick and H. Giliomee, eds., *The Shaping of South African Society 1652–1840* (Cape Town: Maskew Miller Longman, 1989), pp. 472–518.

2. C. Muller, *Five Hundred Years: A History of South Africa* (Pretoria: Academia, 1975), p. 154.

3. William Beinart, *Twentieth-Century South Africa* (New York: Oxford University Press, 1994), p. 46.

4. Nigel Worden, *The Making of Modern South Africa* (Cambridge, MA: Blackwell, 1994), p. 70.

5. Thomas Pakenham, *The Scramble for Africa* (New York: Avon Books, 1991), pp. xxii–xxiii.

6. M. Swanson, "The Sanitation Syndrome: Bubonic Plague and Urban Native Policy in the Cape Colony, 1900–1909," *Journal of African History* 18 (1977): 387–410.

7. E. Koch, " 'Without Visible Means of Subsistence': Slumyard Culture in Johannesburg 1918–1940," in B. Bozzle, ed., *Town and Countryside in the Transvaal: Capitalist Penetration and Popular Response* (Johannesburg: Ravan, 1983), pp. 151–75.

8. Beinart, *Twentieth-Century South Africa*, pp. 118–19.

9. Union of South Africa, *Report of the Native Economic Commission* (Union Government 22: 1932).

10. D. B. Coplan, *In Township Tonight!: South Africa's Black City Music and Theater* (Johannesburg: Ravan, 1985), pp. 90–112; Koch, " 'Without Visible Means of Subsistence,' " pp. 151–75.

11. William Beinart and C. Bundy, *Hidden Struggles in Rural South Africa: Politics and Popular Movements in the Transkei and Eastern Cape, 1890–1930* (Berkeley: University of California Press, 1987), p. 218; S. Marks and S. Trapido, eds., *The Politics of Race, Class and Nationalism in Twentieth-Century South Africa* (London: Longman, 1987), pp. 209–53.

12. P. Christies and C. Collins, "Bantu Education: Apartheid Ideology and Labor Reproduction," in P. Kallaway, ed., *Apartheid and Education: The Education of Black South Africans* (Johannesburg: Ravan, 1984), p. 173.

13. G. Williams, "Celebrating the Freedom Charter," *Transformation* 6 (1988): 73–86.

14. L. Platzky and C. Walter, *The Surplus People: Forced Removals in South Africa* (Johannesburg: Ravan, 1985), p. 107.

15. Nelson Mandela, *No Easy Walk to Freedom* (New York: Basic Books, 1965), p. xi.

16. Nelson Mandela, *Long Walk to Freedom* (Boston: Little, Brown and Company, 1994), pp. 328–29.

17. S. Buthelezi, "The Emergence of Black Consciousness: An Historical Appraisal," in N. Pityana et al., eds., *Bounds of Possibility: The Legacy of Steve Biko and Black Consciousness* (London: Zed Books, 1991), pp. 111–29; Steve Biko, *I Write What I Like* (London: Heinemann, 1978), p. 51.

18. Biko, *I Write What I Like*, p. 21.

19. Pityana, *Bounds of Possibility*, pp. 100–110.

20. T. Lodge, *Black Politics in South Africa since 1945* (London: Longman, 1983), p. 330.

21. Beinart, *Twentieth-Century South Africa*, p. 221.

22. Ibid., p. 186.

23. John de Gruchy, *The Church Struggle in South Africa* (Grand Rapids, MI: Wm. B. Eerdmans, 1979), pp. 118–19.

24. Leonard Thompson, *A History of South Africa* (New Haven, CT: Yale University Press, 1990), pp. 204–5.

25. J. Hyslop, "School Student Movements and State Education Policy, 1972–87," in W. Cobbett and R. Cohen, eds., *Popular Struggles in South Africa* (London: James Currey, 1988), pp. 183–209.

26. Beinart, *Twentieth-Century South Africa*, p. 233.

27. Ibid., p. 186.

28. Robert Mattes, "The Road to Democracy from 2 February 1990 to 27 April 1994," in Andrew Reynolds, ed., *Election '94: South Africa, the Campaigns, Results and Future Prospects* (New York: St. Martin's Press, 1994), pp. 4–5.

2

Racial Separation

Apartheid was separation by race and separation by location. The bureacracy the system required to maintain both types of separation proved to be large, unwieldy, expensive, and ultimately impractical. Different interpretations of the aims of apartheid, the contradictory nature of its ideology, and the eventual economic strain of supporting such a system caused it to reach a crisis point in the 1980s and to collapse in the 1990s. By its very nature, the politics of separation sowed the seeds of its own destruction. An examination of the nature of separation and the tradition of racial divisions before and during the years of apartheid is crucial to understanding the reasons for its collapse.

THE RACES

Central to the system of apartheid was the division and classification of "race" that developed historically with the clashes and migrations of different groups of people in South Africa. These divisions became closely (and often ludicrously) defined with the setting up of apartheid in the 1950s, and this legal classification represented a social hierarchy that underpinned white dominance in a mixed race society. The four classifications separated whites (or Europeans), coloreds (those who were a mixture of different groups including whites), Asians (Indians), and Bantu (African). As complicated as this initial division seems, such classification becomes even more complex when the divisions within each group are examined. None of the categories of race represents a truly homogeneous and separate group, and each is characterized by a certain amount of separation within itself, either created or encouraged by apartheid.

The Whites

The white category represented those people who had descended from Dutch or English settlers in the Cape Colony or Europeans who had migrated to South Africa later on. The major division within this category was between English-speaking whites and Afrikaners. Although generalization is virtually impossible with regard to any classification or division in South Africa, it is fair to say that history and culture caused a marked difference in outlook and character between English-speaking and Afrikaner whites.

Almost from the beginning of Dutch settlement in South Africa, the Boers developed three sources of strength: a rugged and deep desire for independence, a strict Protestant morality, and a shared feeling of destiny. Such determination dominated clashes with both blacks and the English-speaking whites. The relations between the Boer settlers and the Africans in the nineteenth century had been marked first by interdependence and later by exploitation. The Boer society that emerged from these experiences was patriarchal and often harsh, and in the early twentieth century Boer farms became the seedbed of white reaction and racism. This was partly due to fear. The settlers had acquired their land through conquest and held on to it mainly by force, but the blacks outnumbered the whites and the possibility of native rebellion haunted the Boer mind. Because the farmers represented the majority of the Boers, their attitudes influenced Boer politics. Social Darwinist theory of survival of the fittest masked rural fears, and racism remained at the core of Afrikaner society, although it initially defined itself in opposition to English-speaking whites.

The Afrikaans language, closely connected with Afrikaner nationalism, also expressed racism. Dutch began as the official language of the Cape settlers, but a simplified version derived from experiences in Africa quickly dominated by the eighteenth century. This version, which became Afrikaans, tended to place more emphasis on relations between the master and the slave; for example, "man" was a word used exclusively for whites (a black man was called a *jong*), and blacks in general were called *skepsels*, which means "creatures." Thus, the Afrikaner emphasis on cultural purity was directly linked with racial purity.[1]

Boer defeat in the South African War marked an even more determined, intense, and romantic Afrikaner nationalism that became closely linked to the question of language. The former president of the Orange Free State proclaimed after the war: "The language of the conqueror in the mouth of the conquered is the language of slaves."[2] As part of the drive to maintain Afrikaner identity, the Dutch Reformed Church financed the Christian National School as a rival to the English school, and Afrikaners formed "cultural organizations" such as the notorious Broederbond, a secret society founded in 1918 to promote Afrikaner nationalism and culture. The Broederbond grew in numbers and prestige to exert great influence in South African business and politics. By 1985, 12,000 members made up the organization in over 800 cells all over the country. All the prime ministers of South Africa under apartheid were members; all the heads of Afrikaans universities in 1978; and all the Afrikaner cabinet ministers in 1980.

Afrikaners dominated the initial stages of the setting up of apartheid. As right-wing forces gained control over South African politics, the definition of "the government" narrowed to include only an ethnic group representing about 12 percent of the population. The term "nation" was translated by Afrikaners into a group identity based on race and Afrikaner culture. The Afrikaners' stranglehold on South African politics over the next forty years arguably caused much suffering and social fragmentation. As Afrikaners came to dominate state power in South Africa, their sense of identity and destiny increasingly became more racial than cultural. A study carried out among Afrikaners in 1977 illustrated this shift. Before 1948 most of the Afrikaners' focus was on distinguishing themselves from the English-speakers. After 1948, however, the focus changed to race as apartheid based itself on racial distinction and had to be made legitimate.[3]

Among this racially conscious population were many Afrikaner "dissidents" who broke with their own background and traditions to protest the majority of their peers and the basis of their beliefs and society. Bram Fischer is one of many notable examples. The grandson of the prime minister of the Orange River colony, Fischer moved so far from his roots that he wound up as the lawyer defending and advising Nelson Mandela and his colleagues in the Rivonia trial in 1964. The *Sestigerbewing* ("Sixties Movement") represented another prominent example of Afrikaner dissidence. The movement consisted of a group of Afrikaans writers who, among other things, objected to the racial meaning of "Afrikaner." They argued that an Afrikaner was a person whose mother tongue was Afrikaans—which included colored people. Many of these Afrikaners became dissidents through exposure to other cultures and countries, as well as a crisis of conscience. Often well-educated, they came to denounce their own society after studying the ideas and politics of others.

With the establishment of apartheid, Afrikaners came to identify themselves as a group with the first claim to certain privileges (which now included English-speaking whites). They now aimed to keep their position in
society secure. To this end, the old ideas of purity proved useful. H. F. Verwoerd, prime minister from 1958 to 1966, for example, argued that whites
created everything blacks now inherited, and that blacks should view whites
as protectors against violence, disease, and disruption. In the 1970s, in order to place greater social distance between blacks and whites, the government made an effort to unify English and Afrikaners by emphasizing
loyalty to the party in power. This was often expressed as "patriotism" and
was meant to act partly as a bulwark against the rise of the Black Consciousness movement.

In the 1980s, Afrikaners' self-perception became more defensive. Senior
cabinet members in interviews continually stressed Afrikaner identity. P. W.
Botha later warned Nelson Mandela that Afrikaners were not to be "tram-
pled under."[4] During the height of political and social crisis in South Africa
in the mid-1980s, Afrikaners had come to see power as not merely a means
to uphold their system but as an end in itself to support their identity. This is
why, on the eve of change in South Africa, their demands centered on some
form of autonomy that would exclude other ethnic groups. Feelings of victimization surfaced as Afrikaners demanded that their history be recognized
as legitimate and the fruits of their years of labor be acknowledged. Accommodation with the blacks would, they believed, destroy their society. They
also feared retribution, indirectly admitting that the blacks had paid a higher
price than they in the formation of their society. This is one of the reasons
that during the 1980s many lower-echeleon Afrikaners began withdrawing
their support for the National party to join right-wing conservatives and call
for the creation of a white "homeland."

The English-speaking whites, in contrast to the Afrikaners, have a more
complex history, not least because of their own confusion as to identity and
justification of their place in South African society. By the beginning of the
demise of apartheid, this group constituted about 40 percent of the white
population. The majority lived in urban areas and were well-educated and
involved in commerce or some professional occupation. As a whole, they
enjoyed a secure economic base. Their liberal English tradition caused a
large number of them to claim they supported accommodation with South
Africa's black majority. In the nineteenth century, while the Boer Trekkers
completely supported a frontier-style economy, the British colonists supposedly held broader ideas of a world trading empire. This implied a free
market with a more egalitarian thrust. The two different economic approaches

were sharply illustrated in the prohibition of slavery in the Cape, a policy that struck a major blow to the Trekker economy. But after the turn of the century, the English-speaking whites became increasingly accustomed to a passive role in South African politics, as Afrikaners began to dominate the government. The English-speakers tended to refrain from seizing the initiative, carving out a comfortable space for themselves under Afrikaner rule. Racial separation often suited their own desires.

The politics of the English-speaking whites reflected their general position in South Africa. English nationalism was never as strong as Afrikaner nationalism. The English South African identity was more international than that of the Afrikaners, and under apartheid, a typical English-speaking white was strongly materialistic, individualistic, and not often inclined to join with other whites to demonstrate strength through unity. According to one observer, they preferred to live in "comfortable political suffocation."[5] The shapeless unity of the English in South Africa could not compete politically with the monolithic nationalism of the Afrikaners. Unlike the Afrikaners, the English whites had no created tradition or straightforward ideology. Nor did they have a language with roots in South Africa or share a common fear of and outrage towards Africans, coloreds, and Asians. Many represented a vague unorganized white opposition to Afrikaner politics. When asked abroad about the situation in South Africa, they would often blame the government, the National Party, or the Afrikaners as a whole, casting themselves as victims and espousing a liberalism that was not always convincing given the benefits they enjoyed under apartheid. The liberal tradition of the English-speaking whites did make many of them more amenable to change once that process became apparent in the 1980s and 1990s, and a number of them formed white protest parties, such as the Progressive Federal Party (see Chapter 3).

The Coloreds

The "second class" of South Africans established through colonialism and institutionalized by apartheid was the coloreds. The ancestors of this diverse group of people include indigenous Khoisan people and slaves imported from Madagascar, Indonesia, and tropical Africa. Their place in nineteenth-century South Africa ranged from deprived farm laborers to skilled artisans of the cities, and immense cultural differences existed among them. Their religious beliefs were either Christian or Muslim, and the majority lived in the western regions of the country and had, as a group, little contact with Africans. They did, ironically, share a common history, language, and ancestry with the Afrikaner population, and the idea of including coloreds into the same classification as "bruin Afrikaners" (brown Afrikaners) was sometimes raised but never viewed as realistic by white Afrikaners. Under different circumstances, it is possible that the colored population could have merged with the Afrikaners. Mixing across the color line was by no means unusual, and some merging of many people of mixed descent occurred. The predominant race-consciousness of the Boer population, however, limited this process. Despite the nonracial terminology of the 1853 Constitution, white authorities in the Cape Colony regarded colored people as secondary citizens and treated them as such. In 1857 the Dutch Reformed Church of the Cape Colony authorized separation of colored and white congregations and established a separate subordinate mission church for coloreds. By 1861, colored children were prohibited from attending public schools, and any formal education this group received had to come from the missions.

By the beginning of the twentieth century, Cape vernacular—a type of Dutch and a predecessor to Afrikaans—became the primary language of coloreds on the farms and in the cities. Coloreds moved more rapidly to urban areas, and particularly in Cape Town, less evidence could be found of racial division. Only later in the century, with the movement of more Africans to the areas around Cape Town, would that city become more similar to others in South Africa regarding separation of races. Before the Union of South Africa, no legal discrimination against coloreds existed in the Cape Colony; indeed there was hope for a future of greater equality. Legal discrimination increased, however, after the Union, and expanded to the Cape area. With the series of official regulations and administrative initiatives introduced, competition with whites became difficult for the colored population in both the public and private sectors. These circumstances contributed to the growth of a large colored underclass, mostly poor farmers and laborers, and among this class, high rates of illegitimacy, crime, and alcoholism, as well as an infection of white fears and bias towards Africans, emerged. This latter aspect of the colored population is an important reason why ANC moves toward the coloreds in later years were less successful than with other groups. A history of tension existed between the two groups—a prime example of apartheid's "divide and rule" policy—and during apartheid the National Party connected repression of the African population with the comparatively greater identity and privilege enjoyed by the coloreds. The latter, for example, were encouraged to join the Dutch Reformed Church, and from 1949 Africans found themselves unable to compete with coloreds for blue-collar jobs or live in colored neighborhoods as a result of immigration legislation. Thus, although among the first victims of apartheid in its early years, coloreds were the most likely candidates as political allies of the National Party especially towards the end of apartheid.

The Population Registration Act of 1950 classified groups in South Africa in such a way as to cause tragic confusion among the coloreds. No physical "homeland" existed for this population, and an absolute identity for them as the primary working class of the Cape was difficult to define. Political changes in terms of representation also took their toll on the coloreds. In 1956 the National Party moved them to a separate roll and initially allowed them the right to elect whites to represent them in Parliament (something that had been granted to the Africans in 1936); but in 1960 the NP abolished the parliamentary seats of white representatives of both colored and Africans voters.

The Group Areas Act also greatly affected the coloreds. Over a period of thirty years, the act pushed approximately 600,000 coloreds and Indians out of the cities as Durban and Cape Town were reorganized to fit in with the apartheid system. In District Six, an area next to Cape Town that had boasted a thriving colored community since the early nineteenth century, close to 60,000 people were relocated to the wind-swept Cape Flats, and many of the buildings torn down. The area by the 1970s is described by historian William Beinart as a "a city-center wasteland dotted with a few churches and mosques and fringed by new highways." The mass relocation of populations in general created the townships, which were the source of so much deprivation and frustration. Africans, Indians, and coloreds have all at different times testified to the hardship of living one's entire life in "overcrowded conditions, overcrowded houses, overcrowded pavements, overcrowded streets, overcrowded station platforms, overcrowded trains, unending bus queues, overcrowded buses. Day after day, night after night, that elbowing for room, the impossibility of any respite from pressure."[6]

In the 1960s, the coloreds began to make some headway in breaking through the political barriers created by apartheid. In 1968 the government established a partially elected Colored Person's Representative Council that was to control local administration and services in colored areas. Although somewhat insulting, the colored population did not completely boycott the new council, and the new colored Labor Party decided this might be an opportunity to raise opposition within the system. The party won a decisive victory in a 1975 poll and proceeded to demand full citizenship for the colored population. In 1976 a government commission recommended redesigning the parliamentary system, and a president's council was set up in 1980, which led in 1983 to the approval in a white referendum of a tricameral parliament that would include two new parliaments for coloreds and Indians. It was the first time the Nationalist government had allowed nonwhite participation in politics. But most opposition movements viewed it as inadequate through the very nature of its setup.

Racial division still existed within the tricameral parliament—whites still had the majority, and the Africans were excluded, even though they made up 75 percent of the population. Both the Indians and the coloreds were, on the whole, unimpressed with the arrangement. When the time of election to the new parliament came, only 61 percent of colored adults and 57 percent of Indian adults registered; 30 percent colored and 20 percent Indian voted.[7] It was clear to most that the tricameral constitution was an attempt on the part of the Nationalist government to share power without losing control.

By the late 1980s, many coloreds gained middle levels of employment, along with Africans and Indians, and this may have helped their rise in confidence in challenging the structure of the government. Botha miscalculated in assuming that the coloreds would go along with the sectional advantage they gained over Indians and Africans with the new parliament, and he met strong protest when he stated in the Colored House in 1987, "Let me tell Honorable Members something new: if it were not for the very Afrikaner and the National Party the colored population would not be in the privileged position it is in today."[8] In the same year, after strong denunciation of the participants in the new parliament, Allan Hendrickse, the leader of the party controlling the Colored House, resigned from his cabinet position. In 1988 the Colored and Indian houses blocked the government's attempt to pass legislation that would impose stiff penalties for violations of the Group Areas Act.

The Indians

The development of the segregated system that led to apartheid had a strange and disjointed effect on the relations between those groups who were suppressed by the system, most notably the Indians and the Africans. In some instances mutual feelings against the repressive government and a realization of strength through unity encouraged greater solidarity between the two groups; at other times government actions and policies fueled differences and resentment between the groups of oppressed.

Most South African Indians are descended from indentured workers who were imported for labor on the Natal sugar plantations between 1860 and 1911. These immigrants were mainly Hindu. Another form of Indian immigrant began arriving in the 1870s–1890s. Known as "Passenger Indians"—voluntary immigrants who were British subjects and therefore free to move about the Empire—these latter Indians were mainly Muslim, came from the western part of India, and called themselves Arabs to differentiate themselves from Indian laborers and Africans. They tended to move quickly up the social ladder to become shopkeepers, traders, and merchants. The former indentured servants meanwhile began to set up farms at the beginning of the industrial boom in South Africa, but the government soon passed restrictive laws that forced their migration to cities. These circumstances and ensuing legislation caused the breakdown of the caste system among Indians in South Africa early on and increased Westernization of the Indian population.

The consistent development of increased anti-Indian legislation sparked greater organization and resistance among the more sophisticated Indian immigrants. Much of this legislation focused on trade and free Indian immigration. When most Indians were laborers, not many restrictions were imposed on them. The threat came when they were free and trading. From 1894 the Indian population was disenfranchised, and found itself discriminated against racially and commercially in Natal and the Transvaal. The latter region closed its borders in 1899 to all "colored persons coming from Asia."[9]

The position of the Indians worsened with the union of South Africa in 1910. All immigration was forbidden, and whites in the Transvaal and Natal pressured the government to limit the number of trading licenses and amount of land leased to Indians. The recommendations of the 1919 Commission led eventually to the 1946 law that restricted Indian acquisition of land throughout South Africa. Meanwhile, the nationalist Afrikaner government perpetuated the earlier segregationist policies of the British government. The Population Registration Act defined Indians as one of the four racial groups in South Africa, and the Group Areas Act determined their areas of residence, their public social life, and their jobs. Indians were still at this time denied citizenship, and the government did not formally accept permanent residence of Indians until 1960.

Organized resistance to increased restrictions began in the 1890s and continued thereafter. In 1891 Indian merchants protested discriminatory laws aimed at the rising Indian merchant class. In 1894 the Natal Indian Congress was formed, and the South African Indian Congress established in 1923. Resistance based on class among the Indians reflected the influence of the Indian caste division. Initially, merchant resistance did not seek alliances with other oppressed peoples; instead, Indian merchants sought support from the Indian colonial government, leading in 1927 to the appointment of a local agent to represent Indians in South Africa. Much of this early resistance was organized under the leadership of Mahatma Gandhi and took the form of *satyagraha* (soul force and passive resistance)—a form of protest influenced by Western and Hindu thought, although African peasants also had used this strategy.[10] Even though Gandhi's movement concentrated mainly on Indians—particularly merchants—his political talent provided a general guide for Indian resistance and served as a basis for other resistance movements in South Africa. The young Nelson Mandela became influenced, among other things, by the Gandhian approach of his Indian classmates in the university and in the Youth League, and helped lead a passive resistance campaign in 1946. Passive resistance also inspired the mass action of the ANC in the 1950s.

The Pegging Act of 1943 further weakened the position of Indians in South Africa by declaring transactions in Durban illegal. In 1946 Indians in South Africa were offered the franchise but at a great price: strict restrictions on land ownership and land occupancy in return. The South African Indian Congress refused the offer. It appealed to the Indian government to impose sanctions on South Africa and bring the treatment of Indians to the attention of the United Nations (which the Indian government did, leading to a series of debates in the United Nations that presaged that organization's eventual general condemnation of South Africa's racial policies beginning in 1952). The Indian Congress also began a passive disobedience campaign through the occupation of land that had been forbidden to them.

The 1940s also marked the explosion, and then abatement, of tension between Indians and Zulus in Natal when Zulu radicals went on a rampage and attacked Indian families. Both African and Indian communities reacted with great shock, and leaders sought ways to build greater cooperation between Indians and Africans in their opposition to apartheid. After the 1949 riots, African and Indian leaders formed the Joint Action Committee of the ANC and South African Indian Congress to coordinate resistance efforts. Indian leaders helped support the African passive resistance campaign across the country in the 1950s, and the Action Committee sent a joint memorandum to the United Nations that further contributed to the UN's long series of protests against South Africa's apartheid regime.

In 1961 the South African government gave official recognition of Indians as a permanent part of the population and abandoned the policy of repatriation. This was partly due to pressure from the UN and India, but mainly due to realization of the impracticalities of the policy. The government also granted a token form of representation in 1968 with the formation of the South African Indian Council (SAIC), a statutory body of nominated members that became partly elective in 1974 and almost fully elective in 1982. From the time of its establishment, like the tricameral Parliament, the SAIC generated much debate and division as to whether Indians should participate in it or resist until a more democratic process was established.

After the passing of the Group Areas Act, many Indians were resettled in remote townships in overcrowded areas with inadequate facilities. Those who were unable to be resettled (although disqualified from urban areas) were put into camps called "sub-sub-economic housing." In 1972, 1,000 families were sent to camps in Merebank, living in tin houses, sharing communal taps, and using a pail system for toilets. No real effort was made to resettle them. As it did with other groups in South Africa, the forced removal of Indians as a whole led to the breakup of families, poverty, and disruption of children's lives. Mothers were no longer assisted by members of their extended family, and with no money for uniforms, books, or transportation, most children could not attend school. The lack of general parental supervision and amenities fueled a rise in truancy, gangs, delinquency, and crime among Indian youth. Bitterness and resentment also arose among the Westernized youth of the Indian population, and in 1972 the government imprisoned many youths from the Group Areas for encouraging scholars to boycott Republic Day celebrations. Increased oppression, however, led to a push for greater unity with other opposition groups, most importantly the ANC. The Black Consciousness Movement of the 1970s included Indians as well as coloreds, and when full-fledged African unions began to form in the mid-1970s, many Indians joined them, recognizing the advantages to representation by organizations such as the National Textile Workers in Durban. The mass movement formed in the early 1980s included radical members of the Natal Indian Congress, which refused to take part in the elections to the tricameral Parliament. Although still the smallest minority in the 1970s and 1980s (3 percent of the population), the Indians were the most urbanized.[11]

The Africans

The Africans of South Africa constitute the largest group in the country, making up over 70 percent of the population. Much of the history of South Africa deals in one way or another with this group: their early existence in terms of the different peoples who first populated the area of southern Africa, their conquest and dominance by white Europeans, the rise of the apartheid regime to regulate their place in society, and their opposition throughout to white dominance. The history of the Africans in South Africa, like the whole history of the country, is a complicated one reflecting much diversity and some division. But, especially with regard to the Africans of South Africa in the twentieth century, it is important not to underplay African unity. This point was directly expressed by Paul Maylam in *A History of the African People of South Africa* (1986):

Afrikaner Nationalist ideology today claims there is no African majority in South Africa, but rather a whole set of minorities: more specifically, there are deemed to be some ten or so mutually exclusive, culturally and linguistically heterogeneous African ethnic entities, each with their own separate historical roots. This notion is a hollow sham. The present-day "homelands" have shallow roots in history. The notion is also a denial of historical trends in the twentieth century. It is true that there exists some ethnically-based organizations like Inkatha, and that ruling groups in the "homelands" have tacitly acknowledged ethnic differentiations by participating in the system. However, the vast majority of African organizations and movements in the twentieth century have transcended and openly disavowed narrow ethnic differences. This is true of political movements like the ANC and PAC; it is true of trade unions and community-based movements.[12]

In the nineteenth century no such unity existed to block European conquest, but as the whites initially broke down the divisions between African groups in their drive to extend and maintain control, they inadvertently sowed the seeds of unity among the oppressed. This made their attempts at division in the twentieth century, after the groups had been economically and politically crippled, less successful.

The first human communities in South Africa were ancestors of the Khoisan, known to the white settlers as Bushmen and Hottentots. These early groups contributed much to the ancestry of the colored population and, to a lesser extent, to that of the Bantu-speaking population. They also play some part in the ancestry of many officially classified as white. The Khoisan were made up of the Khoi-Khoi, who were pastoralists, and the San, who were hunter-gatherers. The arrival of the Bantu-speakers, often referred to as mixed farmers, between the tenth and fifteenth centuries brought further interaction between these groups. Elements, therefore, of the Khoisan are evident in present-day Africans, such as the clicking sounds of the Xhosa language. Much of the culture of these early South Africans underpins the clashes with white society in the late nineteenth and twentieth centuries. The mixed farmers had no concept of land ownership because land was seen as belonging to the community, not individuals. They formed very hierarchical societies but also encouraged a strong sense of responsibility to family and to the less fortunate. The general system of control among the African communities carried out through the nineteenth century was based on chiefdoms. Populations under these chiefdoms were not exclusive and included groups descended from different ancestors and often aliens. The chief's powers rested on the support of his councillors and the respect of his people.

The latter was probably the most important measurement of power since in most cases the chief had no regular army. This reciprocal power has been summed up in two sayings of the Basotho: "The chief can do no wrong," and "No people, no chief."[13]

With the arrival of the whites came the clash that led to eventual subjugation of these African populations. Divisions within the combatants—the British government, the British settlers, and the Afrikaners marking one set of divisions and the tensions between the African chiefs, commoners, community residents, and aliens constituting the other—complicated the process. The whites, as noted, however, made more successful use of the divisions among the Africans than the latter did in the nineteenth century; plus the whites had a great technological advantage. But while the whites methodically broke down the political power of the tribes through war, disease, and destruction of their means of subsistence, neither the Africans' numerical strength nor their tradition of community was crippled. They continued to exist in far greater numbers than the whites.

The traditional division of Africans became splintered and confused in the nineteenth century, and the division that emerged in the twentieth century was basically a linguistic one. After the upheaval caused by the rise of the Zulu and European conquest, all Africans south of the Limpopo River were classified by whites as either Nguni or Sotho. The traditional center of Nguni territory was the southeast region between the interior plateau and the Indian Ocean (what became Ciskei and Swaziland). The Nguni people shared a broad linguistic uniformity, with some dialectical differences among tribes or clans. The northern Nguni included the Zulu and Swazi, and the southern included the Xhosa, Mfengu, Mpondo, and the Mpondomise. The Sotho consisted of three groups: the western Sotho, or Tswana; the northern Sotho, which included the Pedi and Lobedu; and the southern Sotho, known as Basotho who came to occupy Lesotho. The Sotho shared linguistic and some cultural similarities and were associated with the interior plateau of South Africa.

European conquest of the Africans in the nineteenth century took different forms with different groups of Africans. The Xhosa, for example, were severely crippled not only by external forces—defeat in war and cattle disease—but also by the great cattle killing of the 1850s. This phenomenon in Xhosa history occurred through the vision of a sixteen-year-old girl who claimed that the Xhosa people would recover to defeat the British, or "rise from the dead," if they killed their cattle and stopped ploughing their land.[14] The Zulu nation, on the other hand, rose to great political power, setting off a major series of wars known as the *Mfecane* or *Difaqane*, meaning time of troubles, which led to offshoot communities in modern Malawi, Zambia, Tanzania, and Swaziland. Their conquest by the British was short and sharp. After the famous battle of Isandhlwana in 1879, the Zulu War was launched, but the nation's power collapsed after defeat in Ulundi in 1879. The tranquil society of the Sotho people who formed the kingdom of Lesotho after the *Mfecane* contrasted markedly with the Zulus' aggression. Reconstruction was based on peace as opposed to war, and their leader Moshoeshoe never formed a standing army. Whatever the form of capitulation, by the end of the nineteenth century, all the Nguni and Sotho had lost their independence except for the Sothos in southwest Africa.

African involvement in the South African War, meanwhile, had caused great suffering. Both sides used the Africans, and both have records of mistreatment throughout the course of the war. Thousands of Africans died during the siege of Mafeking, and over 14,000 Africans died in concentration camps. Those Africans who sided with Britain believed that victory would bring their own advancement, but their hopes were almost immediately dashed by the Treaty of Vereeniging in 1902. The question of extending political rights to blacks was delayed, and the pattern of denial of these rights continued through the signing of the Constitution of 1910.

The decline of the African rural economy, beginning at the turn of the century, paved the way for more systematic control by the whites. White demand for land led to large-scale expropriation of African-occupied territory at the expense of African peasant farmers and drove many Africans to wage labor on white-owned farms. The economy that supported apartheid grew from the dramatic transformation in the production relations of rural South Africa during the first thirty years of the twentieth century. The government intervened to support white commercial farming at the expense of the Africans and stunted their potential economic power. According to Paul Maylam, "The result was to leave thousands of Africans in a state of semi-proletarianism, either as labor tenants on white farms or as migrant laborers maintaining a partial dependence on the increasingly fragile rural subsistence sector."[15] With the creation of the reserves came increased division between white and African farmers; within the reserves came infant mortality, malnutrition, disease, debt, crime, prostitution, and violence.

The number of Africans employed in the mines was, in the meantime, ever-increasing, with the reserves, particularly Transkei, acting as major sources of labor. The circumstances of working in the mines served as a further means of demeaning and controlling the Africans. Most African labor lived in the compounds in the mining industries and was kept under control by "police" who worked for the manager. Under these conditions, the captains of industry suppressed unrest while also arranging Africans on the compounds in such a way as to reinforce tribal divisions, thereby limiting any potential solidarity among the workers. The working conditions were severe, especially in the early part of the century, and the mortality rate was high, with many Africans dying of pneumonia due to lack of heat and generally poor living arrangements.

A general increase of the African population in the towns echoed the growth of African labor in the mines. The demand for African labor in urban areas was not immediately matched, however, by government moves to help provide accommodation for Africans. In the mid-1930s only a few formal municipally controlled townships existed for Africans near major cities. Other townships that arose did so without municipal control, as did urban slum yards. Even with the need for African workers in urban areas, segregation remained in force, and this process of separation of African populations through townships continued to the end of apartheid.

Historians often view the Native Administration Act of 1927 as the beginning of a new process of segregation that involved the promotion of African traditionalism and an emphasis on ethnic and cultural separation. The state broadened its support for the chiefly order in the reserves. Having fought against the African chiefs in the nineteenth century, the government now intended to use them as a means of controlling the African population and distancing itself from African resentment. In moving toward greater recognition of the chiefs' courts in the reserves, state policy hoped to prevent African unity and organized resistance by "retribalizing" African society. This was especially the case in Transkei where a council system was set up, often referred to as the Bunga. In Natal the new policy led to an important development in the push to prevent organized resistance due to increased proletarianization in that area. The power of the Zulu royal family, which the colonists had tried to destroy in the nineteenth century, was now being propped up by the South African government as an instrument of control against the rising African working class. The government was seemingly pursuing the revival of semi-independent chiefs to maintain separation and authority. This process would reach new heights with the creation of the Bantustan system.

This policy found greater and more precise definition during the apartheid years in which "separate development" was based on the theory that South Africa had two populations—a white minority and a black majority—but that the country consisted of a whole system of ethnic minorities. Under this approach, the Africans did not present one unified group; rather, they were made up of ten groups, each possessing its own distinctive culture and traditions. Each group was therefore to be given a "homeland" to develop its culture, politics, and economics. One problem with this approach (among many) was that it ignored the intermingling between African groups, as well as the obvious fact that while Africans were regarded as distinctive groups, the whites were seen as one. Furthermore, the Africans were not truly allowed to develop politically or economically. The South African government's destruction of the freehold townships during the years of apartheid, along with the decline of the African peasant farmers in the poverty-stricken homelands, made the Africans victims of severe economic oppression by denying them access to the means of production. Their chiefs, meanwhile, had limited power, remained subject to the authority of the white government, and were encouraged by the white government to promote their personal power and wealth, which often caused them to slide into decadence and corruption.

During the 1980s, P. W. Botha's regime introduced reforms, repealed legislation, and used language that seemed to indicate a change in the Africans' position in society. At one point, Botha claimed that South Africa had outgrown apartheid and Africans would be included in politics at the national level. But it soon became apparent that a real change for the African population was not in the cards. Education remained completely separate. In 1986 the government still spent seven times more to educate whites than to educate Africans; the same was true for health and welfare.[16] Most of the black population lived at or below poverty level, and Africans were still excluded from owning land that was not within the homelands or townships. Even more serious, the government continued to carry out its policy of resettlement of Africans, using the army and police to destroy squatter camps outside Port Elizabeth and Cape Town. Thousands of people languished in solitary confinement without trial and without the knowledge of families, friends, or lawyers. Furthermore, despite all the government rhetoric, no real sign of inclusion of Africans in politics at the national level seemed forthcoming.

The result of this dual policy of the 1980s, as illustrated in Chapter 1, was the social turmoil caused by bannings, arrests, detentions, treason trials, police torture of detainees, and widespread assassination of antiapartheid leaders within South Africa and in neighboring countries. All these actions were part of a policy to regain control over the African townships. But it failed. This failure, along with the conservative white backlash caused by the cosmetic changes made and along with continued African resistance, led to the disintegration of apartheid and a turning away from its claim to be a viable form of government. Botha and his colleagues had, to a certain degree, trapped themselves in a corner by speaking the language of change while refusing any real inclusion of Africans in their government, especially if it led to an African majority government. Despite earlier hints, Botha announced in 1988, "As far as I'm concerned, I'm not even considering the possibility of black majority government in South Africa."[17]

The history of the rise of a dominant white government in South Africa in the twentieth century is matched by a history of African resistance. This resistance was a response to the changed circumstances of the Africans once they had been subjugated by colonial governments. As it became clear in the beginning of the twentieth century that Africans had no real hope of participating in the South African government and that white control over Africans would be tightened through the maintenance of the reserves and urban segregation, urban Africans especially responded with increased militancy in opposition politics and increased radicalism. This became particularly apparent during the 1930s.

The history of African resistance in the twentieth century is probably best viewed through a study of class divisions rather than different groups of Africans. Although a large majority of Africans remained peasant farmers or urban workers, a middle class arose, which consisted of small-scale entrepreneurs, professionals, or those holding clerical positions. The difference between these Africans and the proletariat and peasants was not necessarily economic—the wages of a clerk may have been little more than that of a mine worker. Rather, the difference often lay with self-identification. Middle-class Africans were usually Christian, believed in the principles of self-help and self-advancement through education and saving money, and sought freehold land as their eventual goal, usually to provide for their heavily dependent extended families. Their possibilities of advancement, however, were severely constricted by the state. In the late nineteenth and early twentieth centuries, the middle class took the initiative among Africans in opposition to their treatment. As the mission-educated African elite, they were more eloquent communicators than their peasant compatriots, and they tended to share a vision of a nonracial "civilized" society in South Africa. Several were lucky enough to receive higher education abroad; many found their way to the United States where they were inspired by the thinking of either Booker T. Washington or W.E.B. Du Bois. Many of the early African churches forming at this time had strong political overtones, and many of the church leaders were also involved in political activity. Organized working-class resistance increased with the rising number of Africans working in the cities. The first African industrial unions, for example, formed in 1927.

Class differences often explained the different forms of opposition. In the early days especially, middle-class opposition went no further than mild political protest, with an emphasis on petitions and delegations, as in the first actions of the ANC. Sometimes it would manifest itself in extensive unified passive resistance—for example, the defiance campaign of the early 1950s. At times the resistance was local—defying resettlement or organizing bus, rent, and consumer boycotts. More radical resistance could often be traced to worker organization and proletarian calls for militant action, which developed steadily with the rise of urban African labor. In the ANC, debate with regard to class arose in the 1960s over whether leadership should be restricted to members of the working class, since the ANC by that time was a mass movement and consisted mainly of members of that class. Mandela criticized this approach as undemocratic and pointed out that the movement would lose some able leaders if this argument was carried through.[18] Popular resistance also burst out, as in the protest of Soweto students in 1976. The most significant aspect of opposition strategy came in the changing official view of the ANC and PAC in the 1960s to one that included an armed struggle.

From early on, there were clear signs of a desire for solidarity in resistance; for example, one of the first newspapers started by the ANC (then the SANNC), *Abantho Batho*, contained several articles written in different Nguni and Sotho languages, as well as English. The idea was to build African unity and attract non-African support. More unity came with the Black Consciousness Movement of the 1970s. In the 1980s, the movement fostered solidarity among Africans, Indians, and coloreds in opposition to the South African government. With the development at this time of greater economic and political strength, many Africans, especially the younger generation, became less submissive.

During the 1980s, black workers stepped up increased action. In 1987 alone, 1,148 strikes broke out. The most serious was the National Union of Mineworkers' strike led by Cyril Ramaphosa, which involved over half of the country's miners in all the mining industries and lasted three weeks. As a result of this strike, mine workers received death and holiday benefits and a 23 percent wage increase. Africans also enjoyed greater power at this time as consumers and entrepreneurs and achieved middle levels of employment in industry; a few even reached management level. They also progressed in the informal sector, for example, dominating the transport industry in the townships. The Africans demonstrated their increased confidence in the late 1980s in the municipal elections held in October 1988, still based on segregation. As a demonstration of their refusal to accept superficial reform, African nationalists boycotted the elections and only 3 percent of the African population voted.[19]

As the period of transition began in the 1990s, and it became clear that Africans would play a major role in the new dispensation, the expectations of the Africans rose. Although Mandela urged patience, many Africans believed that the new government would mean a rapid translation of political freedom into jobs, transfers of land, improved housing, electrical services, roads, and agricultural extension. The new government would have quite a job dealing with these expectations. In 1994, 53 percent of Africans lived below poverty level—as compared to 2 percent of all whites—with millions unemployed, 2.3 million malnourished (including 1 million children), and the homes of 80 percent of all Africans needing electricity. One problem that would exacerbate the situation was that the ANC had been persuaded during the negotiation process to promise that white civil servants would not be fired by the new government and their pensions would be kept safe. The cynical hope of many whites, furthermore, was that while the government would become black, the economy would stay white.[20]

The participation of the African population in the first free elections in South Africa was historic. With the collapse of apartheid, an estimated 17 million Africans were eligible to vote. Their economic conditions would see no immediate dramatic change, however. In 1994 the Africans made up 75 percent of the South African population, but owned about 15 percent of land in South Africa and controlled about 2 percent of the nation's wealth. But the election was still of great symbolic importance to the African population. They would now participate in the decision-making process that had affected their lives for hundreds of years. The first African to vote was Nomaza Paintin, the niece of Nelson Mandela, who cast her vote in New Zealand, which had a twelve hours' difference from South Africa. As Nelson Mandela himself cast the first vote of his life in a national election, he stated, "We have moved from an era of pessimism, division, limited opportunity and turmoil. We are starting a new era of hope, of reconciliation, of nation-building."[21]

NOTES

1. J. S. Marais, *The Cape Coloured People 1652–1937* (London: Longmans, Green, 1939), p. 31.

2. Sheila Patterson, *The Last Trek: A Study of the Boer People and the Afrikaner Nation* (London: Routledge and Kegan, 1957), p. 33.

3. Hermann Giliomee, "The Last Trek? Afrikaners in theTransition of Democracy," *South Africa International* 22 (January 1992): 111–20.

4. *Die Burger* (Johannesburg), November 25, 1991.

5. Lawrence Schlemmer, "English Speaking South Africans Today: Identity and Integration into the Broader National Community," in Andre de Villiers, ed., *English-Speaking South Africa Today* (Cape Town: Oxford University Press, 1976), p. 97.

6. William Beinart, *Twentieth-Century South Africa* (New York: Oxford University Press, 1994), p. 147; Pushpa Hargovan, "Apartheid and the Indian Community in South Africa: Isolation or Cooperation," *Journal of Asian and African Affairs* 1 (December 1989): 155–79.

7. *Race Relations Survey 1984–85* (Johannesburg: The South African Institute of Race Relations), pp. 127–28.

8. *Debates of House of Representatives* (Pretoria, 1987), col. 2286.

9. Hargovan, "Apartheid and the Indian Community," pp. 155–79.

10. Beinart, *Twentieth-Century South Africa*, pp. 90–91.

11. Gwendolen M. Carter, "The Coloured and the Indians," in David Mermelstein, ed., *The Antiapartheid Reader* (New York: Grove Press, 1987), pp. 205–6.

12. Paul Maylam, *A History of the African People of South Africa: From the Early Iron Age to the 1970s* (New York: St. Martin's Press, 1986), p. 223.

13. Leonard Thompson, *A History of South Africa* (New Haven, CT: Yale University Press, 1990), p. 26.

14. See J. B. Peires, *The Dead Will Arise* (Johannesburg: Ravan, 1989).

15. Maylam, *A History of the African People of South Africa*, p. 144; E. Hellmann, ed., *Handbook on Race Relations in South Africa* (London: Oxford University Press, 1949), pp. 172–74.

16. *Race Relations Survey, 1985–86*, p. 417.

17. *The Independent* (London), August 19, 1988.

18. Nelson Mandela, *Long Walk to Freedom* (Boston: Little, Brown and Company, 1994), p. 375.

19. *Race Relations Survey, 1987–88*, pp. 103–5, 667–84.

20. Jeffrey Herbst, "Creating a New South Africa," *Foreign Policy* 94 (Spring 1994): 120–35.

21. "Mandela and ANC Claim Victory in South Africa's First All-Race Elections," *Facts on File* 54 (May 5, 1994): 313–18.

3

The Parties and the Process of Transition

The complexity of South African society and history in the twentieth century is reflected in the development of a myriad of political parties. During the years of apartheid, the ideology of each of these parties reached across the political spectrum from right-wing racist extremism to communism. But each party's political outlook and choice of allies became increasingly flexible in many respects through the course of events of the 1980s and 1990s. While some merged with others, a few found themselves left by the wayside, and several, most importantly the ANC, were considerably strengthened by the overall process of change.

BACKGROUND

The African National Congress (ANC)

From the time of its development in 1912, the ANC represented one of the strongest parties of protest against discrimination in South African society and one of the oldest nationalist organizations in Sub-Saharan Africa. Starting out as a moderate movement taking an evolutionary approach to change, it moved over the years toward a more radical position, increasingly replacing its early petitioning methods with nonviolent protest, then open defiance, followed by underground insurgency, which led to its banning and exile until 1990.

The ANC's defiance campaign of 1952 represented the first mass civil disobedience campaign in South Africa, and during this time the ANC formed the Congress Alliance as part of an attempt to broaden its base of support. In the 1960s, the ANC leadership together with white and Indian communists formed a paramilitary sabotage unit known as Umkhonto we Sizwe (MK) signifying the end of nonviolent protest. MK's purpose was to draw attention to the ANC's opposition to apartheid, and to a certain degree it succeeded. The NP government banned the ANC in 1961.

In the mid-1970s the MK launched a low-key insurgency campaign that involved sabotage and attacks on government installations resulting in a few fatalities. In the 1980s, the sabotage strategy became more sophisticated, and the ANC leadership stepped up the overall campaign. Violent action on the part of MK rose sharply in the 1980s, sparked by spontaneous rebellion in the townships, and the military wing of the ANC gained strong popularity, especially with the youth. It suffered a major setback, however, in 1988 when the peace agreement between South Africa and Namibia led to the breakup of MK military bases in Angola and diminished the possibility of guerrilla warfare on a large scale. The damage already done by MK, however, and the international attention it had drawn to black South Africa could not be ignored or eradicated, and this was a factor in the process of change beginning in the late 1980s.

The structure of leadership in the ANC, especially after the establishment of apartheid, was based on a tightly grouped bureaucracy that rose to the challenges of exile and clandestine activity within South Africa. This leadership, from early on, made clear the open approach of the movement stressed in the Freedom Charter and forming the basis of ANC philosophy: that South Africa was a country that belonged to all who lived in it, regardless of color or race. Despite the radical parties and movements stressing a more exclusive approach that arose with the establishment of apartheid, the ANC maintained its philosophy throughout the years following its banning, the arrest of the MK leadership, and the detaining or exile of much of the ANC during the early 1960s. The party became strongly influenced by communism, with its leadership including committed communists such as Joe Slovo. Similar to the general pattern of African and Third World nations that challenged colonial rule, the ANC, from exile, received the majority of its munitions and training from the Soviet Union and other communist European countries. This communist connection was one of the most worrisome aspects of the ANC to conservative whites in South Africa as well to the National Party government. It was one of the major reasons, along with the ANC policy of conducting an armed struggle, that the Botha regime stalled on negotiations with Nelson Mandela.

Despite President Botha's intransigence and increasingly irascible behavior in the 1980s, he eventually agreed to meet with Mandela secretly in

1989 after the ANC leader sent the president a memorandum repeating the request he had made to H. F. Verwoerd twenty-eight years earlier for a national convention. Mandela already had been secretly meeting with Minister of Justice Kobie Coetzee since 1985, and Coetzee had formed a secret committee to conduct private talks with Mandela. The meeting with Botha was cordial, but it accomplished little, and little would be accomplished in terms of full recognition of the legitimacy of the ANC until the dramatic reversal of policy launched by deKlerk when he replaced Botha as president and leader of the National Party.

The National Party (NP)

The National Party of South Africa emerged out of a series of splits and mergers that date back to pre–World War II. When it came to power in 1948 under the leadership of Daniel F. Malan, it proceeded to absorb the Afrikaner party, and established itself as the majority party in 1953. For many years, it maintained a rigid official doctrine of strong anticommunism and separate development, and it remained the leading party during most of the apartheid period. Though not as extremist as smaller white formations, it stuck consistently to the principle of white supremacy until the 1980s.

In the 1960s, a split emerged in the National Party between the *Verligte* ("enlightened") and the *Verkrampte* ("unenlightened"). The *Verligte* tried to reconcile NP policies with promotion of white immigration, solidarity among all white South Africans, and the pursuit of friendly relations with other countries, including black African states. The *Verkrampte* rejected this approach, promoting instead a specifically Afrikaner nationalism and opposing the inclusion of English-speaking whites. Viewed as ultraconservative, the *Verkrampte* estranged themselves from the NP to form the Reconstituted National Party (HNP) under Dr. Albert Hertzog to compete in the 1970 election. It failed to win any legislative seats and the NP went on to increase its majority in 1974. The NP continued to increase support until the 1981 election when its power was marginally reduced.

When Botha came to power as president in 1983, the National Party government began a process of limited change in South Africa. But Botha apparently remained under the influence of his military-security establishment, which was preoccupied with the perceived threat of communism. Because the National Party attempted to match reform with increased security, it failed to please both the right and the opposition movements. In the election of September 1989, the NP kept the overall majority in the House of Assembly, but its vote dropped to less than one-half (48.6%).[1]

When deKlerk came to power, few suspected the announcement of sweeping reform that marked his inaugural address. DeKlerk began as a party conservative who was not even aware until 1988 that the government was holding secret talks with Mandela. But in 1986 his party had accepted the principle of "a single South Africa," and deKlerk went along with this change. His change of heart in 1990, claim observers, came largely from pragmatic motivation and as part of a general change in the NP itself, especially among the younger members of the party who began to see the continuation of the apartheid system, especially in conjunction with the modern global economy, as unrealistic. DeKlerk also was influenced by trips taken abroad during which he met with British Prime Minister Margaret Thatcher and the leaders of Portugal, Italy, and Mozambique, all of whom emphasized the need for South Africa to change. One major and obvious influence was the disintegration of communism in eastern Europe in the late 1980s. This collapse eased worries in the NP government that the black struggle against apartheid was part of a communist conspiracy directed by the Soviet Union. Thus, when deKlerk made his dramatic announcement of the unconditional release of Mandela and far-reaching reform in February 1990, the reaction was profound. But the signs of his party's move toward power-sharing with the black population had been apparent for some time.

The Pan-Africanist Congress (PAC)

When the Pan-Africanist Congress broke away from the ANC in 1959, it claimed to reject the vague socialism and multiracial approach of the ANC. The underlying sentiment of the former ANC members involved a suspicion of the Indian and white communist activities countenanced by the ANC, but the doctrine of pure African nationalism which the PAC embraced marked the most significant difference between the two parties. Founded by Robert Sobukwe and consisting of many former members of the ANC Youth League, the PAC became strongly anticommunist and viewed the ANC Freedom Charter as a betrayal of African nationalism. For a brief period after the Sharpeville massacre and the banning of both parties, the PAC and ANC made an alliance known as the South African United Front. This alliance collapsed, however, soon after its inception because of ideological and personal conflicts.

Throughout its existence, the PAC had to operate largely in the shadow of the ANC. Unlike the ANC, after its banning the PAC was less successful in organizing outside of South Africa. It established its base in Lusaka, Zambia, and set up offices in New York, London, and Dar es Salaam; but from the time of Sobukwe's death from cancer in 1978, the party suffered from weak leadership, dissension within itself, and assassination. A sizable base of support did stay inside South Africa, and its underground affiliate, the Azanian People's Liberation Army (APLA), carried out intermittent guerrilla attacks, although, again, not on the scale of the ANC's MK. After its unbanning in 1990, the PAC joined the ANC and sixty other groups to form the United Patriotic Front, but broke away soon after and opposed the CODESA talks, claiming that it would settle for nothing less than a democratically elected Constituent Assembly.

The Conservative Party (CP)

When J. B. Vorster's influence with the NP quickly faded with the scandal of the 1970s, a conservative wing in the party continued, led by Dr. Andries Treurnicht. After the NP's parliamentary caucus in the Transvaal expelled Treurnicht over the question of power-sharing with the coloreds and Asians, he organized the Conservative Party of South Africa (CPSA). Throughout the 1980s, after merging with other conservative groups, the CPSA (which became known as the CP) cut into government majorities in by-elections. It played on the reaction to Botha's reforms especially among white bureaucrats whose livelihood depended on administering apartheid, as well as white workers threatened by black competition. The party maintained a platform based firmly on Verwoerdian-style apartheid. Its support came mainly from rural voters but included members of the urban lower middle-class, mainly in the Transvaal, Orange Free State, and Northern Cape. The CP often exploited the political and economic insecurity of white farmers.

As the NP began to lose some ground in elections in the late 1980s, the CP benefited. In 1987 the CP vote rose to 26 percent and the party won twenty-three seats in the House of Assembly, taking the lead in opposition from the liberal Progressive Federal Party. In October 1988 the CP won control of the majority of small towns in the Transvaal and came close to a majority in Pretoria. During the early 1990s the CP rejected CODESA's commitment to an "undivided" South Africa and stressed the right to self-determination with the possibility of a white homeland.[2]

The Progressives

In 1959, after the beleaguered United Party attempted to compete unsuccessfully with the National Party on racism by vetoing the purchase of more land for Africans, its liberal members broke away to form the Progressive Party. Throughout the 1960s, this party espoused reform of apartheid and better treatment for blacks through its one representative in Parliament,

Helen Suzman, who maintained strong criticism of government economic policy, human rights violations, and apartheid itself. Unlike the black opposition movements that sought full equality, freedom, and political rights, the Progressives committed themselves merely to a qualified nonracial franchise, but this was still a challenge to the majority of the white population.

Adopting the name the Progressive Federal Party (PFP), the Progressives continued to gain seats in the 1970s. But by the end of the 1980s they suffered as a result of the swing to the right of many white voters. In April 1989 the PFP merged with two other parties to form the Democratic Party (DP) as a challenge to the conservatives as the official opposition in the House of Assembly. But within a month, one of its founders, Willem deKlerk, left the new party to support the NP and his recently elected brother F. W. deKlerk. This defection represented a severe blow to the DP's chances at the September election as the party had hoped to benefit from the younger deKlerk's appeal to the Afrikaner electorate. Eventually in 1992, five DP legislators joined the ANC to give the latter party representation in what was at that time still an all-white parliament.

The South African Communist Party (SACP)

The South African Communist Party emerged in 1953 after the dissolution in 1952 of the original Communist party of South Africa, which had formed in 1921. Throughout the era of apartheid the SACP worked in close coordination with the ANC, and often any division between the two was indiscernible. The two jointly established MK in the 1960s and strengthened their ties in 1969 at the Morogoro Conference with the adoption of a strategy that approved the struggle for a national democratic revolution. The SACP further fought within the ANC to maintain the basic tenets of the Freedom Charter, which endorsed nationalization of the leading industries (including the banks, mines, and heavy industry), land distribution, and a broad social welfare program. But the ANC's overriding concern was consistent opposition to the apartheid system and the overturning of racial oppression and white rule. This approach stressed the attainment of political democracy over improved living and working standards, the concerns of the SACP.

With its unbanning, the SACP viewed its primary role as that of maintaining the left-wing slant of the ANC, mainly through helping its important ally attain power in the new South African government in return for which the ANC would keep its long-term plan of creating a socialist South Africa. This role, ironically, kept the SACP from asserting its own separate identity as most of its activities seemed to be directly connected with the ANC or the other arm of the tripartite alliance, the Congress of South African Trade Unions (COSATU). This loss of identity became even more acute in 1993 with the assassination of Chris Hani, who had become the party's general secretary in 1991 when Joe Slovo was elected party chairman. Hani was the great hope of the SACP; he had a large popular following and seemed ready to fill the inevitable gap left in the predicted disillusionment with the older ANC leadership after the first multiracial election. The hardworking Charles Nzakula replaced Hani, but he lacked the popularity of his predecessor.

The Azanian People's Organization (AZAPO)

The Azanian People's Organization arose in the 1970s as the political base of the Black Consciousness (BC) movement. When the South African government banned most of the important leaders of BC, former members of the ideological movement and of the Soweto Representative Council formed AZAPO. AZAPO kept a low profile in its early years but established itself as the representative of BC philosophy. The party took a nonviolent approach to opposition politics, but its attitude toward negotiating with a white government was inflexible. AZAPO stuck firmly to the principle that unity among the victims of apartheid was paramount, and any moves towards discussions with the ruling class should only come after achievement of this unity. It objected to the inclusion of homeland leaders in negotiations for a new South African government and rejected the idea of an interim government before the elections, as this would legitimize the NP government. These firmly maintained principles kept AZAPO on the margins of influence during the years leading up to the 1994 elections.

The United Democratic Front (UDF)

The United Democratic Front, established in 1983, became the broadest base of political movements in the 1980s, temporarily filling the ideological gap left by the banned ANC. Although the UDF came late to the resistance movement, it possessed deep philosophical origins. The UDF attracted many different groups of people, such as those who supported the ANC but were uncomfortable with the latter party's exile status and its open support of violence, and those who were unhappy with the BC's radical transformation after its banning. Archie Gumede, Albertina Sisulu, and Oscar Mpetha became joint presidents of the new movement with Nelson Mandela, Walter Sisulu, Helen Joseph, Govan Mbeki, and Dennis Goldburg, its declared founders.

The strategy of the UDF was organizing, mobilizing, and educating South Africans to create unity within its support and to act as a representative of its followers' opinions and desires. The UDF based its platform on the Freedom Charter but officially separated itself from the ANC, although there were links with ANC members. Ideological differences with the ANC mainly involved the use of violence, and many of the UDF white supporters maintained a distance from the ANC, feeling uncomfortable with an open connnection. The link, however, was made clear when the UDF disbanded in 1990 with the unbanning of the ANC and other organizations, its role as their substitute being no longer necessary.

The Inkatha Freedom Party (IFP)

The Zulu cultural organization known as Inkatha dates back to 1928, but the organization itself played a fairly low-key role in politics the first half of the century. Its major revival came in 1974 through the dynamic leader Mangosuthu Buthelezi who used Inkatha to avoid legal repression of political activity. Its 1975 constitution defined it as a "national cultural movement" that aimed at abolishing "all forms of discrimination and separation." Its stated objective was to cause change in an "orderly and controllable fashion which will lead to a liberated South Africa which is governable." By 1984 Inkatha boasted approximately 750,000 members, which made it the largest black organization in South Africa's history. Marked by a military-style leadership and discipline that echoed the organization's heritage, Inkatha claimed to be open to all black people, but its membership remained basically Zulu.[3]

Relations between Inkatha and the ANC were cordial to begin with, but by 1979 Inkatha's rejection of violence and Buthelezi's stand against foreign disinvestment and other sanctions caused the friendship to sour. Personal conflict and student clashes in the 1980s caused further distancing between the two. The NP and white conservative groups increasingly became Inkatha's strongest allies during the 1980s, and this helps to account for Buthelezi's bitterness over the NP's perceived "dumping" of Inkatha once it unbanned the ANC in 1990, recognizing the latter as the more powerful black political movement.

Although it built its reputation on remaining a cultural movement, in 1990 Inkatha voted at a general conference to transform itself "from a liberation movement into a political party," which it claimed would be open to all races. Thus, Inkatha became the Inkatha Freedom Party (IFP), but to most observers it remained a means of expressing Zulu interests in KwaZulu. It stayed bitterly opposed to the ANC until 1994.[4]

The *Afrikaner Weerstandsbeweging* (AWB)

The paramilitary organization, the *Afrikaner Weerstandbeweging* (Afrikaner Resistance Movement) was formed in 1973 with the People's State Party operating as its political wing. Defiantly right wing and racist, and using symbols similar to swastikas, it became the most visible of the Afrikaner armed factions against majority rule. It broke up government meetings and made preparations for a revolutionary war against all black factions and the government, as the latter began adopting more reforms in the 1980s. The compelling leader of the AWB, Eugene Terre Blanche, became almost a cult hero with his emotional oratory and appeal to the *Afrikanervolk*, and helped to transform his movement from a fanatical fringe group to a party enjoying substantial support of over 150,000 people and a possible 500,000 more silent sympathizers.[5]

In June 1993, armed members of the AWB invaded the Johannesburg building where talks were being held for the 1994 election, and met with no resistance from the on-duty police. In October 1993 the group was convicted and fined for electoral violence; and in November 1993 Terre Blanche called on whites to arm themselves for civil war. While the speeches, symbols, and sporadic action of the AWB caused considerable concern among antiapartheid groups and the South African government, the degree to which it represented a serious military threat often invited skepticism, and the force of this movement diminished with the approach of the 1994 elections, the collapse of the Freedom Alliance which it had joined, and its failure to preserve the government of Bophuthatswana.

THE PARTIES AND NEGOTIATION, 1990–1994

During the 1980s when Botha was stalling at key moments on the process of reform, white power groups and the ANC expanded contacts with each other. For example, the National Intelligence Service, which was more reformist than the Military Intelligence Department, held several meetings with exiled ANC leaders, as did important members of the powerful Afrikaner Broederbond. During the process of his release, Nelson Mandela maintained that the whites would have to accept majority rule. He made it clear, however, that he was open to the reconciliation of black majority rule and white concerns over this demand.

Many sections of South Africa greeted the unbanning of political parties such as the ANC and PAC in February 1990 with exuberance. But the legacies of apartheid remained, not least that of political intolerance and the entrenched South African belief that blacks and whites could not live together.

Apartheid governments had crushed opposition and discouraged diversity. These legacies often encouraged rigidity and extremism among the parties competing for support and recognition in the post-apartheid system, not to mention confusion.

Although Mandela was released in February 1990, it took until 1991 for negotiations for a new constitution to begin. The ANC and PAC needed to bring their exiled headquarters back to South Africa and make a dramatic re-adjustment to a country that many of their members had not seen for decades. Released prisoners had to join with exiles to form political movements and prepare to negotiate with the NP government. This meant an accelerated mental change from underground revolutionaries to legal party members involved in politics. And things were moving quickly. On June 21, 1990, deKlerk announced that he was ready to negotiate a new constitution to eliminate all aspects of apartheid. On August 7, 1990, Mandela announced that the ANC was suspending its thirty-year armed struggle. In October of that year, deKlerk asked the NP to open rolls to all races. In January 1991 the government and the ANC agreed to convene an all-party conference on the drafting of a new constitution. Moderates in the liberation movement, meanwhile, already had been concentrating on how to reach a compromise on power-sharing versus majority rule. The movement toward a solution eventually came from SACP chairman Joe Slovo, who suggested a "sunset clause" that would provide for compulsory power-sharing for a certain number of years and then fade out. On January 29, Mandela and Buthelezi met for the first time in thirty years. Within days, however, renewed fighting erupted among their supporters.

While black parties struggled with their reemergence as legitimate participants in the political process, deKlerk already was working on his strategy for developing a constitution based on power-sharing as opposed to majority rule. He wanted to build an alliance with Buthelezi, other black political organizations, and coloreds and Indians in order to challenge the potential power of the ANC. DeKlerk preferred negotiation at a convention including all political parties rather than an elected constituent assembly. ANC objections, however, led to the compromise, which emerged as the Convention for a Democratic South Africa (CODESA).

When about 240 representatives from all ends of the political spectrum met at the World Trade Fair outside Johannesburg to begin CODESA, conspicuously absent were AZAPO, the CP, and the AWB. Participants worried that those who opted out might subvert the negotiations and might lessen the legitimacy of the agreements made. But through self-exclusion, the parties created more problems for themselves than for the process of settlement.

CODESA, on the other hand, enjoyed "sufficient consensus" to forge a legitimate settlement. The participants represented a clear majority of whites and the two largest representatives of blacks, the ANC and IFP.

As negotiations began, clear differences began to emerge between the ANC and the NP government. The ANC favored a short term for the interim government, which would prepare the path for an election on the basis of one person, one vote for a constituent assembly for South Africa; it envisioned a time length of eighteen to twenty months for that process. DeKlerk's government, on the other hand, favored a longer period for the interim government: five to ten years of power-sharing with the ANC. The approach of both was based on election strategy. The NP wanted to extend the period of interim government in order to lessen the force and popularity of the ANC as a resistance movement. The ANC wanted to maintain its stamina. General disagreement also arose over the nature of the presidency—the ANC favoring a strong executive and deKlerk favoring a collective presidency of the major parties—and the balance of power between central and regional governments, and between the two legislative houses. Furthermore, deKlerk wanted to hold a white referendum to approve the constitutional changes. The ANC was strongly against any "racial referenda" that would give white voters veto power over reform. Right-wing groups, the PAC, and AZAPO joined the ANC in criticism of the white referendum, albeit for different reasons. The latter two parties demanded the affirmation of a new basic law by a broad-based consituent assembly. The right wing wanted no white affirmation of the end of white rule. Despite these objections, deKlerk held the white referendum in March 1992, and he and his party received an overwhelming show of support for change, thus dashing ultraconservative hopes of preventing the collapse of white rule. But a clash of proposals between the NP and ANC emerged two weeks after the referendum, leading to a deadlock.

The ANC scornfully denounced NP proposals, especially those concerning transitional councils that would only have advisory powers. The NP in turn denounced the ANC's "winner take all" approach, which was largely based on the Namibian model. The deadlock led to the ANC's decision to launch its campaign of mass action to challenge the immobility of the NP government. The ongoing violence throughout the negotiations also raised the tension that led to the ANC walkout. Mandela compared the NP government to Nazi Germany, and the deKlerk administration charged Mandela with deliberate polemics to mask the ANC leadership's inability to restrain its mass support.[6] The impasse, however, was not irredeemable. Looking at the situation practically, the ANC could not conceivably overthrow the NP government, and the government could not conceivably govern without the inclusion of the ANC.

The culmination of the violence in the Boipatong massacre of June 17, 1992, influenced the ANC's breaking off talks with the government, but the Bisho massacre of September 7, 1992—in which Ciskei police opened fire on ANC marchers—brought the two sides back to the negotiating table. The two parties drew up a "Record of Understanding" that revived the constitutional talks, which formally resumed in March 1993. The new set of negotiations involved twenty-six parties, including the PAC and SACP. The participants made major breakthroughs in the negotiation process in May and June 1993 when they agreed upon nonracial elections for a five-year transitional government to be held on April 27, 1994.

The involvement of the PAC in CODESA II came as a result of preparations the party had been making since the end of 1992 to become a part of the negotiations. The previous deadlock between the ANC and the NP, meanwhile, had provided an opportunity for the PAC to come back into the negotiation process and increase its importance. The CP and other conservative groups also joined the second set of talks because of their fear of political irrelevancy. The new talks further involved the Zulu King Zwelethini, whose presence Buthelezi demanded throughout the 1992 talks. CODESA II therefore represented overall a wider embrace of the political spectrum with only the self-exclusion of the AWB and AZAPO. The latter party, however, had decided in principle to participate and was merely waiting for a respectable opportunity to join. But this atmosphere of greater conciliation and compromise would again be shaken by challenges.

The ANC and the NP government, meanwhile, made a bilateral agreement that encompassed a final constitution for a nonracial and democratic South Africa drawn up by a popularly elected constituent assembly of 400 members. The constituent assembly would serve a dual function as a constitution-making body and a transitional government. The transitional government was to last five years, and the parties represented in it would be proportionate to their strength in the constituent assembly. Some viewed the agreement as a sign of great hope, but radicals in the ANC thought it was a risky compromise. Winnie Mandela described it as "a shortcut route to Parliament by a handful of individuals." Others in the NP government saw the agreement as appeasement of the ANC and a betrayal of the IFP. Two de-Klerk officials, Jurie Mentz and Hennie Bekker, defected to the IFP after the signing of the agreement, and parties on the outside accused the NP and ANC of collusion.[7]

The division that emerged in the second round of talks differed significantly from the first. The ANC, NP, and PAC represented one side, which supported a new constitution drafted by an elected constitution-making body for the sake of legitimacy. Buthelezi's IFP led the other side, which claimed that an elected body would result in the majority party dominating the process and building up its own strength; instead, the IFP insisted, the new constitution should be drafted by a multiparty conference made up of constitutional experts. All the parties involved in CODESA II favored regionalism (except the PAC), but the ANC envisaged a system in which the balance of power rested ultimately with a central government. The other parties, not surprisingly, supported a division of power more favorable to regions with local governments holding certain inviolable powers.

CODESA II also introduced two provisions that challenged the strength and concerns of the IFP: the fencing off of hostels that had become centers of violence in Witwatersrand, and the ban on the carrying of "cultural weapons" by Zulu demonstrators. Buthelezi angrily denounced these two provisions as well as the Record of Understanding altogether, claiming that the negotiators were ignoring the IFP on issues that concerned its members. Many of South Africa's 220 hostels were controlled by the IFP, which had captured them in an unofficial war with ANC supporters. To the ANC, these hostels were IFP garrisons that formed bases of attacks on the residents of black townships and assisted the IFP in setting up areas under its control and creating chaos. The ANC's final aim was to dismantle these hostels. But the IFP claimed that the hostels gave poor rural people accommodation and wanted them upgraded rather than destroyed. To the IFP, the hostels served as garrisons against attacks on Zulus by ANC supporters. Buthelezi claimed on South African television that Mandela and deKlerk had no right to interfere with the hostels because neither relied on the hostels for support. He accused deKlerk of appeasing the ANC regarding the hostels and of ignoring the ANC's refusal to dismantle its underground army.[8]

Feeling that the major parties of CODESA were increasingly pushing his party to one side, Buthelezi walked out of the talks in July, accusing the ANC of being dominated by the Xhosa and of carrying out a policy of "ethnic cleansing." He further criticized all the negotiators for ignoring a "nation," and the IFP publicly protested the concept of "sufficient consensus." The Record of Understanding was not necessarily the primary catalyst for Buthelezi's recalcitrance. A week before the agreement, Buthelezi, in traditional Zulu dress, had addressed three mass rallies and warned his Zulu audience that they were under threat from their enemies whose aim was to wipe KwaZulu "off the face of the earth."[9]

The bilateral agreement between the ANC and NP represented the end of hopes among other factions for a multiracial alliance between the NP, CP, and IFP occupying a central position and posing a strong challenge to the ANC. Not soon after the deal was made public, the former chief of the South African Defense Force, General Constand Viljoen, brought together the fractured elements of the right-wing Afrikaners and disillusioned NP members to form the *Afrikaner Volksfront*, or Afrikaner People's Front (AVF). The new movement introduced an aura of respectability and legitimacy to the vast range of right-wing groups in South Africa, shading the images of thuggery and racism connected with groups such as the AWB.

In October 1993 the AVF joined with the CP, IFP, and homeland leaders of Ciskei, KwaZulu, and Bophuthatswana to form the Freedom Alliance, and publicized their demands for a federal system of government. Buthelezi and Viljoen called for the securing of the boundaries and powers of federal states that would include an Afrikaner *volkstaat* and a KwaZulu state before an election. It seemed that Buthelezi had increasingly taken on the role of "spoiler" of negotiations. He threatened unilateral action in establishing the KwaZulu state and continued to attack the ANC. The IFP leader also appeared to be hinting at civil war: "As a leader it is my prerogative to warn people about the dangers. . . . The clouds are gathering and there is a storm brewing. I'm not saying I'm brewing it." The IFP further exploited discontent among NP members and recruited them to its party. Seven cabinet ministers were apparently unhappy over the Record of Understanding, which they viewed as a miscalculation and abandonment of the IFP.[10]

The forces of the AVF and IFP were not sufficient to force a settlement, but they did represent potential damage. The AVF had links with deKlerk's security forces, especially the part-time commando units; and the IFP was used to wooing right-wing white factions. Right-wing U.S. constitutional experts also advised the IFP, while some private security companies (including ex-special forces soldiers and disillusioned members of the South African police and South African defense force) began moving their offices to KwaZulu, where the government exercised less control over their actions. To the pragmatists of the right-wing factions, the blacks now represented less of a threat than the communism connected with the ANC.

DeKlerk and the ANC took the matter of the IFP and AVF's Freedom Alliance very seriously. DeKlerk entered into negotiations with Buthelezi, whereas the ANC already had begun talks with the AVF. The purpose of the AVF/ANC talks was to agree upon a "strategic alternative" to separate Afrikaner states, and they involved the assumption that the AVF would take part in the elections and a proposal to use the AVF vote to elect an *Afrikaner Raad*

(Council) to represent Afrikaner national interests in establishing an Afrikaner state. The ANC made concessions that moved the proposed system closer to federalism.[11]

The AVF leaders started out agreeing to the proposal, but rank-and-file nationalists responded angrily. Viljoen was jeered at a rally and labeled a "coward" and a "traitor." Right-wing hard-liners such as Ferdi Hartzenberg, who assumed leadership of the Conservatives after the death of Andries Treurnicht, and Terre'Blanche attacked any compromise with the ANC, and the talks deteriorated. In September 1993, the AVF called off the negotiations, ostensibly because it felt that deKlerk and Mandela did not support a separate Afrikaner state. The real reason was probably pressure from the right.

On April 8, 1994, deKlerk and Mandela held a summit meeting with Zwelethini and Buthelezi that ended in a deadlock. Mandela tried to sway the Zulu king from his dependence on Buthelezi by offering him a guarantee of special status of the Zulu monarchy after the election. The offer was not immediately successful, but Zwelethini seemed sympathetic to the idea. A foreign mediation team led by former U.S. Secretary of State Henry Kissinger and former British Foreign Minister Lord Carrington also tried to effect a compromise, but the team left South Africa fairly soon after its arrival because of the inflexible postion of Buthelezi. With all these divisions and tensions building up around the IFP in the months before the election, the politics of KwaZulu/Natal disproportionately affected the process of transition to a post-apartheid system. The greatest challenge to negotiations was the forces of the IFP, Zwelethini, the Kwazulu government led by Buthelezi, and the Freedom Alliance. An underlying factor in the importance of this area centered on ANC/IFP competition for African votes.

In the final days before the election, neither the AWB nor the CP participated. The CP believed the NP government was selling out to the ANC and SACP. AZAPO, too, stayed away because its leaders felt the ANC was making compromises that would lead to trickery and manipulation by the NP and failure to achieve "true liberation." The PAC was in a complicated position. It had started out as a participant in the preliminary meetings over procedure, but through pressure from its rank-and-file members it had suspended its involvement. Eventually, however, the PAC decided to participate, fearing the risk of being sidelined.

Buthelezi remained aloof, but the IFP door was kept open. Other elements of the Freedom Alliance—the AVF and homeland leaders—splintered bitterly after the failed right-wing defense of the Mangope leadership in Bophuthatswana collapsed (discussed later). In March, Viljoen launched another party to revive the beleaguered efforts of the FA, its stated objective being a confederated South Africa based on the "inalienable and non-negotiable" right to self-determination for Afrikaners and all other groups. It came in fourth in the April elections, winning 2.2 percent of the vote and welcomed Mandela's proposal in June 1995 of a consultative referendum to be held to find out the Afrikaners' view on a separate state.

In the last week before the elections, Buthelezi called off the IFP boycott and allowed the inclusion of his party on the ballot for both the national assembly and provincial legislators. With his demands unfulfilled, his position in the political arena increasingly isolated, and IFP popular support dwindling, Buthelezi had found himself "staring into the abyss of political irrelevance." Under pressure from Inkatha moderates as well as Zwelethini, the IFP leader decided at the last minute to participate. He therefore signed an agreement with deKlerk and Mandela that guaranteed the ceremonial status of the Zulu king and promised that foreign mediators would examine Inkatha's claims to more autonomy in the Zulu area. The agreement strengthened legitimate consensus for the elections and the new South African government.[12]

CAMPAIGNING: THE NP AND ANC

While struggling with negotiations to dismantle the apartheid system, the two strongest parties, the ANC and NP, also had to cope with the more strategic concern of winning support in the eventual elections. Both had to reexamine traditional party ideology and traditional support. Whereas the ANC eventually maintained its widespread appeal, the NP struggled but made major gains in certain areas, winning a surprising victory in the western Cape. The first challenge met by the NP was a reassessment of party strategy by its younger members, concerned as much over their own careers as the future of the party. They "did not want the albatross of apartheid around their necks."[13] To them, the strategy of alliance with the IFP or other such groups to fight the ANC seemed increasingly senseless. Thus arose the division between those supporting Buthelezi and those wanting closer ties with the ANC.

Just after the March 17, 1992, referendum, the NP began campaigning aggressively among the colored, Indian, and African populations, claiming 54 percent support from the coloreds and 52 percent from the Indians (as compared to 7 percent and 8 percent of these populations, respectively, supporting the ANC). But only 5 percent of the Africans supported the NP as compared to 67 percent supporting the ANC.[14] White confidence in deKlerk dropped in the opinion polls from 60 percent to 40 percent between April and December 1992, and by 1993 his estimated overall support was down to 12 percent. Upper-level officers in the South African Defense Force were unhappy, mainly over the downgrading of their institution, the cuts in defense spending, and the reduction of military service from two years to one. Many of those who had fought in Angola and Namibia felt betrayed by the politicians. There was anger and resentment in the party ranks directed toward many of the main (often younger) negotiators such as Roelf Meyer, Minister of Constitutional Affairs, and Leon Wessels, Minister of Manpower. These party tensions seemed to be one of the reasons deKlerk began publicly showing greater interest in federalism and opened talks with the IFP.[15]

The NP enjoyed its biggest success in the Western Cape, mainly due to the support of the Cape coloreds. The coloreds in that area especially feared the Africans, more particularly since the elimination of the Western Cape's status of "Colored Labor Preference Area," with rigid controls over African labor, and the lifting of influx control. The NP took note of this fear and resorted to scare tactics to win the vote of the Cape coloreds. An "Adult Education" program covertly launched by military-intelligence funding operated through youth, women's, and church organizations to turn coloreds against the ANC and its communist allies. When the ANC and DP called for certain prisoners to be released to vote, the Cape Town NP rushed out a campaign ad with the photo of a serial sex killer of township boys, asking, "Can you imagine the Cape Strangler having the vote? The ANC and DP can." The man in the picture had African features, although the suspect arrested just before the election turned out to be colored. The Cape NP meanwhile transformed the image of deKlerk from apartheid leader to symbol of security and free enterprise.[16]

In 1992 the ANC enjoyed 70 percent of African support, but only 50 percent overall support including whites, coloreds, and Indians. The ANC also had to deal with the NP's stressing communism in the ANC. In 1992 a debate arose within the ANC over its goal to nationalize banks, mines, and industries as part of its commitment made in the Freedom Charter of 1955. Mandela acknowledged a parting of the ways with the SACP once apartheid was formally ended. Another problem for the ANC was that the whites had the benefit of experience in campaigning for the elections; they knew how to influence the media and how to get out the vote. The key to the ANC's success would be in getting the rural vote—hence, the need for greater organization. All the black parties faced the challenge of how to prepare a population that had never participated in a national election before. To combat this problem, the Washington-based Mandela Freedom Fund, private

South African businesses, and Scandinavian money set up the Matla Trust (Sesotho for "empowerment"). The Trust encouraged political tolerance between supporters of different political organizations, and provided education on democracy, voting, and the acceptance of the verdict of the elections. Other civic groups such as the women's antiapartheid group Black Sash and the YWCA also educated voters, and formed the Independent Forum for Electoral Education. These nonpartisan efforts worked to the advantage of the ANC nationwide, but the party made mistakes in the Western Cape that benefited the NP. For one thing, it took colored opinion for granted. The ANC also misjudged the fears of the coloreds with regard to African encroachment and communism, and failed to make a major effort in the Western Cape to counter NP propaganda.

Like the colored population, much of support from the Indians for the ANC came from the middle class, whereas Indian workers often felt more threatened by an African majority than what might emerge from the new NP. Major figures in the Indian community, prominent in cultural, religious, professional, and sports organizations, stood publicly in full support of the ANC, but they were unable to sway a vast majority of Indians. Though much of the Indian population was opposed to white domination, this did not lead naturally to complete support for a nonracial democracy. The NP encouraged the fears of the Indians, a task made easier by tension that arose over African occupation of houses allocated to Indians, rising crime and violence, and the hoarding of food in trepidation of the outcome of the election. The tradition of antipathy between the Indians and Africans in Natal also contributed to the conservatism of Indian voters, and support for deKlerk over Mandela among Indians was consistently established by surveys taken before the elections. Years of manipulating division by the apartheid government, which had scarred both the colored and Indian populations, worked to the benefit of the NP.[17]

THE PRESSURE OF VIOLENCE

The tensions built up by the system of apartheid left a legacy of violence that those intent on creating a new state had to face. Violence had contributed in many ways to the decision to abandon apartheid, and now violence dogged the parties involved in the negotiation process that led to the elections of 1994. A youth culture arose in the townships that formed gangs out of frustration and fear, and with no direct means of expressing its anger. The ANC leadership tried to keep a check on those youths who interpreted politics in terms of violence, but it was hampered by division within the party itself. Some blamed Winnie Mandela for this division. By 1992 she was estranged from the leadership of the ANC due to her controversial actions and outspokenness. But she continued to receive considerable support among the militant youth and some MK members who allegedly set up an underground army, and she maintained a high profile in the townships, visiting war-torn areas and building up her popularity. This was in direct contrast to the increasing distance of the ANC leadership from daily struggles in urban areas. Thus, in the spring and summer of 1992, the ANC faced the problems of an army of frustrated youths who ignored the calls of discipline from party leadership, a conflict between returning exiles and local leaders, dissension with ANC-led community based "defense units" that were taken over by criminal elements, and the continued popularity of Winnie Mandela. The hostility between the ANC and Inkatha provided the primary fuel for violence in the townships, however. In 1992 the IFP enjoyed between 1 and 3 percent of black support but was able to raise its status as a political party through violence.[18]

Although both the ANC and IFP signed the National Peace Accord, the violence continued. In KwaZulu, intense political repression reigned. KwaZulu government officials had to be members of the IFP, and the ANC could not openly campaign in this region. The KwaZulu police force became little more than the private army of the IFP. Durban struggled under the influx of refugees fleeing from KwaZulu, and IFP warlords, who acquired power through the backing of the police, increased in numbers. In early January 1994 Cyril Ramaphosa and Joe Slovo visited the East Rand to bring attention to the violence near Mazibuko hostel. The visit backfired, however, when the ANC representatives found themselves the target of gunfire from the hostel.

In March, deKlerk and the Transitional Executive Council (created in September 1993) declared a state of emergency in KwaZulu/Natal, sent troop reinforcements, and gave security forces more power. The death toll continued to rise, however, and the tension spread to Johannesburg. Zulu royalists led a march through the city that sparked shooting in the streets. Over fifty deaths resulted, mainly Zulus, including eight shot dead outside ANC headquarters. The two sides blamed each other, with the IFP calling the incident a massacre. Violence and tension between the ANC and IFP continued until Buthelezi decided to rejoin negotations and allow the IFP to take part in the elections. While widespread conflict died down considerably, the fear of violence still overshadowed the election process.

The role of the NP government in the outbreaks of violence throughout the process of negotiation was cloudy and controversial. From early on in the process, the deKlerk administration was caught up in "Inkathagate" and the revelations of SADF involvement in providing military training to the IFP. Many viewed the pattern of violence in relation to political advances and setbacks of the NP as suspect. Observers pointed out that the violence in Natal and the Transvaal escalated with each dramatic political event such as the National Peace Accord of September 1991 and the white referendum of March 1992. When deKlerk began his antisanction tours, however, the level of violence dropped significantly, a circumstance noted by both the Community Agency for Social Enquiry (CASE) and the Human Rights Commission (HRC), both of whom closely monitored the violence in South Africa. Both agencies argued that the violence in Natal and Transvaal acted to the advantage of the NP government and the IFP and would erupt at times most detrimental to the ANC and its allies. But, as previously noted, many members of the NP had doubts over deKlerk's strategy of building an anti-ANC alliance, and the wider effects of the violence and implications of government involvement were that they harmed the image of the NP and the national economy. Of further concern to the NP government was the contrast between itself and the ANC in confronting the violence of the past. Though the ANC Commissions Report admitted frankly to torture and brutality in the detainee camps of its underground operations during the time of apartheid, deKlerk maintained ignorance of many of the past violent acts of the government despite Inkathagate and revelations concerning the secret military "special operations" unit operating since 1985 and known as the Civil Cooperation Bureau (CCB).[19]

The negotiating parties also had to contend with violence from the right and its threats of sabotage and armed resistance. Many of these threats were mere grandstanding, but they were not empty. The right-wing extremists received significant support in the armed forces, ranging between 80 and 90 percent in the South African Police Force and between 70 and 80 percent in the South African Defense Force. Throughout CODESA the AWB openly boasted that it would physically crush any "takeover" by the ANC, and right-wing extremists called on whites to take up arms to resist threats to their "homeland."[20]

Terrorist attacks by the right wing grew significantly during the 1990s, with groups focusing on the bombing of public buildings and random shooting of blacks. In April 1993, right-wing extremists also assassinated Chris Hani, whom many had viewed as a successor to Mandela. The right wing gained further attention by storming the World Trade Center in Johannesburg during constitutional talks in June 1993. The culmination of right-wing violence came with the attempt to protect the Bophuthatswana government from rising opposition and the bombing attacks launched on the eve of the elections in 1994. In March, the AWB and other Afrikaner paramilitary groups invaded Bophuthatswana to protect Chief Lucas Mangope, an ally in the Freedom Alliance, from ANC-led protests against his decision to boycott the elections. After exchanges of fire between the right-wing forces and the Bophuthatswana police force, the NP government sent in the SADF, which quickly restored order. On March 12 a delegation from the South African government formally informed Mangope that he had been deposed. The embarrassing retreat of the right-wing commandos from Bophuthatswana caused bitter exchanges between Viljoen and Terre'Blanche and resulted in Viljoen's resignation to form a new party, and the disintegration of the Freedom Alliance. The fall of Mangope's government also influenced the collapse of the other homeland ally in the Freedom Alliance, Gqozo's government in Ciskei.

Between April 24 and 27, 1994, bombs exploded across South Africa killing twenty-one people and injuring over 145. The first bomb exploded with no warning in downtown Johannesburg and killed, among others, Susan Keane, the white ANC candidate for the Johannesburg region's provincial legislature. It was the deadliest bombing since 1983. On April 25 more than twelve bombs exploded, several at the black taxi terminals and planned polling sites. On April 27 the government arrested thirty-one white right-wing extremists, several from the AWB-based Ventersdorp region, in connection with the bombings. Terre'Blanche announced on April 28 that the AWB would continue its bombing campaign if Afrikaners were not given their own autonomous homeland. But the arrests dealt a crippling blow to the right-wing leadership and threw the extremist groups as a whole into disorder. The bombing campaign also failed to prevent the 22.7 million eligible voters from going to the polling stations.

The Azanian People's Liberation Army (APLA), the military wing of the PAC, further contributed to the cycle of violence that plagued the negotiation process. Its targets were often white civilians, but it also launched an aggressive campaign to eliminate policemen, mainly black policemen, in townships. These attacks raised the profile of the PAC, but not surprisingly they did not increase suppport for that party. The attacks on whites sparked white anger, and the campaign against policemen was not a popular move in the townships. The apparent strategy of the APLA was to take advantage of the ANC's suspension of the armed struggle and assert itself. Joe Slovo sarcastically observed that the PAC's post-1990 military action marked a formal end to the "thirty-year ceasefire." In early 1994 the PAC announced it was abandoning the armed struggle so that it could register for the April election and the APLA could be included in the new National Peacekeeping Force (discussed below).[21]

One mitigating factor in the pattern of violence from 1990 to 1994 was the serious attempts made by the major players to cooperate in curbing sporadic outbursts and attacks. Much of this stemmed from the Record of Understanding of September 1992 and the creation of the Transitional Executive Council in September 1993. A core group of business and church leaders who believed that the fate of South Africa could not just be left to the politicians set up the National Peace Accord. It consisted of a National Peace Committee, a National Peace Secretariat to manage the eleven Regional Peace Committees (RPCs) and eighty Local Peace Committees (LPCs), and the Goldstone Commission, which had powers to investigate public violence. The LPCs became a forum for people of widely different backgrounds and a major force in negotiation. When the ANC withdrew from the peace accord structures after the Boipatong Massacre in 1992, the Vaal LPC worked hard to get the ANC back in and organized a weekend retreat in which all signatories of the Peace Accord renewed their pledges.

As South Africa showed signs of serious strain after the assassination of Chris Hani in April 1993, Mandela and other leaders counseled restraint. The ANC meanwhile worked with the NP toward the creation of a "super cabinet" whose powers would include monitoring the various armed forces from the South African Defense Force to the armies of the ANC and PAC, and the overseeing of a force whose sole aim would be to restrain violence. The National Peacekeeping Force (NPKF) emerged, which was made up of many different organizations, partly as a means of inclusion of all parties in the peacekeeping process, partly as recognition that the South African police and South African Defense Force were not reliable sources of security. The force was hindered by deKlerk's touchiness over allowing any direct involvement of foreigners in the NPKF and problems of organizing its participants. The NPFK further suffered from reports of disorderly conduct, desertion, drunkenness, and tension within its ranks. But the elections were carried out relatively peacefully. This was as much due to the peacekeeping efforts on the part of the main negotiators as it was to the last-minute participation of the IFP.

The political parties of South Africa, despite their disparity, managed during the period leading up to the elections to overcome tremendous odds in working out an arrangement that allowed for the relatively fair participation of all factions in South Africa. This was no mean feat given the violence that plagued the process, the extreme divisions among the parties, and the internal conflicts that also threatened to weaken their positions. Although the emerging system was not completely free from divisiveness and sporadic violence, the political negotiations that led to change managed to hold the country together. Such cohesion was achieved partly through a willingness to compromise, partly through determination, and largely through the will of the majority of the country to make the new experiment work.

NOTES

1. Allister Sparks, "The Secret Revolution," *New Yorker* 70 (April 11, 1994): 56–78; Arthur S. Banks, Alan Day, and Thomas Muller, *Political Handbook of the World, 1997* (New York: C.S.A. Publications, 1997), p. 768.

2. *Race Relations Survey, 1987–88* (Johannesburg: The South African Institute of Race Relations), 103–5; *The Times* (London), October 28, 1988.

3. Helen Kitchen, ed., *South Africa: In Transition to What?* (Westport, CT: Praeger, 1988), pp. 43–45.

4. Banks, *Political Handbook of the World*, p. 772.

5. "The Major Organizations," *Weekly Mail and Guardian* (Johannesburg), March 31–April 7, 1994.

6. Patrick Laurence, "Deadlocked," *Africa Report* 37 (July–August 1992): 55–57.

7. Patrick Laurence, "Finding Common Ground," *Africa Report* 38 (May–June 1993): 25–27.

8. Patrick Laurence, "Buthelezi's Gamble," *Africa Report* 37 (November–December 1992): 13–18.

9. Alexander Johnston, "The Political World of KwaZulu-Natal," in R. W. Johnson and Lawrence Schlemmer, eds., *Launching Democracy in South Africa: The First Open Election, April 1994* (New Haven, CT: Yale University Press, 1996), p. 175; Phillipa Garson, "Drowned in Blood," *Africa Report* 38 (September–October 1993): 43–44.

10. Garson, "Drowned in Blood," pp. 43–45; Patrick Laurence, "The Diehards and Dealmakers," *Africa Report* 38 (November–December 1993): 13–16.

11. "NP the Only Winner with New Concessions," *Weekly Mail and Guardian*, February 25–March 3, 1994.

12. Martin J. Murray, *The Revolution Deferred: The Painful Birth of Post-Apartheid South Africa* (London: Verso, 1994), pp. 205–6.

13. Sparks, "The Secret Revolution," pp. 56–78.

14. Patrick Laurence, "Competition or Coalition?" *Africa Report* 37 (May–June 1992): 64–67.

15. Patrick Laurence, "Temperatures Rising," *Africa Report 38* (March–April 1993): 29–31; Laurence, "The Diehards and Dealmakers," pp. 13–16.

16. Denis Herbstein, "DeKlerk's Big Win," *Africa Report* 39 (July–August 1994): 20–22.

17. Yunus Carrim, "Minorities Together and Apart," in Wilmot James, Daria Caliguire, and Kerry Cullinan, eds., *Now That We Are Free: Coloured Communities in a Democratic South Africa* (Boulder, CO: Lynne Rienner, 1996), pp. 47–49.

18. Sparks, "The Secret Revolution," pp. 56–78; Philippa Garson, "The Third Face," *Africa Report* 37 (May–June 1992): 68–71.

19. *Sunday Times* (London), April 28, 1991; Murray, *Revolution Deferred*, p. 88; Patrick Laurence, "Exposing the Past," *Africa Report* 38 (January–February 1993): 51–53.

20. *Africa Confidential* 33 (1992): 5–6; C. Erasmus, "The Far Right Vows a Fight to the Death," *World Press Review* 41 (March 1994): 12–13.

21. Philippa Garson, "The PAC Enters the Fray," *Africa Report* 37 (November– December 1992): 19–22; Laurence, "Temperatures Rising," 29–31; Garson, "Drowned in Blood," pp. 43–45.

4

Internal and External Pressure

The decision by the South African government to reform and eventually abandon the apartheid system came largely as a result of immense strain on South African society arising from both within and outside the country. The creation of the Bantustans and townships eventually backfired in terms of developing a prosperous white society enjoying separation from blacks as well as security. The South African economy felt the oppressive weight of segregation impinging its freedom, and by the 1980s international criticism and pressure exacerbated its problems to the point of decline and social disruption.

It was to a large degree the uneven distribution of wealth and prosperity created by the apartheid system that eventually put overwhelming pressure on the economy of South Africa as a whole, and the formation and maintenance of the homelands was the perfect expression of this imbalance. In 1970 the South African government passed the Bantu Homelands Citizenship Act Number 26, which provided that all Africans in South Africa were to be given citizenship of one of the Bantustans, and each would be issued a certificate of citizenship. The act immediately aroused fear among urban Africans that they would lose their remaining rights under Section 10 of the 1945 Urban Areas Act and become migratory laborers. Their fears were realized by the statement of the Minister of Bantu Administration and Development regarding the Section 10 rights, "I am going to remove all and every one of them."[1] By the end of 1972, self-government status had been conferred on the homelands of Ciskei, KwaZulu, Lebowa, Venda, Gazankulu, Bophuthatswana, and QwaQwa. Nominal independence was now being promoted, and one Johannesburg newspaper noted cynically, "With a dismal record of new jobs created, and economic advancement in the homelands in general less than successful, the Nats would welcome the smokescreen of political independence."[2]

This comment touched on the crux of the matter in terms of the effect of the homelands policy on Africans. The policy resulted in forced relocation of Africans on a large scale. The South African government removed an estimated 3.5 million people from their homes under the Group Areas and Separate Development legislation between 1960 and 1983. This massive relocation was comparable in many cases to genocide because much of the African population was moved to empty and unproductive areas and away from any means of employment. The whole process of removal followed a regular pattern: The South African police forcibly removed people and destroyed their homes, the South African government gave them no compensation, and the new site of settlement often had no accommodations except sometimes tents, with inadequate water supplies and sanitation, and no basic social institutions. Forced removal became a major feature of African daily life, and the threat of resettlement affected almost every African in South Africa.

The homeland economies were, meanwhile, extremely poor. They suffered from a growing dependence on migrant labor, and many economic operations in these areas were monopolized by agencies of the South African government who abused the trust, as for example, when these agencies set up enterprises that exploited the fact that no minium wage existed in the homelands. Botha's ambitious plan of reforming the townships in the 1980s to entice middle-class blacks into the system was carried out at great cost to the homelands. Pretoria offered financial incentives to bring in investment capital to "growth points" in the homelands, and companies of newly industrialized countries came in at the expense of the health, wages, and working conditions of the local work force. The European and Asian companies often paid local labor less than two dollars a day. Unemployment rose to about 50 percent of the economically active population, and an estimated 70 percent of households lived below the poverty line with widespread disease and malnutrition. According to one observer of the 1980s, the homelands had developed into "poverty-stricken fiefdoms, ruled by well-paid politicians who have demonstrated little tolerance for opposition."[3] The homelands, therefore, existed as little more than economic wastelands. The widespread poverty and starvation in these areas was only marginally alleviated by black workers finding employment in white South Africa.

A study made in the early 1970s attempted to assess the attitudes of Africans in the Bantustans. Fifty-eight percent of those questioned appeared to be in favor of the homelands because of their supposed freedom from whites. But the more-educated residents were adamantly critical of every aspect of the homelands. This criticism represented a profound suspicion of white motives, and bitterness over the ultimate control of the homeland administrations by whites and over forced removals. The greatest resentment was expressed with regard to the economic and social stagnation in the homelands, and many critical residents accused whites of exploiting homeland Africans for cheap labor and maintaining the backwardness of Africans through the homeland system.

The ANC and PAC, meanwhile, consistently condemned Bantustan policy and denounced the homeland chiefs as collaborators. In 1976 Jimmy Kruger, the South African minister of prisons, twice visited Nelson Mandela on Robben Island and presented him with the offer of freedom with the stipulation that Mandela move to Transkei, the place of his birth, and recognize the legitimacy of the Transkeian government. Mandela refused, stating that he rejected Bantustan policy. As he remarked in his memoirs, "It was an offer only a turncoat could accept."[4] This criticism was connected to another aspect of the homelands. By setting up local authorities in these regions, the South African government could also distance itself from the frustration of the homeland dwellers. The immediate symbols of oppression were Africans as opposed to whites, and violence against authorities could thus be represented as tribal strife.

Although the South African government viewed the homeland system as a successful method of segregation and curtailing opposition, the white population as a whole was less enthusiastic over the policy. In the late 1960s, during an active government campaign for establishment of homelands, 50 percent of whites expressed their opposition to granting independence to Transkei, and 40 percent felt that the government was spending too much on the development of homelands. The party also feared the presence in white South Africa of millions of African immigrants acting as "a gigantic fifth column" of politically dissaffected workers.[5] Many whites complained of the physical deterioration of areas designated as homelands where whites had lived and dominated before "self-government."

The cost of maintaining the homelands did stretch the coffers and resources of the South African government, and developments in the homelands challenged its authority. Pretoria not only financed educational and government institutions in the homelands, but also sent military protection at times of instability. The ANC and other groups thrived as underground protest movements in several of the homelands, most notably Transkei, confirming white suspicions of the Bantustans as "hotbeds of sedition." The nominal independence and rising black middle class of these areas also strengthened black confidence in opposing the apartheid system. With the relaxation of pass laws in the 1980s, much of the homeland population flooded into the cities, further exacerbating problems of the industrial economy and labor policies of apartheid.

The stress on and complications to South African society brought on by the homeland system culminated in confusion in these regions at the end of the 1980s and in the early 1990s. The initial excitement in the homelands over the release of Nelson Mandela in February 1990 developed over the next series of months into anger directed at the leaders, viewed as puppets of Pretoria. Within the space of about ten days, the homelands became scenes of vast disruption. In Ciskei, Brigadier Oupa Gqozo launched a coup that overthrew Lennox Sebe while the latter was secretly trying to make a deal with the NP. This event was followed by street celebrations and riots in Mdantsane, Ciskei's largest township, and Fort Jackson, both symbols of the once-powerful Sebe family. In Bophuthatswana, Lucas Mangope suppressed demonstrations for his resignation by declaring a state of emergency and ordering his police to shoot to kill, and in Venda rebels overthrew the president, Frank Ravele. In Transkei, a coup attempt against Holomisa failed. The botched affair ended with a shootout in the main government building; the leader of the rebels was shot and bundled into the trunk of a car while Holomisa's army chased the resisters through the streets of Umtata. The rebel leader's wife had meanwhile apparently spent the day at the hairdresser's in optimistic preparation for her new role.[6]

The homeland that presented the biggest problem in the process toward change was Bophuthatswana. Bophuthatswana contained one-third of the world's platinum and chrome deposits and was in possession of larger reserves of other scarce minerals. There were also the problems of the notorious Sol Kerzner's gambling parks built in this homeland as an outlet for gamblers from the republic (where gambling was illegal) and of Sun City (also referred to as "Sin City") and Lost City, which both attracted large numbers of visitors. The latter boasted a 338–room Palace Hotel and casino, a pool with six-foot waves, five water slides, and a sixty-acre jungle. It was often compared to Xanadu, as "nothing in it is real."[7] Bophuthatswana, however, was largely dependent on South Africa economically and would eventually succumb to the general breakup and reincorporation of the homelands, especially after the fall of the Mangope ruling dynasty. The region itself remained unsettled and the source of post-apartheid controversy.

While the homeland system increasingly put strain on the economy and order in South Africa, the situation in the cities further contributed to the crumbling of apartheid. Often serving as the bases of mass protest and organized opposition, the cities also represented one of the best examples of the conflicting interests of segregation and a capitalist economy. The policies of apartheid were designed to separate blacks from whites geographically, but the demands of industry required the cheap labor of blacks who needed to live in reasonable proximity to the places of employment. The black population migrated in increasing numbers to the cities while the apartheid system struggled to balance the demands of industry with a policy of separation. As the blacks swelled the cities, they formed unions and gained confidence in bucking the system through protest, demonstrations, and strikes. The rise of the cities, the development of the townships to cope with the increase in black urban population, and the concentration of protest in the cities all had a direct effect on the crises of the 1980s that led to the downfall of apartheid.

The 1960s and 1970s marked the growth of both a middle class and a semiliterate, semiskilled class of Africans in the cities. The former adopted the manners and style to distinguish themselves as a separate elite and could be found in their free time involved in church activities. Some of the latter began to aspire to the middle classes, but many younger members turned from these aspirations to start their own trends and criticized the affectations of the elite. Township life often possessed an American flavor in the cigarettes, movies, jazz, and rock music that dominated the youth culture. In the late 1970s the music of Bob Marley became an expression of urban youth protest, and reggae music as a whole continued to reflect the society of opposition in the 1980s. In time, some of these youths became a strong political force in the cities and part of the Black Consciousness movement of the 1970s. All these developments increasingly challenged the status quo of the apartheid system.

In the 1980s, under increased pressure, the government began repealing apartheid law and by 1986 had undone much of the legislation attempting to control the urban population. Durban grew to twice its size, and its population rose to about 3 million in less than ten years. Cape Town also expanded at a rapid rate. The new area known as Khayalitsha and surrounding makeshift locations on the Cape Flats—an area hardly inhabited in 1980s—grew to a population of 750,000 also in a decade.[8] Despite the repeal of many discriminatory laws such as the ban on multiracial political parties and interracial sex and marriage, and the desegregation of certain types of restaurants, hotels, trains, buses, and public facilities, resentment and crime in the townships continued. This was largely due to social frustration linked to the lack of funding for the Community Councils formed by urban reform, and the inability to pay the increasing rents that provided the councils with their main source of income.

One of the major forces in the urban rebellions was the militant youths who rose to the forefront as the power of the state-created authorities diminished. Known as "comrades," or *amaqabane*, their philosophy centered basically on creating anarchy in the townships. As apartheid began to unravel, many of these youths later turned to straightforward crime and became known as *comtotsis*. Their competing gangs transformed the townships into warring camps. Often the *comtotsis* were pitted against ANC activists now trying to maintain discipline and order in the urban areas. The mass killing of close to forty-five people by a group called the "Five Star Gang" in Sebokeng at a funeral vigil for an ANC member in January 1991 provides one example of this tortuous conflict.

The townships in South Africa, throughout their history, reflected the superficiality of apartheid as a valid state form. These periurban locations acted as poor renditions of the cities themselves and highlighted the social and economic inequality that accompanied the political inequality set up by apartheid. They were, by definition and geographical position, metropolitan, but they enjoyed few of the benefits and suffered all the worst aspects of a metropolitan area: no space; no electricity; no running water; no sewage system; no paved roads; no proper police force; no security; and despite their closeness to the cities, no proper transportation system. The continued deterioration of living conditions in the townships throughout the 1980s led to greater tension, crime, and general confusion as patterns emerging from years of protest rose to a crescendo.

THE ECONOMY AND SANCTIONS

From the time of its formation, the apartheid system of South Africa caught the attention of the rest of the world, and increasing condemnation arose from international agencies, governments, and public opinion. Pressure on South Africa to reform, however, was uneven and not usually coordinated in such a way as to be consistently effective. Those who argued against economic pressure in the form of sanctions often claimed that the natural pattern of economic forces would undo apartheid, and that "constructive engagement" as opposed to isolation of the South African government made better sense. Those who supported strong pressure in the form of economic sanctions and disinvestment criticized their opponents for disguising "business as usual" with moral hypocrisy while foreign companies reaped large profits from cheap black labor. Because the history of outside pressure against South Africa is marked by some weakness due to flaws in the wording, interpretation, and carrying out of sanctions, it is still difficult to decide the degree to which it influenced the fall of apartheid and rise of democracy, and whether internal economic pressure brought on by the system played a bigger role. Nevertheless, there can be no doubt that the isolation experienced by the South African government through international pressure had an important impact on the decision to change. Internal developments in the business and industrial sectors also made their mark.

Although ostensibly strong in the 1950s and 1960s, the South African economy from the beginning of apartheid was vulnerable in three ways: It was dependent on a large amount of foreign capital; it lagged behind in advances in technology except in mining, and had to import heavy machinery and transportation equipment; and it had no natural oil. Except after the Sharpeville killings of 1960 and the Soweto uprising of 1976, the United States and Western Europe provided South Africa with enough capital and equipment to keep her economy stable. When the Organization of Petroleum Exporting Countries (OPEC) imposed an oil embargo on South Africa in 1973, it was unable to enforce its decision, and South Africa continued to receive most of her oil from Iran until 1979 when Mohammad Reza Pahlavi (the shah of Iran) fell from power. Recognizing the country's potential vulnerability in these areas, the South African government began to reduce its dependence on imports in the 1970s and created its own supply of petroleum products.

But the mid-1970s can been seen as a turning point. The oil crisis of 1973, the collapse of the Portuguese colonial empire in Africa in 1974, the rise of black worker militancy, and the Soweto revolt all contributed to the decline of growth and spurred the South African government to reconsider its direction. The severe skill shortages, technological dependence, and lack of competitivenes that became clear in the 1970s strengthened the case that apartheid hurt growth and that rates of development would have been higher without it. Capitalists within South Africa began to attack apartheid more vigorously, not necessarily because of a moral awakening but because apartheid labor policies challenged their own interests. A spiral of decline emerged when the economic problems (especially high unemployment) fueled the political unrest of the mid-1980s, which in turn worsened economic problems. All these developments occurred under the growing shadow of international condemnation and coercion.

In many ways, the pattern of pressure on South Africa to reform should be examined in the context of the development of international law and behavior against racial discrimination. The development of international human rights law forms the basis of the radical change in international attitudes from 1946; for example, the Universal Declaration of Human Rights, the International Convention on the Elimination of All Form of Racial Discrimination, and the International Convention on the Suppression and Punishment of the Crime of Apartheid. The International Law Commission characterized apartheid as an international crime in its Draft Articles on State Responsibility, and by the 1980s, the norm of nondiscrimination had become part of customary international law. From the 1940s, South Africa became a special case at the United Nations, which officially condemned the apartheid system for violation of accepted norms of international law. From the time of the first presentation of violations against a population by the government of India, the UN consistently criticized South Africa's apartheid policy and demanded that it be dismantled and replaced with the right of self-determination for all peoples of South Africa.

Both the Security Council and the General Assembly in the UN imposed sanctions against South Africa. In 1962 the General Assembly passed a resolution requesting its member states to break diplomatic relations with South Africa, close ports to ships flying the South African flag, prohibit their ships from entering South African ports, boycott South African trade, and refuse landing and passage facilities to all aircraft belonging to the government of South Africa or companies registered there. In 1963 the Security Council made a call for a ban on arms sales to South Africa and shipment of equipment and materials for production of arms and ammunition in South Africa. In ensuing years the General Assembly adopted resolutions that called for further sanctions. In 1977, following the death in detention of Steve Biko, the Security Council declared that the activities and policies of the South African government constituted a danger to international peace and security and imposed its first mandatory arms embargo on South Africa. Although in the past, the United States, Britain, and France opposed or abstained from Security Council resolutions concerning pressure on South Africa, they did not in this case.

In 1985, after the South African government declared a state of emergency and news of more repression and casualties in South Africa reached the international public, the Security Council passed a resolution urging UN member states voluntarily to impose sanctions against South Africa. Included in the resolution were a call for voluntary termination of new investments in South Africa and a ban on the sale of Krugerrands, suspension of export loan guarantees, a ban on nuclear contracts, and an end to the sale of computer equipment that might be used by the South African military. The resolution was adopted but with the abstention of the United States and Britain. Despite the urgent appeals to carry out these sanctions, no efforts in these areas succeeded, and in 1987 the General Assembly failed to get the Security Council to act immediately to apply comprehensive and mandatory sanctions against South Africa.

Much of UN censorship of South Africa focused on its aggressive policy toward neighboring African states. In 1966 the UN General Assemly ended South Africa's mandate over Namibia, and the UN viewed the continued South African occupation of Namibia as illegal. In 1971 the International Court of Justice gave the advisory opinion that South Africa should withdraw from Namibia. The UN Security Council agreed and called on member states to conform to pressure on South Africa. In June 1985, the UN Security Council warned South Africa that failure to cooperate with the UN Transition Assistance Group (UNTAG), established in Namibia in 1978, would cause the Security Council to consider passing measures under its charter against South Africa.

In the 1980s, South Africa launched a campaign of destabilization against the so-called frontline states: Angola, Botswana, Mozambique, Tanzania, Zambia, and Zimbabwe—a campaign that cost Pretoria between 10 and 60 billion dollars from 1980–1987. In the UN General Assembly's thirty-ninth session in 1984 the Angola representative accused South Africa of "armed aggression, massive invasions, and military occupation of parts of its territory, a sustained battering at the Angolan government institutions, infrastructure and people."[9] In December 1983 and January 1984 the Security Council passed resolutions that demanded that South Africa unconditionally surrender the military forces occupying Angola. But even after South Africa's withdrawal from Angola in 1988, Pretoria still supported guerilla movements such as the Mozambique National Resistance Movement and the Lesotho Liberation Army. It also continued to support the National Union for Total Independence of Angola (UNITA). The South African army further made several direct military raids on neighboring countries, including Mozambique in 1981 and 1983, Angola in 1981 and 1982, and Lesotho in 1982. Pretoria's reason for launching the invasions was to eliminate ANC and SWAPO activity in South African territory.

The success of multilateral sanctions, like the success of the UN as a peacekeeping institution, depended on the cooperation and agreement of sovereign governments to take concerted action. Many of these governments were for many years and many reasons reluctant to impose sanctions on South Africa, most notably Britain and the United States. Britain historically enjoyed especially close connections with South Africa, even after 1961 when the South Africa declared itself a republic and left the British

Commonwealth. Many white South Africans were born in Britain, and many more had family connections there. The culture of English-speaking South Africa focused on Britain, and the South African economy was more important to Britain than any other country. In 1978 Britain accounted for approximately 40 percent of all foreign investment in South Africa. British banks such as Standard Chartered and Barclays International controlled 60 percent of South African bank deposits.

Some South African émigrés, both white and black, tried to organize a major antiapartheid movement in Britain, but from 1965 to 1980 British attention focused more on white Rhodesia's unilateral declaration of independence. Both the Conservative and Labour governments in Britain publicly denounced apartheid, but even the Labour government vetoed sanctions against South Africa in the UN Security Council. President Botha was particularly fortunate regarding the danger of potential sanctions from Britain when Margaret Thatcher became British Prime Minister in 1979 (as he was fortunate with Ronald Reagan's election to the American presidency in 1980). Although Thatcher's government became involved in the negotiations that led to transfer of power to blacks in Zimbabwe, the prime minister maintained strong opposition to sanctions against South Africa, and steadily rejected demands by other Commonwealth countries that Britain join them in taking strong economic measures against apartheid.

The Thatcher government's approach adopted the argument that market forces would take care of apartheid and that sanctions would hurt blacks in South Africa more than whites. In a discussion with the Eminent Persons Church Group (ECPG) consisting of prominent clergy members in South Africa, British Foreign Secretary Sir Geofrey Howe stated, "It is a market issue—in fact [South Africa's] debt is self-inflicted by the policy of apartheid." The ECPG reminded Howe that when the British government was sufficiently outraged as in the cases of the Falklands, Poland, or the Soviet invasion of Afghanistan, it did impose sanctions "without any debate on whether the peoples of those countries would suffer or not. It did not wait for opinion polls on sanctions from those countries."[10]

The lack of coordination between countries that hindered the effectiveness of sanctions is best illustrated in the case of the United States, which failed to coordinate sanctions policy both in its own policies and in conjunction with other counties. From 1964 the United States complied with the voluntary arms embargo authorized by the UN, but loopholes linked to divided responsibility in the American bureaucracy in implementation arose in compliance with the embargo and other sanctions, and U.S. adminstrations gave a low priority to the South African embargo, in comparison with embargoes against other nations. The gradual evolution of the ban from voluntary to mandatory gave South Africa time and opportunity to find alternative suppliers and to build up its own self-sufficiency.

Operating from the Cold War perspective, the United States, along with Western Europe, was reluctant to rock the boat in South Africa for fear of creating a situation that would encourage a communist revolution there. From the business perspective, the stakes that the West had in South Africa made it easier to assume that economic growth would kill apartheid. The South African economy was very attractive to both American and European business and defense interests. In 1948 Britain had the closest business ties with South Africa, but throughout the years trade with Western Europe and the United States grew dramatically and by 1978 the United States was South Africa's main trading partner, with Japan not far behind. Much of the involvement came through direct investment in South African subsidies or affiliates of American companies such as Ford, General Motors, Mobil, and Caltex Oil. Indirect investment came through U.S. and European bank loans and shares in South African gold mining and other stock.

Like Britain, the United States consistently opposed UN imposition of mandatory sanctions against South Africa—an ironic position, because the United States had always seen itself as the champion of international human rights and a staunch proponent of the rule of law in the international arena. The United States defended its position by stating that sanctions did not work, although critics pointed out that the United States did impose sanctions against Cuba, Libya, Panama, and the Soviet Union. The United States, however, did not oppose all sanctions and joined the call for voluntary sanctions and the mandatory arms embargo, undertaking these measures on its own, and her position did change in the 1980s.

Under President Dwight D. Eisenhower, the United States conducted relations with South Africa as an ally, and the Pentagon and CIA had contacts with South Africa's military and security services. The administration also oversaw cooperation between the two countries in nuclear research. The John F. Kennedy and Lyndon B. Johnson Administrations were more critical of apartheid and committed the United States to stop selling arms to South Africa, but both rejected economic sanctions proposals. Presidents Richard Nixon and Gerald Ford moved away from the antiapartheid lobby and fairly liberal African Bureau toward the Pentagon and big business. In a review of U.S. world policies ordered by Secretary of State Henry Kissinger in 1969, the Nixon Administration chose the option that stated, "The whites are here [in southern Africa] to stay and the only way that constructive change can come about is through them. . . . We can, through selective relaxation of our stance toward the white regimes, encourage some modification of their current racial and colonial policies."[11] The policy led to increased official relations with white South African officials, pro-South African UN votes, and the appointment of an ambassador to South Africa who seemed to care little for the sufferings of blacks and was reported to have gone hunting on Robben Island using political prisoners as beaters.[12]

The Jimmy Carter administration moved away from the Nixon-Ford position and viewed South Africa as a liability to the Western alliance, as opposed to an ally. It regarded black nationalists as the future of South Africa, deciding that the United States needed to come to terms with them, and Vice President Walter Mondale told South African Prime Minister John Vorster that the United States supported the principle of majority rule with universal suffrage, in concurrence with the ANC. In 1978 the United States government toughened its arms embargo on South Africa and placed restrictions on which South African government agencies could buy high technology items such as computers. American computers, however, still found their way to the South African military and police who could use this equipment to control South Africa's black community. In 1979 Carter banned Eximbank loans for the South African government and parastatals (companies owned and controlled partly or wholly by the government), and restricted export credits to companies in South Africa.

United States policy toward South Africa changed again during the administration of President Ronald Reagan in the 1980s. Conflict in the American government over South African policy hurt the effectiveness of sanctions and the clarity and coherence of American dealings with South Africa. Ignoring the rising antiapartheid lobby in the United States, the Reagan administration opposed sanctions, and Assistant Secretary of State for African Affairs Chester Crocker spent most of his time engaged in long diplomatic efforts to evacuate Cuban troops from Angola in exchange for liberation of Namibia by the UN. Supporting the approach of "constructive engagement," the Reagan adminstration encouraged the South African government to reform apartheid, and refrained from making any contact with antiapartheid organizations such as the ANC. Reagan accepted the rhetoric of Pretoria at face value, remained uninformed over the actual situation in South Africa, and was biased in favor of the white population. In 1985, at the height of disruption and repression in South African society, he claimed that South Africa "has eliminated the segregation we once had in our own country."[13]

The antiapartheid lobby in United States, however, grew larger and louder. Between 1984 and 1986, 6,000 Americans were arrested while picketing the South African embassy and consulates. A large number of state and city governments and universities sold investments in companies that did business in South Africa, and American companies themselves began to withdraw from South Africa: forty in 1985 and fifty in 1986. In July 1985 Chase Manhattan Bank refused to roll over short-term loans to South Africa, and other banks followed this example, creating a financial crisis in South Africa. In 1985 American public opinion was strong enough to put pressure on Congress to take more direct action against South Africa. Aware of this development, Reagan preempted Congress from passing a sanctions bill by imposing limited sanctions on South Africa. In July 1986, in a major public address, Reagan urged the South African government to negotiate over reform of apartheid, but he opposed sanctions as a "historic act of folly," drawing bipartisan criticism for the lack of significant initiative toward South Africa. Pretoria, meanwhile, praised his speech.

In September 1986, as the level of awareness of the turmoil in South Africa grew in the United States, the U.S. Congress adopted an antiapartheid bill (known as the Comprehensive Antiapartheid Act—CAAA) despite Reagan's veto. Important elements of the act included a banning of new investments and bank loans to South Africa, the ending of air links of South Africa with the United States, prohibition of a variety of South African imports, and a threat to cut off military aid to allies suspected of violating the international arms embargo against South Africa. The act also included financial assistance through scholarships for "victims of apartheid," grants for community organizations in disadvantaged communities, and assistance for political detainees and families. The act directed the Eximbank to aid black businesses in South Africa and make sure that American businesses stuck to a defined code of conduct on fair employment practices for black employees. Several congressmen introduced further bills proposing legislation on sanctions in 1988 and 1989, but these failed to pass. Charles Rangel, Democratic Representative from New York, however, sponsored a scarcely noticed amendment to the Budget Reconciliation Act of 1987 that withdrew tax credits for taxes paid by American companies to the South African government. The amendment raised the state of taxation 58–72 percent, a development that influenced Mobil Oil, Hewlett Packard, St. Paul Companies, and Goodyear Tire and Rubber to pull out of South Africa in 1989.

Two hundred U.S. companies pulled out of South Africa between 1984 and 1989, and sanctions became tougher through the CAAA, but the latter was not as effective as it could have been due to the methods of its interpretation and implementation; for example, Congress allowed the president to prepare a list of "strategic minerals" that would be exempted from the ban on imports from South African parastatals. An executive-wide definition of "strategic minerals" resulted in the exemption of a large number of exports. Definition problems also arose over noncomprehensive sanctions, and in general the Reagan adminstration tended to interpret the loose wording of amendments to the CAAA in a manner that undermined their intent. Furthermore, there was no regimen of vigorous enforcment of the terms of the act. The act, however, did force the Reagan administration to reexamine its position favoring the South African government. It reflected the real expression of American public opinion against the apartheid system and the dissatisfaction of Congress with the administration's method of dealing with the South African government's policies of both repression and regional destabilization.

When George Bush became president in 1989, his administration moved its position closer to that of the antiapartheid lobby. When the Eminent Persons Church Group met with U.S. Secretary of State James Baker, he claimed that the Bush administration was "in a reflective mood with respect to problems in South Africa," and admitted that in the past the United States government had not made "vigorous efforts in the multilateral foray to muster international support against apartheid." He further made the suggestion that it was time to act. On the other hand, Baker claimed that unilateral sanctions were ineffective and that up until then sanctions against South Africa had not worked and "as a result, in South Africa, the right wing is getting stronger." The EPCG responded by stating, "the right wing was never a factor. It was used as a factor only by those looking for excuses not to adopt tough economic measures against South Africa."[14] Meanwhile, the U.S. Assistant Secretary of State for African Affairs Herman Cohen stated, "Sanctions have had a very major impact, I believe, on the development of new thinking in South Africa."[15]

By 1986 foreign countries as a whole were putting strong pressure on the South Africa government. Many different countries televised the violence of the townships in South Africa, showing South African police and soldiers shooting and beating unarmed blacks. The South African government stopped journalists from reporting these occurrences in its crackdown in 1985, but South Africa could not escape from being a strong focus of international attention. In 1985 and 1986 the European Community adopted measures that included a suspension of new direct investments in South Africa, a ban on exports of arms, petroleum and certain high-technology products to South Africa, and a ban on imports of Krugerrands, iron, and steel from South Africa. The Nordic countries of Europe imposed sanctions that also involved an end to new investment South Africa, tightening of visa requirements, and the ending of sports ties and oil connections. The Commonwealth countries joined the ban on new investment; ended air links with

South Africa; prohibited imports of South African coal, iron, steel, and uranium; and withdrew its consulates from South Africa. International banks imposed financial sanctions on South Africa in 1985, refusing to roll over loans to South Africa and forcing the South African government to agree to stringent repayment terms.

Margaret Thatcher tried hard to prevent Britain and the Commonwealth countries from initiating joint action against apartheid, but early in 1986 the Eminent Persons Group, a collection of seven senior Commonwealth politicians led by former Prime Minister of Australia Malcolm Fraser, visited South Africa and conducted a round of talks with the white regime and underground black liberation groups. It drew up a suggested negotiating plan that included the release of political prisoners, removal of the military from the townships, provision for freedom of assembly, suspension of detention without trial, the release of Nelson Mandela, and a lifting of the ban on the ANC and other black organizations. A report of Commonwealth nations issued in 1989 stated, "Sanctions are a diplomatic tool. They are a spur to the negotiating process, not an alternative to it. . . . We see the role of sanctions as making it increasingly difficult to maintain even a 'reformed' apartheid, thus forcing white South Africans to realize that fundamental change must take place."[16] Remarkably, those countries that most consistently called on the international community to implement sanctions were the southern African states—those most affected by Pretoria's policy of destabilization. Even the most vulnerable such as Lesotho spoke out.

An important element to consider in the imposition of sanctions is the reactions and opinions of the black South African population with respect to sanctions policy and disinvestment. The ANC supported sanctions from the beginning and even through the negotiating process when the outcome of these was uncertain. The Congress of South African Trade Unions (COSATU) also supported sanctions and disinvestment. Overall black opinion is less clear. In a survey of black production workers conducted in 1984, Laurence Schlemmer concluded that about 75 percent were opposed to disinvestment and about 25 percent were in favor. Other studies produced more mixed opinions. In a 1985 study of black opinion undertaken by Mark Orkin, 24 percent supported disinvestment, 26 percent opposed, and 48 percent supported conditional disinvestment. When asked if they would still support disinvestment if it resulted in serious job losses for blacks, 26 percent replied yes, 26 percent replied yes if only a few jobs were lost, and 48 percent opposed any loss of jobs.[17]

Some blacks appeared to support the Reagan administration's opinion that the main impact of sanctions was to mobilize and unify whites in resistance to change. Others supported sanctions using a long range argument, as illustrated in the following comments of a worker supervisor in a private organization:

In the short term it will harm blacks but in the long term it will bring liberation. White people will also suffer because firms will close down. If I lose my job I will be pleased because the white man will also be in trouble; because I will become a criminal and deal with the white man directly. Whenever he is at work he will have to employ a guard at home. . . . He will realize that he is forced to do all this because of government policy.[18]

In two sets of interviews of a cross section of urban black South Africans carried out in 1986, a widespread and sharp rise in hostitily toward the United States was noted. The majority of those interviewed regarded the Reagan administration as detrimental to black liberation. Inkatha supporters were the main exceptions. There was also criticism of U.S. failure to make any high-level official contact with the ANC, Reagan's continuous call on the ANC to renounce violence (viewed as ill-informed and hypocritical), and overt U.S. support for UNITA, which was seen as a military alliance with the South African government. Blacks also became disillusioned with the process of disinvestment, feeling that it was a public relations trick. One black businessman remarked, "We are seeing management buy-outs, which have not included blacks. Top White guys in management have become instant millionaires and blacks remain sloggers as before. . . . Kodak is the only exception."[19] (Kodak had removed itself completely from South Africa instead of selling to management).

Archbishop Desmond Tutu, in a speech calling for international sanctions, launched an attack on the hypocrisy of Western countries rejecting economic sanctions for the reason that they would hurt blacks most of all:

It is amazing how solicitous for blacks and such wonderful altruists everybody has become. It is remarkable that in South Africa the most vehement in their concern for blacks have been whites. Few blacks have repudiated me for my stance. . . . They are not stupid. They know whether they are going to suffer. . . . Two recent surveys have shown that over 70 percent of blacks support sanctions of some sort.[20]

Foreign countries' relations with South Africa changed substantially once President F. W. deKlerk came to power and began dismantling the pillars of apartheid. In September 1993, the UN Secretary-General Boutros Boutros-Ghali met deKlerk in New York to congratulate him on the South African Parliament's "historic" decision to establish the Transition Executive Committee and further conveyed support for the August 16 agreement to transfer the South African enclave at Walvis Bay to Namibia (it had been under South African administration since 1922). On September 24 Nelson Mandela called for the lifting of all economic sanctions, in order, as he stated, to create the best social and economic conditions for the victory of democracy. Mandela, however, called for the maintenance of mandatory sanctions concerning arms and nuclear materials until South Africa had elected a democratic representative government.

The lifting of sanctions had already begun in 1990 when deKlerk announced his intention to end apartheid. The European Community, Japan, and the United States lifted bans on trade and investment. The Commonwealth (except for Britain) and the Organization for African Unity (OAU) lifted only "people to people" sanctions, but both kept their trade and financial sanctions until transition agreements were made. From 1993 the U.S. Congress made it possible for South Africa to start receiving International Monetary Fund loans and urged the removal of state and local sanctions. Following Mandela's call for the end of sanctions, the Commonwealth, OAU, and UN announced the lifting of remaining trade and investment sanctions. Mandela's motive in ending sanctions was to get the international community to help prevent the new South Africa from sinking into social and economic chaos. According to Mandela, years of apartheid had left a "swath of disaster" in its wake.[21] He hoped foreign investors would help regenerate the economy.

THE EFFECTS OF PRESSURE

Both internal and external pressure took their toll on apartheid. The South African government's political problems of the mid-1980s were made worse by a deteriorating economy, partly due to political uncertainty and withdrawal of foreign investment. The annual rate of inflation rose from 11 percent in 1983 to 18.6 percent in 1986. Real growth per capita declined between 1985 and 1986, while unemployment rose steadily. South Africa had gained some experience in getting around trade sanctions, but her stricter exclusion from international capital markets, disinvestment, and the arms embargoes were harder to deal with.

By 1989 many long-term conditions that undermined apartheid became apparent. One condition was demographic: By official census reports the percentage of white population to black had dropped from 21 percent in 1936 to 15 percent in 1985, while the rise of the African population, influx to cities, and deterioration of homelands continued without pause. The rise in the number of Africans, coloreds, and Indians reaching middle levels of employment by the 1980s marked a second condition stretching the limits of apartheid. The decline of white dominance in education marked a third condition, and the extravagance of the apartheid system was an important fourth condition. With three parliamentary chambers and ten different departments of education, health, and welfare (one for each "race" and one for each nonindependent homeland), the apartheid system had set up expenses that could not be maintained under economic strain. During the 1980s, a government park in Durban found itself facing closure due to maintenance costs. An Indian woman wrote to the local paper suggesting that doing away with the separate entrance to the park for nonwhites, complete with separate guard, might be one way for the park to save money. Her suggestion was met by a barrage of personal threatening letters from whites.[22]

Opponents of sanctions continued to argue that the result of economic pressure would be a movement of whites to the right in South Africa. Import sectors did in fact move to increase the numbers of the Conservative party, but no convincing evidence that this was due to sanctions exists. Most indicators reveal that by 1989 the white community was more bitterly divided and bewildered than at any time in the history of apartheid. Draft evasion was high. In 1985, 25–40 percent of whites conscripted did not report for duty. Morale in the armed forces was very low; and in 1988, 344 members of the South African Defense Force attempted suicide, triple the number in 1985.

The piecemeal application of sanctions increased to a certain degree the resentment and confusion of South African whites. Although many companies left South Africa between 1985 and 1989, disinvestment revealed itself to be more a business move in reaction to protest in home countries and economic instability than a factor in national policy. Companies' reasons for leaving were not unified, and all had different approaches to the method of pulling out. Antiapartheid messages became lost in the confusion. The lack of clarity in disinvestment and sanctions accounts for the cynicism and defiance among many South African whites. The South African government could (with some measure of truth) interpret the sanctions policies as the actions of foreign politicians under pressure from their constituents and with no real comprehension of the situation in South Africa. Quite a few South Africans viewed disinvestment as a sham. Although sometimes the names were changed, many products and services were still available after companies had supposedly pulled out.

Disinvestment nonetheless affected South Africa on a broad level: It removed much-needed capital and technology from the country and created a debilitating sense of isolation. According to one observer, disinvestment "contributed to an overall atmosphere of uncertainty which has been damaging to the confidence required for earnings and investment to flourish."[23] Financial sanctions also hurt South Africa's access to capital. Their implementation meant that the South African government had to attain large balance-of-payments surpluses to meet its international debt and interest payments, and would therefore have to restrict imports with tariffs (in a sense, imposing sanctions on itself), an action creating hardship as its export markets were suffering from world trade sanctions on South Africa and the dropping gold price. Because South Africa's economic health depended on external capital and goods, these import restrictions represented a strong check on growth. The *Financial Mail* referred to the process as "our progressive impoverishment."[24] To counter the effect of sanctions, consumers had to pay higher premiums, taxes rose, and many workers in export-related industries lost their jobs. The pattern of rising costs, lost investments, and technological isolation—all connected with outside pressure—was slow but steady. The president of the South African Foundation stated at the end of 1987, "There is no doubt that the [sanctions] package has had an adverse effect on domestic confidence. The lack of confidence is again and again emerging as the most important single factor inhibiting growth in this country."[25]

Although some white South Africans remained defiant, many in the business sector began facing the fact that Africans would eventually acquire a major share of political power in South Africa. A pattern of business leaders meeting with the ANC outside South Africa emerged, starting with a group of businesssmen led by the chairman of Anglo American Corporation Gavin Relly, who met with Oliver Tambo and other opposition leaders in Zambia. In July 1987 sixty-one white South Africans, mostly Afrikaners, traveled to Dakar, Senegal. Led by F. van Zyl Slabbert, founder of the Institute for a Democratic Alternative for South Africa (IDASA), the group engaged in three days of talks with seventeen members of the ANC led by Thabo Mbeki. The meeting ended with a joint communiqué that expressed unanimous support for a negotiated settlement. South African business executives lobbied their government in the late 1980s for change and moved to find common ground with antiapartheid groups and trade unions. Henri de Villiers, Chairman of Standard Bank Investment Corporation argued, "In this day and age there is no such thing as economic self-sufficiency. . . . South Africa needs the world. It needs markets. It needs skills, it needs technology and above all it needs capital. . . . It is imperative that we do not adopt poses of defiance and bluster." He added that the business community had a special responsibility to push consistently for speedy political changes.[26]

The cultural boycott, which involved exclusion of South Africa from worldwide participation in sports, music, academia, and plays put further pressure on South African society. Cultural resistance, meanwhile, in the form of protest plays, concerts, and literature within South Africa escalated in the 1980s and became a major source of opposition to apartheid. This made it necessary for the representatives of the antiapartheid struggle to alter the original pattern of cultural boycotts so that they did not suppress cultural activities. The policy of the 1980s continued the isolation of apartheid institutions but established direct contact between antiapartheid groups inside and outside South Africa. Known as the "culture of liberation," this direct contact became widespread and increased the psychological isolation of the apartheid system in the 1980s.

By 1990 polls indicated strong pessimism among whites over the future of South Africa, and fear regarding their own security. The reactions, however, were splintered and did not lead to a rallying around the government. The Dutch Reformed Church divided over the morality of apartheid, the Broederbond split over national strategy, and the National Party debated political strategy. The 1984–1985 uprisings and their aftermath accounted for a large part of this reaction and division, but sanctions and disinvestment also played a part. None of these pressures apparently led to unity and structured defiance among whites. Confusion and vulnerability were the more obvious result of steady coercion inside and outside the country. Among all these factors in the fall of apartheid, the decline of communism in eastern Europe played an essential role. The end of the Cold War acted as a major influence on the South African government's increased comfort in meeting with antiapartheid leaders and adopting a more visionary outlook toward reforming or dismantling apartheid, as it also ended the rationale of the United States and Britain for not being more forceful in pressing for change in South Africa. The fear of dangerous outside forces undermining South African society could no longer hold water, and a growing sense of urgency among many whites toward change, most notably in the business sector, replaced it.

EXTERNAL INVOLVEMENT IN THE ELECTIONS

Considering the norm in such situations, less international presence was apparent during the elections process in South Africa in 1994. It was, however, substantial and active. The preoccupation with potential violence determined the nature of outside involvement in polling, and the UN Observer Mission for South Africa (UNOMSA) formed to defuse potential violence threatening to disrupt negotiations. The European Community and OAU also sent observers, and a network of nongovernmental organization (NGO) observers connected with the church community arrived. Security Council Resolution 894 extended UNOMSA's mandate to include election observation, and a technical task force joined with the Independent Electoral Commission (IEC) and coordinated UNOMSA's collection and analysis of information on the election. An estimated 5,000 international observers came to South Africa, as well as a wide variety of organizations, including the Association of Western European Parliamentarians, Central Electoral Commission of the Russian Federation, and the pan-African group Pollwatch Africa. Many American organizations came, most operating under the Lawyers' Committee for Civil Rights under Law.

The foreign presence at the elections actually stretched beyond observation, and operated at many levels, from international commissioners sitting on the IEC to foreigners working as technical advisers. International influence could sometimes be abrasive and intrusive, but it was made more acceptable by the presence of Third World country observers from African, Asian, and Latin American countries who could identify with South Africans overwhelmed by the new process of election and politics and explain it clearly and sympathetically. These observers played a significant role in balancing the large number of technical advisers from North America and Western Europe. The security role of international representatives during elections, however, was kept to a minimum, as security remained a touchy subject with the South African government.

Overall, the international community viewed the elections as vital and their actual occurrence as encouraging. A voter education specialist from Zambia summed up her feelings, and captured the sense of other observers', during the elections process, remarking on the "outstanding" parallels and insights she and her colleagues gained, and observed:

Elections are the midwives of the political transition. And the breakthroughs made between South Africa, [the] Philippines and other countries in the elections could be the basis for working through the more difficult tasks ahead—governing. Perhaps South-South exchanges in relation to governance are some of the things that should be put on the agenda for the next six years.[27]

Through pressure within and without the country, South Africa had moved from pariah of the international community to a strong symbol of peaceful change and the democratic process. In 1993 Archbishop Desmond Tutu remarked that South Africa was a microcosm of the world, encompassing all the global issues of white, black, rich and poor, developed and underdeveloped: "Once we have got it right, South Africa will be the paradigm for the rest of the world."[28]

NOTES

1. Barbara Rogers, *Divide and Rule: South Africa's Bantustans* (London: International Defense and Aid Fund, March 1976), p. 21.

2. *Financial Mail* (Johannesburg), April 23, 1971.

3. "South Africa: What Future for the Homelands?" *Africa Confidential* 29 (1988): 1–3; Miriam Lacob, "Homelands: The New Locus of Repression," *Africa Report* 29 (January–February 1984): 44.

4. *The Star* (Johannesburg), December 7, 1974; Rogers, *Divide and Rule*, pp. 12–13; Nelson Mandela, *Long Walk to Freedom* (Boston: Little, Brown, and Company, 1994), p. 240.

5. *Cape Times* (Cape Town), June 30, 1969; *The Star* (Johannesburg), August 26, 1974.

6. L. W. Michie, "Personal Journal of Events in Transkei and South Africa 1989–91" (in author's possession).

7. Richard Stengel, "Dinosaurland," *The New Republic* 208 (January 4–11, 1993): 11–12.

8. William Beinart, *Twentieth-Century South Africa* (New York: Oxford University Press, 1994), pp. 238–39.

9. *UN Chronicle* 21 (1984): 21.

10. *South Africa: The Sanctions Mission: Report of the Eminent Church Persons Group Prepared by Dr. James Mutambirwa* (London: Zed Books, 1989), p. 59.

11. Mohamed A. El-Khawas and Barry Cohen, eds., *The Kissinger Study of Southern Africa: National Security Study Memorandum* 39 (Westport, CT: Greenwood Press, 1978), pp. 105–6.

12. *South Africa: Time Running Out* (Berkeley and Los Angeles: Study Commission on U.S. Policy toward South Africa, 1981), p. 353.

13. Pauline Baker, *The United States and South Africa: The Reagan Years* (New York: Praeger, 1989), p. 25.

14. *South Africa: The Sanctions Mission*, pp. 88–89.

15. *Newsweek* 45 (September 25, 1989); *Washington Post*, October 4, 1989.

16. Robert E. Edgar, ed., *Sanctioning Apartheid* (Trenton, NJ: Africa World Press, 1990), p. 15.

17. Laurence Schlemmer, *Black Worker Attitudes: Political Options, Capitalism and Investment in South Africa* (Durban: Center for Applied Social Sciences, University of Natal, 1984), pp. 33–41; Mark Orkin, *Disinvestment, the Struggle and the Future, What Black South Africans Really Think* (Johannesburg: Ravan Press, 1986), pp. 12–13.

18. David Hirschmann, "The Impact of Sanctions and Disinvestment on Black South African Attitudes toward the United States," in ed., *Sanctioning Apartheid*, p. 98.

19. Ibid., p. 101.

20. Desmond Tutu, "A Plea for International Sanctions," in S. Prakash, ed., *The South African Quagmire: In Search of a Peaceful Path for Democratic Pluralism* (Cambridge, MA: Ballinger Publishing Company, 1987), p. 164.

21. "Mandela Calls for Lifting of Economic Santions," *UN Chronicle* 30 (December 1993): 14–15.

22. Michie, "Personal Journal of Events in Transkei and South Africa 1989–91."

23. *South Africa's Relationship with the International Financial System* (Toronto: Commonwealth Secretariat, August 1988), p. 55.

24. *Financial Mail* (Johannesburg), September 2, 1988.

25. *Financial Times* (London), November 11, 1987.

26. *The Star* (Johannesburg), July 20, 1988.

27. Francis A. Kornegay, Jr., "A Little Help from Friends," *Africa Report* 39 (July–August 1994): 24–28.

28. Allister Sparks, "The Secret Revolution," *New Yorker* 70 (April 11, 1994): 56–78.

Riot police arrest Soweto demonstrator, 1978. Courtesy of Amnesty International

Nelson Mandela at a rally in Umtata, June 1990. Author's collection

Winnie Mandela. Courtesy of Amnesty International

Mangosokho Buthelezi. Courtesy of South African Embassy, Washington, DC

Demonstrators at a strike in Butterworth in the Eastern Cape. Author's collection

Demonstrators "toi-toi" in Butterworth. Author's collection

Nelson Mandela at a rally in Umtata, June 1990. Author's collection

ANC "army" at a rally. Author's collection

F. W. deKlerk. Courtesy of the South Africa Embassy, Washington, DC

5

Challenges of a New Democracy

On December 16, 1997, in an address to the ANC, Nelson Mandela announced his resignation as president of the party. It was six years after his appointment as ANC president, and three years since he had been elected to lead the Government of National Unity—the new democratic government that had signaled the end of apartheid. The post-apartheid government had faced many challenges since its election, and Mandela's resignation speech drew attention to these challenges. It was particularly harsh in its criticism of both ANC opposition and the ANC itself.

Mandela accused the white opposition and the white media of trying to undermine recent reforms to secure their own racial advantages. He warned that the security networks of the apartheid era had not been completely dismantled and that these still threatened stability and democracy in South Africa. Although not directly declaring the certainty of racial conflict, he did suggest its possibility. He spoke of a counteroffensive "that would seek to maintain the privileges of the white minority," and whose power had yet to be tested by new democratic attempts to tear down the legacies of apartheid. He further criticized South Africa's parties for deciding against "the pursuit of a national agenda," choosing instead to pursue a "reactionary, dangerous and opportunist" position against the ANC. Mandela was referring, in particular, to the National Party's decision to withdraw from the government in 1996 to become the formal opposition to the ANC government. He further accused whites of using racist symbolism to gain political ground by highlighting South Africa's high crime rate and encouraging the idea that a black government was doomed to fail. Mandela also pointed out that the apartheid economy remained entrenched in South Africa; apartheid patterns still influenced where South Africans lived, worked, and went to school.

Mandela then turned on his own party, claiming that the ANC had failed to create a set of common national goals to transform South Africa's political culture from one of apartheid to that of a democracy. He pointed out that the ANC suffered from creeping careerism, corruption, and indiscipline. He further cited the damage made by philosophical divisions between socialist elements in the party and free market supporters over the economic policies pursued by the ANC.[1]

Mandela's criticism encompassed many of the problems his post-apartheid nation had faced over the last three and a half years: increased crime, challenges from the right, divisions within the ANC, economic problems, and changes in the media. These criticisms related to further problems: reform of the police force, corruption, the position of African nationalism in the new dispensation, the position of the old tribal chiefs, and disruption in KwaZulu/Natal. The connecting point for all these problems was the need for unity, and crucial to the achievement of unity was the success of the newly created Truth and Reconciliation Commission.

As demonstrated in earlier chapters, the ANC won an overwhelming victory in the 1994 national elections, with Northern Transvaal emerging as the most solid ANC bastion. In one example of the pursuit of unity, the ANC included representatives of Constandt Viljoen's right-wing party, the Freedom Front, in Northern Transvaal's provincial cabinet. Mandela also engaged in talks with the Conservative party while the new Minister of Justice Dullah Omar met with the right-wing Afrikaner Weerstandsbeweging (AWB). Both meetings attempted to address demands for a separate Afrikaner state and amnesty for right-wing political prisoners.

On assuming office, Mandela immediately put his ambitious Reconstruction and Development Plan (RDP) into action, receiving cautious approval from leaders of the business community. RDP projects included free medical care in state hospitals and clinics for pregnant women and children under the age of six; a plan to electrify 350,000 houses; and the initiation of a public works program to fight unemployment and restore services in black townships. The government also set to work on creating a new constitution for South Africa, signing an interim constitution in the meantime.

In mid-1995, the government passed a law known as the Promotion of National Unity and Reconciliation Act. The act spawned the Truth and Reconciliation Commission, which linked truth over brutalities committed during the apartheid era with reconciliation, national unity, and nation building. The commission was given several jobs, including establishing as clearly as possible the gross violations of human rights from March 1, 1960 (the day of the Sharpeville massacre) to May 10, 1994 and granting amnesty to those who made full disclosure of the necessary facts relating to acts carried out with a political objective. The commission, after carrying out a series of hearings over the next few years, was to make a final report by June 1998 when its mandate expired.

In December 1996 South Africa's new constitution was certified by the new Constitutional Court (similar to the U.S. Supreme Court) and signed into law. The Constitution defined a majority-rule government whereby the party that won more than half the seats in parliament was given the power to choose the president. The president would then form his cabinet. The new constitution included a bill of rights that guaranteed the right to adequate housing, food, water, education, and health care. It further banned discrimination on the basis of race, gender, sexual orientation, age, pregnancy, or marital status. The constitution and Truth and Reconciliation Commission, in theory, transformed the South African government from a morally backward and repressive system to one of the most progressive in the world.

The passing of the constitution also marked the end of an era in South African politics. From that time on, parties became focused on the 1999 election, future leaders, and party alignments. One month later, deKlerk's NP left the unity cabinet to form the opposition party. Although both Mandela and deKlerk publicly declared it a normal development for a multiparty system, the move upset Mandela's carefully created coalition. From the time of the NP's break from the government to the resignation of Nelson Mandela from the ANC, divisions between and within the parties began to challenge the unity that had been the aim of the interim government. These divisions added to and were fueled by the other challenges facing the new South Africa.

CHALLENGES TO THE NEW REGIME

The legacies of apartheid left overwhelming social and economic challenges. In 1994 the per capita income of South Africa was $2,800 per year, ranking South Africa among the upper middle income of developing countries. But social conditions measured by the human development index put the country behind Thailand, Botswana, Cuba, and Albania. During apartheid, 87 percent of South Africa's land was reserved for South Africa's 5 million whites. The repeal laws of 1990 had not done much to change this. Whites earned, on average, 9.5 times more than blacks. Three percent of all managers were black, and black-owned companies comprised about 2 percent of the Johannesburg stock exchange. South Africa's budget deficit was at approximately $8.5 billion and represented 6.8 percent of her gross domestic product, much larger than the 3 percent mark preferred by international finance institutions.[2]

The early days of the new government saw a rise in trade union militancy. One factor in the strikes was the controversy over the large salaries accepted by ANC members of parliament. Desmond Tutu wryly remarked that the ANC had stopped the gravy train only long enough to climb aboard. One perpetrator was Winnie Mandela who, after her cabinet appointment, charged the state for private hotel expenses and accepted an expensive gift (the use of a luxury house) from a businesswoman with a criminal record. Workers observing the perks and increase in government salaries demanded higher salaries for themselves. The boycott mentality, meanwhile, persisted, with many blacks refusing to pay rent in arrears. The government's decision to write off millions of rands by scrapping debts merely created further problems. Coloreds demanded that their arrears also be done away with, and even whites demanded a flat rate of 45 rands per month. Unemployment was high, the departure of many whites from the country caused a capital drain, and the income gap between Africans and whites was still large.[3]

The nature of South African cities was changing. Johannesburg was fast becoming Africa's capital with traders coming from Zaire, Nigeria, and other African states. Rich Germans bought Cape Town property, and affluent South African whites flooded into Cape Town, the only region still ruled by the NP, resulting in a great property boom. Squatters and poor blacks also poured in from the Eastern Cape, putting greater pressure on the city.[4]

Foreign elements in the cities were matched by foreign influence on the media, which was also undergoing major changes. Mandela's criticism of the media in his resignation speech echoed criticism he had made the previous year of "senior black journalists." It also supported the views of his successor as ANC president, Thabo Mbeki, then deputy president, who had become a major critic of the media. Mbeki believed that the press was unsympathetic to the ANC's nation-building plan and that it employed too many knee-jerk radicals. He further believed that black writers lost their roots when they went to work for large corporations.[5] The ending of apartheid's strict control and censorship of the press caused rapid developments that probably fueled ANC worries over communicating a sense of unity to the public. A large number of the English-language papers were taken over by Tony O'Reilly, an Irish tycoon, and a consortium led by Cyril Ramaphosa, who had left his ANC government post for a career in the private sector. Apart from the criticism of bias from the ANC, the greater access to the media and its greater freedom created other conflicts. One division concerned the cultural influence of imported programs, encouraging the Afrikaners, in particular, to feel that their own culture was under attack, not least because most of the imported television programs were in English.[6]

The dramatic changes in politics brought on by the ending of apartheid also changed the expectations of different sections of the South African population, the groups with which they identified, and the forms and levels of protest. After the 1994 elections, the pattern of trust and confidence in the government among Africans compared to whites was reversed. Black South Africans generally felt less deprived after the first year of the new government, but the new government also led to a rise in their expectations. This would, in many cases, develop into frustration. Housing, jobs, and education replaced political rights as grievances, and these were difficult areas for the government to tackle and produce immediate results. Whites generally mistrusted the new government, and colored and Indian trust diminished during the first year of the new democracy. In political terms, trust was restricted mainly to ANC and PAC supporters. Trust was, of course, related to group perception of its own situation. The Africans saw the most immediate changes in their social conditions but wanted more. Coloreds saw not much change in their own situation. Indians were slightly more satisfied but were concerned over education and safety. The whites were most satisfied in terms of their social and economic situation but had become more concerned over education and health care than during the apartheid era.

Identification among different groups in South Africa also changed. As political identification eased off, language and ethnic group took prominence as forms of identity. Generation and gender also gained significance. Rearrangement of group identification changed the form of protest. Protest remained high in the first year of the new government, but its constituents and character were different. Violent protest decreased as did collective action, but peaceful protest continued. Preparedness to take part in peaceful demonstrations was still high among Africans and increased among coloreds. Africans, due to their tradition of protest during the years of apartheid, were still the most prepared to take action.

Whereas political violence declined in South Africa, violent crime rose. In January 1995, 279 police were murdered—one of the highest rates in the world. The rise in crime fueled and exacerbated the problem of reforming the police force in South Africa. One legacy from the apartheid area that made this problem difficult was public perception of a police force that had been so brutal. One of the first things the interim constitution did was to change the official name of the police from South African Police "Force" to

South African Police "Security." During apartheid there had been a strong military aspect to the South African Police, and the police were connected in black minds with stirring up violence as opposed to restoring law and order. Much of the dirty work of the South African police force was carried out in the homelands by black policemen. Another legacy was discrimination in the police force. Sixty percent of policemen were black, but 95 percent of the senior officer corps were white.

Reform of the police in South Africa began with amalgamation of the eleven police forces into one national police force, and obligatory police and community forums set up at all police stations. An independent complaints mechanism replaced the system whereby police reported on their fellow officers. This was all part of an overall community approach to the police system that would encourage greater trust between police and the public. The new training course at the Pretoria Police college involved a close study of the new constitution, especially the bill of rights, and relied heavily on role-playing.

One worrying question from the beginning of reform of the police was how much real support would be given for these new progressive concepts. Police Commissioner Johan van der Merwe outwardly cooperated with the new Minister for Safety and Security in Sydney, Mufamadi, but one foreign police expert associated with the reform process noted that the former apartheid policeman had been "very technical, very correct about everything, showing no enthusiasm for the changes being proposed."[7] The police themselves were reluctant to carry less-lethal weapons than previously, which undermined attempts to demilitarize the system. The technical work of combining the eleven police forces also had revealed enormous problems: different pay scales, conditions of service, and the corrupt system of promotions in the homelands. Former apartheid officers had trouble respecting the seniority of officers from the homelands. The general difficulties of affirmative action to redress the balance in the South African police also made themselves felt. The reform of the police in South Africa represented yet another area where progressive change struggled against a repressive legacy.

Connected in the minds of many in South Africa with the rise in crime was the increase after the end of apartheid of illegal immigration into the country. By regional standards, South Africa was well off, with a gross domestic product that was twenty times that of Zimbabwe, the next richest member of the Southern African Development Community (SADC). The lifting of apartheid made South Africa an attractive country for migration, and immigrants began increasing in number. Buthelezi, as the new home affairs minister, took a hard-line approach to illegal immigration, linking it directly to crime. He was supported in his approach by Defense Minister Joe Modise and Chief of the South African National Defense Force General Georg Meiring. Meiring claimed that his soldiers, with police, arrested over 23,000 illegal immigrants between January and July 1997, and seized about 23,000 kilograms of *dagga* (the local marijuana), with a street value of over 3 million rand, and 2,660 tablets of Mandrax (a barbiturate). Meiring further claimed that 929 illegal weapons were captured, 1,840 criminal suspects, and almost 200 stolen vehicles and 426 stolen cattle were recovered. Police claimed that 14 percent of crimes involved illegal immigrants.[8]

Early in 1997 Buthelezi commissioned a green paper on international migration from a nine-member team chaired by Wilmot James, Executive Director of the Institute for a Democratic South Africa. The commission's findings and recommendations most likely disappointed the home affairs minister. The commission rested its findings on the basic assumption that because South Africa was much richer than her neighbors, immigration would continue. It recommended a system of temporary admission for SADC workers with full rights granted to due process, administrative review, and information to migrants. In this case, Buthelezi and his supporters were taking the old approach to immigration as the commission attempted to follow the new progressive line. Unity was again a problem, along with struggles with the leftover psychology of apartheid.

One problem the ANC also had to face was getting African approval for those policies that appeared to contradict African nationalism, an element that had been crucial to opposition to apartheid. The ANC increasingly felt pressure from the Black Consciousness movement to take on a more African identity to get support for its policies. Some of this was linked to the continued economic disparity between blacks and whites.

One major example of the attempt to connect African tradition with government policy was the emphasis placed on *ubuntu*, an African concept purposely defined by the ANC as humanity, community, and compassion. Respect for human dignity and solidarity were also wedded to *ubuntu*. The postamble of the 1993 Interim Constitution stated, "There is a need for understanding but not for vengeance, a need for reparation but not for retaliation, a need for *ubuntu* but not for victimization." The passage also appeared in the preamble to the 1995 National Unity and Reconciliation Act to establish the Truth and Reconciliaiton Commission. *Ubuntu* was employed to defend the controversial decision by the Constitutional Court to get rid of the death penalty in South Africa.[9] In this particular challenge to the new South Africa, progressivism appealed to African tradition in order to combat both black and white conservative opinion.

Another sticky problem connected with African identity was what to do with the traditional leaders of African groups, such as the chiefs of the former homelands. In ANC circles before the election, it was assumed that the position of chiefs of homelands would not survive the post-apartheid era. But the African traditional leaders' position had always been flexible, and instead of being phased out, the chiefs began reasserting themselves, mainly by appealing to tradition and representation of rural areas. They allied with the ANC and combined their traditional background with the language of liberation politics and development. They further formed the Congress of Traditional Leaders of South Africa (Contralesa), whose aims were uniting all traditional leaders in South Africa to fight for elimination of the bantustan system, and to "school the traditional leaders about the aims of the South African liberation struggle and their role in it." Contralesa received ANC approval, but the alliance made many ANC supporters uncomfortable. As one observer put it, "The picture of venerated ANC leaders wining and dining with bantustan leaders and paying homage to chiefs was thoroughly upsetting for rural activists." Many did not like the idea of the ANC being swamped with yesterday's enemies.[10]

Both the interim and the final constitutions provided for recognition of traditional leaders, but the language concerning traditional leaders was watered down in the final constitution. National legislation, it stated, could set up these institutions but was under no obligation to do so. Involvement of traditional leaders and the customary law they represented clashed with the newly recognized women's rights encoded in the new constitution. The rights under the new constitution, the government decided, should prevail over customary law. This decision apparently sat well with general public opinion, which generally approved the institution of traditional leadership, but favored more female participation. The position of traditional leaders as ex-officio members of local government was guaranteed until 1999, but it appeared likely that the chiefs' traditional role would diminish afterward.

One of the thorniest issues in the question of traditional leadership was the role of chiefs in the new local governments. This issue became prominent in yet another major challenge to the new democratic South Africa: continued conflict in KwaZulu/Natal. The 1994 elections brought stability to South Africa and an end to political violence everywhere in the nation except in KwaZulu/Natal. Throughout 1995 and 1996, a monthly toll of fifty to eighty deaths caused by political violence still plagued the area. One main issue to resolve was the status of the contested election in KwaZulu/Natal in 1994. The local ANC would not respect the results, which gave control to the IFP; and the IFP wanted the results officially recognized. It was only strong pressure from the ANC's national leadership for the sake of unity that prevented the provincial ANC leadership from challenging the election result in court.

On November 1, 1995, local elections were held in all designated areas of South Africa except KwaZulu/Natal because of unsettled disputes over the new local government structures. These disputes involved the place of traditional authorities in rural local government structures and whether certain tribal areas should be included in Greater Durban. Central to the disputes was the continued conflict between the ANC and IFP. Local elections in KwaZulu/Natal consequently were postponed three times and finally took place in June 1996. The result was that the IFP stayed the majority party in KwaZulu/Natal but lost a great deal of support in urban areas. The ANC enjoyed a sweeping success in Durban, Pietermaritzburg, and smaller towns, but the IFP was boosted by a large turnout in rural areas and captured 44.54 percent of the overall vote. Neither the ANC nor the IFP disputed the 1996 elections, and this implied acceptance of the 1994 elections.

A peace process launched in March 1996, which involved meetings and discussions between ANC and IFP leaders to improve the atmosphere between the two, continued after the local elections in KwaZulu/Natal. Militant mid-ranking leaders, including "warlords," made public avowals of their commitment to peace. In August 1996, however, the negotiations broke down. The IFP officials had grown angry over the Truth and Reconciliation Commission's linking of its top officials to hit squads of the late 1980s and refused to participate in the proceedings of the commission.

At the beginning of 1997, the ANC proposed a peace package that included an offer to Buthelezi of the position of Second Deputy President in the Government of National Unity. It also tried to accommodate IFP objections to the Truth and Reconciliation process by offering to replace public disclosure of past crimes with private disclosure of the hit squads' networks. But Buthelezi pushed for more, demanding resurrection of lost constitutional battles and tacit agreement that KwaZulu/Natal would remain an IFP province. His demands could be partially explained by a purge of the moderates in the IFP at a meeting of the IFP's National Council in January 1997. Buthelezi was apparently trying to encourage a traditionalist rise in the IFP, a faction that pushed for replacement of "deadbeat" parliamentarians with "grassroots" party leaders—a term that often translated into "local warlords."

To further complicate the peace talks, a cycle of revenge killing in KwaZulu/Natal, which seemed to be dying down in 1996, rose up again in 1997. The question of who exactly was behind the violence gave weight to Nelson Mandela's accusation, in his resignation speech, of networks threatening the stability and democracy of South Africa. Fears arose of a sinister "Third

Force" of white right-wing groups trying to encourage black-on-black vio-lence. At a funeral in August 1997 held for five killed in KwaZulu/Natal, Nelson Mandela claimed that the deaths proved the existence of organized efforts to undermine South African democracy. Mandela made his opinion clear over the violence: "We are dealing with a highly coordinated network of people deployed in state organs, such as the army and police. They are driven by the desperate attempt to arrest the democratic transformation of our country."[11]

THE TRUTH AND RECONCILIATION COMMISSION

The Truth and Reconciliation Commission was an aspect of the new South Africa that captured the most attention worldwide and that became the focus of much South African hope and criticism. Established to investigate abuses under apartheid, offer reparations to victims, and give amnesty to perpetrators, the commission was influenced by the "movement for account-ability" in Latin America that had led to close to twenty truth commissions set up in that region from 1974 to 1997. The idea of accountability dated back to the Nuremberg trials after World War II. The concept was based on a Jewish quote, "To remember is the secret of redemption," and the psycho-logical theory that it is as bad for nations as it is for individuals to suppress the memory of a sad or evil thing in their past. What was most original and particularly controversial about the South African version of truth and ac-countability was that the object of the exercise was not judicial punishment; instead, a full confession would lead to amnesty. The desire was to move through "truth" to "reconciliation." Some ANC members had originally wanted "Nuremberg Trials" for former apartheid leaders. But with the peaceful transition of the 1994 elections, Nelson Mandela led a movement for placing strong political emphasis on reconciliation and national unity. In-vestigation into the past was to lead to reparation as opposed to revenge.[12]

The commission also had a specific commitment under agreements made in 1993 whereby the Afrikaner police, security, and military chiefs de-manded amnesty as the price for allowing the country to proceed peacefully to a free election. The constitution of 1993 stated, "Amnesty shall be granted in respect of acts, omissions, and offences associated with political objec-tives and committed in the course of the conflicts of the past." The new gov-ernment of 1994 was bound by that commitment. Thus, in return for telling the truth of past atrocities in front of the commission, former perpetrators would not be criminally charged, provided the commission was convinced that the crimes were related to the political situation. The extended deadline for amnesty applications was May 10, 1997, and anyone not applying for amnesty, in theory, could still be prosecuted. Those who did not apply included top military personnel from the apartheid era, most senior NP politicians (including P. W. Botha), almost all members of the IFP, and ordinary ANC members involved in violent acts such as "necklacing."

Nelson Mandela appointed the commissioners for the Truth and Reconciliation Commission after careful televised public examinations. Archbishop Desmond Tutu chaired the commission, with Alex Boraine, a former Methodist minister and MP, as deputy chairman. The commission included lawyers, human rights activists, churchmen, doctors, and psychologists. It also represented all groups of South Africans: English-speaking whites, Afrikaners, coloreds, Indians, and Africans; and concerned itself with activities that occurred in the period from March 1, 1960, to May 10, 1994. The hearings involved the testimony of victims of brutality during apartheid, victims' families, and those implicated in carrying out the brutality. The latter category included agents of the apartheid regime as well as former ANC underground activists. The Reparation and Rehabilitation Committee would focus on the victims. It could order immediate support, treatment, or counseling, but its main task was to make recommendations on the method of reparations. Efforts at compensation included tombstones for a murdered family member or scholarships for surviving children of a victim's family. The less wealthy mostly wanted some sort of material recompense. One observer noted, "The poor can't eat tombstones."[13]

As with truth commissions in Latin America, there existed a strong element of political theater in the proceedings of the Truth and Reconciliation Commission. Archbishop Tutu would often weep with those testifying the details of their sufferings. A certain amount of drama was evident in the confessions of policemen over their brutality. Those in attendance would encourage or jeer the testimony of those being questioned by the commissioners. The more-prominent cases drew large crowds, and media attention remained focused on the hearings of the commission.

Reactions to the proceedings of the commission and the whole concept of amnesty were mixed. While the constitutional court judge Richard Goldstone claimed, "Making public the truth is itself a form of justice," others were not satisfied, especially when it came to their own personal cases. One African woman, after listening to evidence of how her husband was killed, was asked if she could forgive the man responsible. Through her interpreter, she replied, "No government can forgive. No commission can forgive. Only I can forgive. And I am not ready to forgive."[14]

Many of those involved in former brutalities came forward to confess mainly through fear of prosecution. Officials from the apartheid regime who testified ranged from ordinary policemen to former President deKlerk. In August 1996 deKlerk testified to the commission that he never authorized "assassination, murder, torture, rape, assault, or the like." Witnesses stated that they "seriously doubted" the truth of this statement. Colonel Eugene de-Kock, who had run a security-police hit-squad at a converted farm near Pretoria until 1993, claimed that deKlerk ordered a 1993 attack on the homeland of Transkei in which five children were killed. DeKlerk's response to this accusation was made to the Truth Commission: that he did use "unconventional strategies" to combat what his government regarded as Soviet-backed terrorism, but "within my knowledge and experience, they never included the authorization of murder, torture, rape, assault, or the like." In October 1996 senior policemen of the old security forces appeared before the commission and gave evidence that shed light on the chain of command that led to crimes such as the abduction of ANC members. Their evidence implicated both deKlerk and former president P. W. Botha.[15]

DeKlerk, at that time, was in an awkward position. The former Nobel Peace Prize winner (shared with Nelson Mandela) and hero of the end of apartheid was now being questioned about his own role in former atrocities. He needed to cooperate in the mood of reconciliation through truth to maintain the trust of the black population. He also needed to maintain the trust of his own party, which was largely white and wanted to see no admission of weakness from their party leader. DeKlerk the visionary struggled with deKlerk the politician and ended up disappointing black South Africans. His testimony also contributed to further political rifts in the carefully structured unity of the new South Africa (discussed later).

One controversial case for the commission was investigation into the death of former Black Consciousness leader Steve Biko. Those police officers involved in his death were granted amnesty in return for their testimony, despite efforts by Biko's family to stop them. Even when granted amnesty for truth, former policemen were still often reluctant to give full revelations. The original story of Biko's death was that he had gone wild and possibly hit his head while being subdued. The apartheid regime had declared his death an accident. The five officers who came forward to the Truth Commission in January 1997 gave new evidence that Biko was injured a day earlier than previously known and that his documents had been altered because a doctor had not been called for twenty-four hours. But the officers still claimed that Biko's death was mainly the result of an interrogation that got out of hand because of Biko's aggressive behavior. One officer, Harold Snyman, had difficulty looking up during his testimony and nervously folded and unfolded his hands. At the prompting of his lawyer he stated, "I feel very badly about these actions." Many of the large audience that came to the Biko hearings hooted and whistled at Snyman's answers.[16]

The Truth and Reconciliation Commission could subpoena witnesses to testify at its hearings, and P. W. Botha was the only person to ignore his subpoena. Botha did file 1,700 pages of written answers to questions put to him by the commission, but he would not come forward in person, claiming that the commission was trying to humiliate him and that he would not apologize for apartheid. Brought to trial for his refusal to testify, Botha, in fact, defended his regime as a "struggle against the Marxist revolutionary onslaught." Botha often expressed contempt for the new South Africa, and in a long speech to reporters, he called on those "opposed to the forces of chaos, communism and socialism" to unite. Botha's written replies did not fully answer the Truth Commission's questions, particularly knowledge of and possible complicity in state-sponsored acts such as the bombing of a church, torture in prisons, and raids into neighboring countries.[17] In August 1998, Botha was found guilty of contempt for ignoring his summons to appear before the Truth and Reconciliation Commission, given a suspended jail sentence of one year, and fined $1,500.

Despite the apparent self-protection as the motivation behind many former perpetrators of violence coming forward to testify to the Truth and Reconciliation Commission, there were also many who came forward with great difficulty and faced more directly their former crimes. These included ANC activists and apartheid agents. Senior representatives of the ANC had to answer questions about the ANC's part in past human rights violations, including executions in their frontline camps, bombings involving deaths of innocent civilians, and attitudes to necklacing once endorsed by Winnie Mandela. One police officer and former interrogator from the apartheid regime cried during his testimony and confessed that he had no explanation for his actions. His psychiatrist testified that, after years of never discussing his work, the policeman was full of self-loathing and suffered acutely. He was still in the police force but was shunned by many officers after his testimony and held an obscure job at Cape Town International Airport. One of his former victims, now a police superintendent, remarked that he was ambivalent toward his former torturer and in a strange way felt sorry for him: "He came out and we exposed him. What's it really going to serve now, not to give him amnesty?"[18]

The overall influence of the Truth and Reconciliation Commission was difficult to gauge in the year that it had still to produce its report. (The hearings ended on July 31, 1998, and a preliminary report on the Commission's findings was given to Mandela in October 1998.) There is no doubt that it caused revelations to many people of incidences that had greatly affected their lives. Truth was definitely and dynamically pursued, and in some cases a measure of reconciliation achieved. National reconciliation, however, was a tall order, and much bitterness remained. The commission was an original and progressive experiment, and like many such experiments, its success depended upon the desire of all those involved to make it work. It did succeed in preventing a pervasive and socially divisive revenge mentality from disrupting the progress of the new South Africa. It did not, however, completely satisfy all those who had suffered under apartheid, nor did it force all those who had committed brutalities to face up to their former crimes. It was, however, a bold experiment that challenged the Western tradition of a punitive justice based on revenge.

POLITICAL DIVISIONS

The new constitution of May 8, 1996, received overwhelming support from the majority of South Africans, but some parties expressed their worries that, under the terms of the consitution, too much power would be given to the governing party. Although he decided to support the constitution, deKlerk expressed his fears over the lack of powers for minority parties. Thirty-one groups including farmers and white mine-workers unions representing Afrikaners made a public statement of their position: "We see no salvation in this constitution for the Afrikaner people or for any other nations."[19]

Despite government efforts for national unity, divisions remained between political groups and grew within the ANC. The Truth and Reconciliation Commission was ironically one source of division. As already noted, the situation in KwaZulu/Natal was another. ANC economic policy created a third source of division, and continued controversy surrounding Winnie Mandela was a fourth. Africanist and Afrikaner unhappiness over the new government's ignoring their own aspirations made for further division. All these sources of disruption of the new South Africa manifested themselves to varying degrees between 1994 and 1997.

DeKlerk's appearance before the Truth and Reconciliation Commission stirred up strong emotions over that leader's sincerity and the motivations of the NP. The NP president's testimony began with a strong apology for apartheid and declaration that it was wrong. But when his cross-examination began, he became ambivalent and defensive. The main point of the cross examination was to determine the level of knowledge and authorization of the series of killings, bombings, and examples of torture taken mainly from the 1980s. DeKlerk claimed in a written submission to the commission that the crimes were committed by "a handful of operatives of the security forces of which the [National] party was not aware and which it could never have condoned." He further argued that abnormal means were needed to combat the ANC strategy of creating chaos in South Africa during apartheid, and pointed out that the other side also had committed crimes.

The reaction of many who were present at the deKlerk hearings was one of indignation and belief that he was lying. Two senior ANC politicians called deKlerk "a disgraceful coward," and at a press conference the following day, Archbishop Tutu said he was close to tears in having to hear deKlerk basically contradict his own apology. How could deKlerk claim he did not know of the brutalities? Tutu asked. "I *told him*."[20]

As noted earlier, deKlerk, in his public testimony, had to consider his constituents, as at that time he was still party leader. The Afrikaners at that time were feeling particularly disgruntled. They saw their language reduced to the same status as Zulu or Xhosa, and their perception of the Truth and Reconciliation Commission was that of an ANC strategy to maintain the moral high ground against the NP until the next election. Support for deKlerk from his own electorate was therefore unlikely if he cooperated with the commission more than was legally required. DeKlerk also might have felt resentful of the burden of responsibility placed on him for apartheid while Botha retired virtually unharmed. The South African historian R. W. Johnson noted, "Questioning deKlerk about the 1980s was rather like asking Khruschchev to answer for the crimes of Stalinism—while Stalin himself sat quiet in his dacha in Tbilisi."[21]

After his testimony, deKlerk immediately demanded an apology for public criticism of himself and his statements. The Truth Commission refused after three weeks of deliberation, and deKlerk withdrew his party's cooperation and started a lawsuit against the commission for bias. On September 5, 1997, the day the legal arguments were to begin for the case, Tutu formally apologized to deKlerk, stating that it was time to "reach out to the National party to serve a cause greater than either body."[22] In the months leading up to the apology, the commission had been attacked by all the opposition parties, who claimed that it was acting merely in the interests of the ANC. The IFP basically boycotted the commission from the beginning, charging it with bias, although KwaZulu/Natal truth commissioners worked hard to get the IFP involved. The IFP remained suspicious. One IFP member described the commission as "a circus presided over by a weeping clown."[23] The loss of the NP's support for the commission would not change its investigations, but it would have an important symbolic influence on the commission's credibility, particularly among white South Africans. It would also hinder the commission's overall success in promoting reconciliation. DeKlerk, meanwhile, announced his retirement as party leader on September 9, 1997.

There did exist an ANC bias in the Truth Commission, and leading ANC members made political capital out of the commission proceedings. But the commission tried to be as tough in its questioning of one side as the other. ANC leaders under examination were not allowed the simple defense that because they supported a just cause they had fought a just war. Thabo Mbeki, for example, had to explain the township liberation chant, "Kill the boer, kill the farmer." (He claimed it was merely a piece of African folk tradition as opposed to a statement of policy.) But the commission's final report was bound to be more critical of the NP than of the ANC because the NP had been in power and had run the apartheid system. This will likely lead to greater separation between the ANC and NP.

The ANC was, meanwhile, increasingly plagued by its own divisions, most notably within the "tripartite alliance" formed with the Congress of South African Trade Unions (COSATU) and the South African Communist party. Controversy was centered on the ANC's economic policy, with COSATU and the SACP criticizing Finance Minister Trevor Manuel's macroeconomic program, launched in June 1996. COSATU and the SACP also wanted the ANC to be restructured, giving more political control to the alliance as a whole. Criticism from COSATU stemmed from a deep-rooted ideological division based on the wide gap in living standards between the broad population and the prosperous white minority, and the rapidly growing prosperous black minority. SACP criticism was grounded in a feeling of betrayal by the ANC of former political and economic policies.

Both COSATU and the SACP viewed the ANC's economic program, which rested on a set of orthodox free market principles sanctioned by the International Monetary Fund and World Bank, as a neoliberal betrayal of the alliance's socialist origins. The new program based itself on fiscal discipline, but COSATU and the SACP wanted an economic policy that involved more government spending on development and infrastructure, heavier taxation of the rich, reduction of interest rates, and curbing the independence of the South African Reserve Bank.

Critics in the ANC meanwhile questioned the value of the socialist partnership. Peter Mokaba, Deputy Minister of Environmental Affairs and Tourism, called the SACP a parasite on the ANC, and advised it to quit the alliance. Mokaba rejected socialism as sterile and went so far as to call it "racist" because it argued that black capitalism was misguided. SACP Deputy General-Secretary Jeremy Cronin and SACP Acting Chairman Blade Nzimande retaliated by calling Makaba a "capitalist" and redefined the ANC's December conference as a clash between capitalists and socialists.[24]

Not long after such criticism, Nelson Mandela declared that the ANC's economic policy was not "set in stone." Most observers believed that the "tripartite alliance" would hold together at least for the near future. The ANC needed union votes and the organizational talent of the SACP. The SACP and COSATU needed the ANC's power and influence. Fragmentation of the alliance would probably be detrimental to all the parties in it. Public criticism from within, however, again shook the ANC's attempt at nation building.

Another challenge to the strength of the ANC was the division between supporters and detractors of Winnie Mandela. Dismissed by the government as Deputy Minister for Arts, Culture and Science, Winnie Mandela held on to her position as head of the ANC Women's League and to a large degree to popularity among the poorest and most militant South Africans. In November 1997 she entered the race for Deputy President of the ANC and threw down the gauntlet to her former husband, accusing him of instructing the police to "dig up as much dirt" as possible on her before the ANC conference in December. She further challenged the ANC leadership by calling for a referendum on the return of the death penalty.[25]

To complicate matters, Winnie Mandela was at the same time summoned before the Truth and Reconciliaton Commission to answer questions concerning her role in the murder of fourteen-year-old Stompie Seipei and of the Soweto doctor who treated the boy. In 1991 Winnie Mandela had been convicted in the kidnapping and assault of Stompie, but her charge was later put aside and her prison sentence reduced to a fine. The controversy over the killing was renewed when a former member of her entourage claimed that he was ready to testify that he saw Winnie Mandela stab Stompie.

Winnie, at first, lashed out at her accusers, denying the charges. She threatened to ignore the subpoena and then asked to testify in public, claiming she had nothing to hide. She was eventually questioned by Archbishop Tutu and Truth commissioners in a crowded auditorium in Johannesburg in December 1997. After Winnie consistently denied allegations of murder, torture, and other crimes, dismissing her accusers as liars, lunatics, and apartheid-era collaborators, Tutu became visibly frustrated and gave an emotional personal plea to her as an old friend to confess. Winnie then made an admission that "things went horribly wrong" during her participation in the antiapartheid struggle of the late 1980s. She said she was deeply sorry and issued apologies to the families of Stompie and the doctor who attended to him.

Winnie Mandela's apology, although accepted by some with skepticism, helped to mend breaches in the ANC and South Africa. One of the commissioners of the Truth Commission stated that her apology did not get her off the hook, but it was still important for many South Africans to hear. "One does not underestimate the meaning of apologies for victims," the commissioner said. "One can't discount that the people of this country never had a formal apology from the apartheid state." Winnie Mandela further healed division in the ANC by withdrawing her nomination as Deputy President of the ANC at the party conference. The announcement of her withdrawal was greeted by cheers, demonstrating appreciation that the party had avoided a showdown over its most controversial figure, as well as the depth of the party's rank-and-file belief in unity. One delegate noted that, in stepping aside, "she was a good comrade."[26]

The ANC had, meanwhile, painstakingly built support for party candidates in preparation for the party conference in order to achieve consensus. Nelson Mandela's resignation was part of a generational shift within the ANC. Younger members were expected to replace older ones in several executive postions. Thabo Mbeki, Mandela's successor, increased the number of his staff from 97 to 161, and the new job description of party president implied increased centralization and full commitment to the ANC's economic policy. In the months before his resignation, Mandela did his best to negate public perception of himself as the strong figure holding the new system together by increasingly easing Mbeki into the spotlight.

ECONOMIC AND FOREIGN POLICY

Of all the regions in Africa after the end of apartheid, southern Africa possessed the greatest potential for success in trade, investment, political cooperation, and peace. The African Development Bank claimed that the region stood "on the threshold of a new era."[27] A solid macroeconomic framework for the future economic growth of southern Africa in particular existed, with the lifting of price controls, reduction in government deficits, easing of strict control over money supply, trade liberalization, and privatization programs. General economic improvement in the region raised hopes of a common financial market in the next seven years after apartheid ended, although South Africa was privately skeptical on this point. Although the dramatic political change in South Africa had drawn the countries of that region closer together, they were still a long way from uniformity.

After the 1994 elections, South Africa joined the Southern African Development Community (SADC). During apartheid, the SADC had received a great deal of sympathy and donations from other continents, most notably Europe, but overseas positions hardened after apartheid ended. The Scandinavian countries, for example, claimed that it was time for the SADC to raise its own money and not wait for handouts. This was a particular problem for South Africa. The nation had recently experienced economic growth after ten years of recession, but still fell short of her growth target. Foreign help and investment were crucial.

A cloud of misunderstanding hung over the unfinished negotiations between South Africa and the European Union on rules for trade. Just before the 1994 elections, European politicans promised generosity once South Africa's system was transformed. South African policymakers trusted these promises to the extent that they began negotiations on the assumption that the European Union would help in South Africa's economic transformation. But in the years following apartheid, the European Union did not offer special help to South Africa on the grounds that it possessed one of Africa's most advanced economies. Regional concerns in Europe also constrained active help for South Africa. At the beginning of 1997 the *South Africa News* spoke of "betrayal" and a "U-turn" on the part of Europe since 1994. Sources in Brussels viewed South Africa's position as "aggressive and disappointing."[28]

By 1997 two issues that dominated the South African economy were external criticism by the International Monetary Fund of the South African Reserve Bank's intervention to protect the rand, and internal criticism of government policy from mainstream business. The latter criticism focused on high interest rates, while COSATU continued to criticize the ANC's rush to "liberalization" in its economic policy. The ANC's macroeconomic policy document "Growth, Employment and Redistribution" (GEAR), published in 1996, outlined a free-market strategy for fast growth and more jobs. The perceived weakness of GEAR was its optimistic growth projections of 6 percent annually by the year 2000. The projection seemed to be unrealistic and provided COSATU with ammunition to accuse GEAR of not being equipped to provide jobs for the rapidly increasing work force. Jobs would be the main issue in the years ahead, and much of the increased crime in South Africa could be attributed to the speedy rise in unemployment in the last ten years. Internal criticism of economic policy remained loud, and in the long term the rand seemed likely to stay vulnerable. Uncertainty over the smooth transition from Nelson Mandela to Thabo Mbeki caused volatility in the economy.

Compared to other emerging market currencies under speculative pressure, however, South African fundamentals were sound. Foreign investor opinion on the health of the South Africa economy was mainly positive, if not wildly enthusiastic, and outsiders bought South African equities in response to the country's improving financial outlook. More economic recovery was expected in 1998, and a permanent fall in the currency appeared unlikely.

Although a certain dependency on foreign aid and investment was necessary for maintaining the economic health of South Africa, Nelson Mandela made it fairly clear that his government would determine its own foreign policy despite pressure from countries such as the United States. In October 1997, for example, Mandela visited Libya to present Muammar el-Qaddafi with the South African award, the Order of Good Hope, to thank Libya for backing the ANC during its struggle against apartheid. While in Libya, Mandela announced support for calls by the Organization of African Unity that the two Libyans suspected of bombing the plane that crashed over Lockerbie, Scotland, in 1988, be tried in a neutral country. Mandela further appealed to the United Nations to review sanctions that were generally hurting Libyans. When U.S. officials criticized his visit to Libya, Mandela became indignant. "How can they have the arrogance," he asked, "to dictate to us where we should go or which countries should be our friends?" Others in his delegation criticized the West's "hypocritical finger pointing" when several European countries contracted billion dollar deals with Libya's oil sector.[29] The new South Africa's foreign policy basically combined openness to diplomatic relations with all countries with a determination to remain as independent in all final decisions as the government had been during the years of apartheid.

CONCLUSION

South Africa always has been and remains a complex country. Operating under contradictory forces such as violence and compassion, openness and bigotry, retribution and forgiveness, beauty and squalor, political suppression and creative freedom, it emerged as a country that could experience both a Sharpeville massacre and a Truth and Reconciliation Commission. Suppression and disruption have plagued South Africa for several centuries, and many were surprised that apartheid ended without a civil war. One might argue, however, that a civil war was fought throughout the 1980s, by the end of which the more farsighted apartheid politicians such as deKlerk realized that it could not continue and that change was not only a moral but a practical necessity.

The biggest underlying challenge to South Africa in the process of dismantling apartheid was and still is the legacy of division. Separation of peoples is so deep-rooted in South African society that progressive attempts to create unity and a new sense of nationhood constantly come up against lingering fears and prejudices. One of the most controversial commissions formed under the new constitution was the Commission for the Promotion and Protection of the Rights of Cultural, Religious and Linguistic Communities. Pressure from the right-wing Freedom Front caused the creation of the commission, mainly because of the determination of Afrikaners to achieve some form of self-rule. The stated aims of the commission include promoting respect and tolerance for all the country's cultural, religious, and linguistic communities. But many have worried that the commission will encourage groups to mobilize on the basis of their differences and further promote separation rather than reconciliation.

During the local elections of 1996, several racial incidents indicated continued division. One particularly disturbing incident was when Mandela was called a *kaffir* by NP supporters at a school in Mitchells Plain, a colored area in the Western Cape. The NP did not discipline its members, but Mandela responded with dignity. "I know they are victims of racist indoctrination and I have no hard feelings," he stated.[30] Division is not only social but also psychological, and the new government will have to meet this challenge to unity and nationhood by creative means. The Truth and Reconciliation Commission represents one creative attempt, but this brought division as well. Greater economic equity is another method of breaking down social and psychological barriers, but this is a slow and difficult process with conflicting notions on the best way to achieve overall prosperity.

The eventual achievement of unity and nationhood crucial to the well-being and peaceful evolution of the new South Africa depends ultimately on the same factor that caused the peaceful end of apartheid: collective determination on the part of the majority of South Africans to make it work. Alliances already have been formed across the divisions of the apartheid era, and attempts continue to be made by the government and individuals to carry through that process and promote unity. Economic and social welfare are definitely important factors in the continuation of peaceful change, but a shared vision among South Africans that transcends their differences will be the key to making such a progressive new nation work.

NOTES

1. *The Denver Post*, December 17, 1997; *The Boston Globe*, January 19, 1998; *The Philadelphia Inquirer*, December 18, 1997.

2. Anne Shepherd, "The Task Ahead," *Africa Report* 39 (July–August 1994): 38–41.

3. Patrick Laurence, "Mandela's First 180 Days," *Africa Report* 39 (July–August 1994): 63–67.

4. *The Philadelphia Inquirer*, January 18, 1998; R. W. Johnson, "Diary," *London Review of Books*, July 17, 1997, p. 29.

5. *Africa Confidential* 38 (January 31, 1997): 4–5.

6. Ibid.; *The Philadelphia Inquirer*, December 2, 1997.

7. Colleen Lowe Morna, "Reforming the Police," *Africa Report* 40 (January–February 1995): 32–35.

8. *Africa Confidential* 38 (July 18, 1997): 5–6.

9. Richard Wilson, "The Sizwe Will Not Go Away," *African Studies* 55:2 (1996): 1–20.

10. Ineke van Kessel and Barbara Oomen, " 'One Chief, One Vote': The Revival of Traditional Authorities in Post-Apartheid South Africa," *African Affairs* 96 (October 1997): 561–85.

11. *New York Times*, August 11, 1997.

12. Timothy Garton Ash, "The Truth about Dictatorship," *New York Review of Books* 65 (February 19, 1998): 35–40; Ash, "True Confessions," *New York Review of Books* 64 (July 17, 1997): 33–38.

13. Ash, "True Confessions," pp. 33–38.

14. Ibid.

15. *The Economist* 340 (September 28, 1996): 50; *The Economist* 340 (October 26, 1996): 54.

16. *New York Times*, September 11, 1997.

17. Ibid., January 28, 1998.

18. Ibid., November 9, 1997.

19. *Winston-Salem Journal* (Winston-Salem, NC), May 9, 1996.

20. Ash, "True Confessions," pp. 33–38.

21. Ibid.

22. *New York Times*, September 6, 1997.

23. Ash, "True Confessions," pp. 33–38.

24. *Africa Confidential* 38 (November 7, 1997): 5–6.

25. Ibid.

26. *The Denver Post*, December 5, 1997; *The Philadelphia Inquirer*, December 18, 1997.

27. Colleen Lowe Morna, "New Era of Cooperation," *Africa Report* 40 (May–June 1995): 64–67.

28. *Africa Confidential* 38 (March 14, 1997): 7.

29. Ibid. (November 7, 1997): 8.

30. Wilmot James, Daria Caliguire, and Kerry Cullinan, *Now That We Are Free* (Boulder, CO: Lynne Rienner Publishers, 1996), p. 140.

Biographies: The Personalities Behind Apartheid and Its End

Stephen Bantu Biko (1946–1977)
Black Consciousness Leader

Steven Biko's Black Consciousness Movement (BC) of the 1970s arguably set the stage for the turmoil of the 1980s. Biko believed that God had purposely intended the creation of blacks and that blacks should therefore take pride in their heritage, culture, and philosophy. The BC movement instilled in the black youth of the 1970s a new confidence that aggressively challenged apartheid officialdom and continued to do so after Biko's violent death.

Biko was born in King Williams Town in the Cape Province on December 18, 1946. In 1963 he took exception to his school, which was run by the Bantu Education Authorities, and transferred to a Catholic school in Natal. He later entered the "non-European" section of the medical school at the University of Natal in 1965. In 1969 Biko and his fellow black students formed the South African Students Organization (SASO) in a break from the National Union of South African Students due to the fact that the latter organization's executive committee was all white. From 1971 on, Biko became increasingly involved in political activity, and in the same year his course was terminated. He immediately went to work for the Black Community Programs in Durban and helped found the Black Consciousness Convention (BCP). In March 1973 he was banned, along with seven other SASO leaders, and restricted to his home in King Williams Town. Biko continued to work tirelessly for his movement and founded the Eastern Cape Branch of the BCP. He carried out his duties as branch executive until an extra clause was inserted into his banning order at the end of 1975 that prohibited him from working for the BCP.

The use of the word "black" to denote Africans, coloreds, and Indians became part of Biko's philosophy of a unified nonwhite identity. The constant use of this term by those involved in the BC movement eventually influenced P. W. Botha's government to drop the term "bantu" and apply "black" (at least to Africans) in the 1980s. Much of the language of the BC movement had been fueled by black power movements in the United States in the 1960s. Biko wrote in 1971, "Black consciousness is in essence the realization by the black man of the need to rally together with his brothers around the cause of their subjection—the blackness of their skin—and to operate as a group in order to rid themselves of the shackles that bind them to perpetual servitude."[1]

In 1976 Biko was detained for 101 days under section 6 of the Terrorism Act, but he was released without being charged. He was charged many times under security legislation but never convicted. In January 1977 he was appointed Honorary President of the BCP for five years. On August 18, 1977, Biko was again detained under section 6 of the Terrorism Act. There was no charge, but the ANC believed that Biko was arrested because he was planning to meet with ANC president Oliver Tambo. This meant the possibility of greater unity between BC and the ANC—a possibility feared by the apartheid government. Biko was taken to Port Elizabeth and kept manacled and naked, eventually dying from a blow to the head (he was presumably rammed against a wall) during interrogation by South African police on September 12, 1977.

Biko was regarded as the father of the BC movement. The anniversary of his death was celebrated every year by blacks and many whites throughout the years of apartheid, and the circumstances of his death as uncovered by the Truth and Reconciliation Commission in 1997 aroused much public attention. The story of his friendship with *The East London Daily Dispatch* editor Donald Woods was told in the book *Biko* (1987) and the movie *Cry Freedom* (1987).

Pieter Willem Botha (1916–   )
Prime Minister and President of South Africa

Vilified by many South Africans as the last repressive apartheid leader, P. W. Botha's direction and intentions throughout his political career are full of contradictions that cause the character of the former South African president to remain something of an enigma. He gave the impression of supreme loyalty to his party regardless of his own private thoughts, which made him instrumental in the formation of apartheid policy in the 1950s. But he was later ready to attempt reform as the mood of many of his constituents changed in the late 1970s and early 1980s.

Botha was born on January 12, 1916, in the Orange Free State, where he later attended the state university. He became an MP for George in 1948 and remained its MP until 1984. From 1948 to 1958, he held the post of Chief Secretary of the Cape NP, during which time he took part in the crucial debates over the policy of separation of races. At one point he declared that to achieve a clear picture of the position of "non-Europeans," the NP should answer the question, "Do we stand for the domination and supremacy of the European or not? . . . For if you stand for the domination and supremacy of the European, then everything you do must in the first place be calculated to insure that domination."[2]

In 1958 Botha became Deputy Minister of Home Affairs, and in 1961 Minister of Colored Affairs, Community Development, and Housing. It was during these appointments that one example of his contradictory stances stood together with his purported party loyalty. At first he had appeared open to colored representation in the NP government, but later he declared that he would fight any proposal for direct representation of coloreds in parliament. When questioned by his biographers on this change, Botha replied that what he had first meant was that coloreds would be better represented by coloreds than by whites, but he had to go along with his leader. "This does not mean that in my heart I have not felt otherwise," stated Botha, "but I have said that a good party member must stand with his leader."[3] Botha was a vigorous defender of his leaders, particularly John Vorster, and one fellow minister noted that Botha would be a formidable opponent in future leadership struggles due to his experience and knowledge of the inside workings of party politics. Until he became party leader, Botha had established a reputation as a "hawk" and a hard-liner.

Botha had some reason to be a hard-liner because he had served as secretary of the Sauer Commission whose report in 1947 had formed the blueprint of the NP's apartheid policy. He had even been praised by the commission chair for his personal contribution to the report. After his post dealing with colored affairs, he served as minister of defense from 1966 to 1980, and added to his tough reputation. But by 1978, when he became prime minister of South Africa as head of the NP, Botha appeared to have reconsidered his views. In 1975 he stated at the provincial congress of the NP, "I will not lead you if you do not subscribe to the principle that all people are equal creatures before God," and on becoming party leader he referred to apartheid as a "recipe for permanent conflict," and warned the white electorate to "adapt or die." He also directly criticized the very system he had helped to legislate, by stating, "We have built a wall of legislation, behind which we have sought cover. . . . We have to change our mentality and to fortify our inner strength."[4] This is not to say that his tough character had changed. Botha kept his drive and quick temper; the latter trait, in fact, seemed to worsen during his terms as prime minister and State president.

While Botha made clear his intentions for reform, it soon became apparent that these would fall short of expectations and would be accompanied by the stepping up of security measures, with Botha himself as Minister of National Security from 1978 to 1984. Elected president under the new constitution in 1984, Botha also remained stubbornly opposed to any incorporation of the "independent" homelands and envisioned an eventual confederation of Southern African states that would maintain advantages to whites enjoyed under the apartheid regime. Jacobus Coetzee, Botha's Minister of Justice, noted, "P.W. was not a man for concessions. He never wanted to show any sign of weakness."[5] This was why, after making the offer to release Mandela on the condition that the ANC renounce violence and Mandela's refusal to accept under that condition, Botha remained stuck in a position from which he could not (or would not) extricate himself. Botha's disastrous policy of reform and repression, meanwhile, brought strong international censorship and sanctions in the mid-1980s, and his own country to the brink of civil war.

In 1989 the damaging leadership struggle within the NP just before the election coupled with Botha's suffering a stroke marked the decline of the South African president. Somewhat ill-tempered before the stroke, Botha became even more irascible and tried to stay on as president when F. W. deKlerk was elected party leader. The five-month power struggle between the two became increasingly acrimonious with Botha refusing to attend NP functions in his honor and attempting openly to discredit deKlerk's governing style. When Botha finally resigned in August 1989, he publicly implied that deKlerk had behaved treacherously because of his meetings with Zambian leader Kenneth Kaunda. South African historian R. W. Johnson observed, "It is not often that one sees a retiring president accusing his duly chosen successor—on prime time television—of being a liar and a virtual traitor."[6] In an attempt to limit the damage caused by Botha, Foreign Minister Pik Botha implied discreetly that his former boss was suffering from senility.

During the negotiations for a new government in 1992, Botha publicly aligned himself with the "No" campaign of the right wing in response to deKlerk's white referendum in March. Botha called CODESA a "Tower of Babel," claiming that the government's negotiations would lead to abdication and suicide on the part of the whites and dominance of an ANC-SACP alliance in South Africa. He continued after the 1994 election to voice harsh criticism of the new government, and in 1998 he was charged with ignoring subpoenas from the Truth and Reconciliation Commission. He meanwhile remained in retirement in South Africa in the appropriately named Wilderness.

Mangosuthu Gatsha Buthelezi (1928–   )
Inkatha Leader

Like P. W. Botha, the character and intentions of KwaZulu leader Mangosuthu Buthelezi are complex, and many of his stances of the 1960s and 1970s were contradicted by his actions in the 1980s and 1990s. His shifting platforms hinged largely on his changing relationship with the NP and his increased cooperation with the apartheid government as a Bantustan leader after years of rejecting the policy of geographic separation for Africans. His relations with the ANC also changed over the years from close coordination of protest policy to fierce and violent competition. Much of this change was due to his own increased power as political leader of one of the most dominant African groups in South Africa. In the 1980s, he was embraced by the NP and conservatives as the moderate alternative to the radical and communist-tainted ANC. In the 1990s, when he was seemingly cast off by the NP in favor of negotiations with the ANC, he allied with potentially disruptive right-wing groups and used the threat of escalated violence in Natal to maintain a prominent position in the political arena.

Born on August 27, 1928, in Zululand, "Dr. Mangosuthu Gatsha Buthelezi" was heir to the chieftainship of the Buthelezi tribe. He was educated in Natal and in 1948 enrolled at Fort Hare University where he majored in history and bantu administration. During this time he joined the ANC Youth League as a contemporary of Nelson Mandela, and became active in the protest movement against apartheid. When Buthelezi became head of the KwaZulu homeland, he acquired the standard limited powers of local authority under apartheid but at the same time rhetorically challenged the legitimacy of the system. While playing on his followers' strong sense of Zulu pride, he also voiced wider African grievances about the oppressiveness of apartheid. Eventually, he formed his own national black following, clandestinely supported by the ANC in the 1970s, when the ANC hoped to use the platforms provided by the homelands for mobilization toward mass movement.

In 1975 Buthelezi reconstituted the cultural organization Inkatha, which dated back to the 1920s, into a political movement open to all Africans. The movement under Buthelezi's leadership quickly established a strong presence in Natal and began attracting national and international attention. Still backed by the ANC, Buthelezi made his position at the time very clear. In 1976 he stated, "The whole world must be told that we despise what some people euphemistically call 'a separate development' or 'separate freedoms' . . . South Africa is one country; it has one destiny and it has in fact one economy."[7] In 1978 Inkatha joined with the colored Labour party and the Indian Reform party to form the South African Black Alliance (SABA) with Buthelezi as chairman. When the question of P. W. Botha's proposed new constitution creating a tricameral parliament for limited Indian and colored representation arose in 1983, Buthelezi advised the coloreds and Indians not to accept it but to keep negotiating. The Labour party, however, decided to use the constitution as a forum to continue the fight for civil rights for all South Africans. Buthelezi felt betrayed and voiced his bitter disappointment in a series of speeches. In the 1980s, the NP government cabinet, recognizing the strength of Buthelezi's movement, tried to persuade the Inkatha leader to accept independence. "I have told Inkatha and I have told the KwaZulu Legislative Assembly," Buthelezi responded, "that I cannot be persuaded to think about independence for KwaZulu now or at any time in the future."[8]

But Buthelezi and Inkatha were becoming increasingly isolated from other antiapartheid groups at this time. Their participation in the predominantly Black Consciousness National Forum Committee was blocked because the BC movement viewed Inkatha and Buthelezi as tainted by their participation in Bantustan politics. Relations between Buthelezi and the ANC soured in the 1980s due to Buthelezi's opposition to school boycotts and other ANC-supported campaigns in South Africa, his well-publicized stand against sanctions, and his open attacks on ANC "terrorism." Buthelezi's increasingly strident opposition to underground ANC activities continued to distance him from the mainstream antiapartheid movements, and Inkatha-supported township violence in the mid-1980s widened that distance, as did Buthelezi's growing personal ambitions.

Buthelezi's opposition to sanctions in the 1980s and his public espousal of a free-market economy made him popular with overseas conservatives. With the increased disruption and recognition of the need for change in South Africa, the idea emerged in South African big business and with the West that Inkatha, as an independent and conservative critic of apartheid, might become a potential partner in a right-of-center alliance. Buthelezi took note of this interest and used it to maintain his position of power. His strength in KwaZulu as head of Inkatha as well as chief minister and minister of police also increased. His legislative assembly allowed no serious opposition, and in 1990 Buthelezi transformed Inkatha into the national political organization, Inkatha Freedom party, in a bid to meet new political challenges and to claim national as opposed to regional status.

Having been scorned by the BC and deserted by the colored Labour party in the 1970s, and distanced from the ANC in the 1980s, Buthelezi in the 1990s found himself and his party being dropped by the NP. This led to his courting of the desperate right-wing on the basis of self-determination and federal status for his region and for the Afrikaners. Gone were the bold statements of the 1970s against separatism and for majority rule. As Buthelezi scrambled to keep his role as a major political player in a changing South Africa, his image became tarnished at home and among overseas moderates. Investigations in 1991, for example, revealed a conspiracy between security police and Inkatha to fuel the latter's rivalry with the ANC and promote Inkatha as an alternative to the ANC. The *Weekly Mail* published secret police and bank documents that indicated several meetings between Buthelezi and security police to revive decreasing support for Inkatha, as well as secret funding of Inkatha by the police starting in 1990, just after Mandela's release from prison.

As Buthelezi became more belligerent and unpredictable in the 1990s, the ANC continued to denounce and challenge the IFP. Mandela, however, managed to keep the door open to the Inkatha leader for some kind of agreement that would secure a peaceful election. When the Freedom Alliance between the right-wing parties, the IFP, and the leaders of Ciskei and KwaZulu fell apart in 1994, Buthelezi used the threat of disruption in Natal to keep his position in the negotiation process and appealed to his followers in March of that year to boycott the upcoming election and defend the sovereignty of KwaZulu. Only when it became clear that he would be left out in the cold if he and his party carried out their threat of nonparticipation did Buthelezi join, at the last minute, in the elections of April 1994.

Buthelezi was given a post in the cabinet of the new government of national unity, but he was not appeased and continued with the IFP to challenge the ANC in various ways: by denouncing and boycotting the Truth and Reconciliation Commission, by causing delay in the KwaZulu/Natal local elections, and by avoiding overtures from Nelson Mandela, including the call for a merging of the ANC and IFP in December 1997.

Frederik Willem deKlerk (1936–   )
President of South Africa and National Party Leader

When F. W. deKlerk stepped up to the podium on February 2, 1990, to open his first parliamentary session as president, it was expected that he would declare some form of reform for South Africa. Not even his supporters, however, were prepared for the far-reaching and radical statement that he made. But deKlerk, according to one of his closest friends, had always had a great sense of timing. He had come to the realization that this was the moment to seize the initiative from his opponents as well as to rescue South Africa (and his government) from sinking further into the quagmire of revolt and economic decline. According to colleagues, he also had experienced some sort of conversion that had evolved gradually between the time he was made leader of the NP in Transvaal and when he was elected president. Before that time, his reputation had been that of a conservative, a party loyalist, and a pragmatist. The pragmatism had remained, but his statements suggested radical liberalism.

The action taken by deKlerk on becoming president was particularly ironic, coming as it did from the son of Jan deKlerk, one of the architects of apartheid policy. The elder deKlerk had been a cabinet minister in the NP that came to power in 1948 and later president of the Senate. F. W. deKlerk's grandfather also had been an important Nationalist politician and a friend of Paul Kruger, the Afrikaner leader during the South African War. Nothing in deKlerk's early life or career had given any indication of a leader prepared to tear down the system built up by his family and his people and to end up maneuvering himself and his people right out of power. But in his inaugural speech, deKlerk announced the legalization of the ANC, Umkhonto we Sizwe, PAC, and SACP, and the release of Nelson Mandela. He further stated that he was ready to negotiate with all these parties to create a new constitution that guaranteed equal rights for all.

DeKlerk was born on March 18, 1936, in Johannesburg and attended the conservative Potchefstrom University in the Orange Free State. He worked in a law practice from 1961 until 1972 when he became a member of the House of Assembly and proceeded to hold several posts in the NP government. At age fifty-three, he became the youngest chief executive in South Africa's history. In 1993 he shared the Nobel Peace Prize with Nelson Mandela.

Until deKlerk's presidential inauguration, his image had been fairly conservative. In 1982, when Andries Treurnicht broke from the NP to form the Conservative party, deKlerk had been the party's natural choice as Transvaal NP leader to challenge Treurnicht in his stronghold. In 1985 deKlerk resisted Botha's abolition of the Immorality Act, which prohibited interracial sex, demonstrating that he still supported the harsher aspects of apartheid. But in 1986, the NP accepted the principle of "a single South Africa," a principle also accepted by deKlerk who later stated, "Once we had gone through the process of reassessment, I took a leap in my own mind, more decisively than many other National party politicians, that power-sharing with blacks was the right cause for a new political dispensation." DeKlerk's brother Willem pointed out that deKlerk's change of heart also came from his experience of having to campaign against the Conservative party in Transvaal: "Listening to their arguments, their ideologies, their stubbornness, he realized it was a matter of racism rather than identity. He reacted against and I believe it was the beginning of an estrangement between F. W. and the conservative part of the NP."[9]

DeKlerk, before his presidency, also became involved in a policy think tank run by the minister of constitutional development Chris Heunis. It was the first time deKlerk had had to face the problem of incorporating the black majority into the political system. Through this experience, deKlerk was exposed to reformist thought in the NP. By the time he was elected NP leader, deKlerk was much less of a conservative or party loyalist. He reached the conclusion that he would have to impose a personal stamp on government policy, and he even retreated for a few weeks to consider his choices. Rejecting the models of the policy think tank, deKlerk decided that his new policy would have to be grounded in protection of minority rights; the blacks would be recognized as the majority in a new political dispensation, but minority protection (of whites, for example) would be provided by a bill of rights. DeKlerk was further influenced by his trips abroad, and most significantly by the situation in eastern Europe. The falling away of the Iron Curtain and the reforms introduced in the Soviet Union by President Mikhail Gorbachev eased NP fears over an ANC supported by communist countries and paved the way for a bolder proposition for South Africa.

There remained, however, the sudden motivation for immediate sweeping change that caused deKlerk to make the startling pronouncements of his inaugural speech. Friends say he spoke of being seized by a powerful sense of religious "calling" on that day and was deeply moved by the inaugural sermon preached by his favorite pastor Pieter Bingle. The speech deKlerk gave was one he had written himself and had kept the text secret to avoid any leaks to the press. "I didn't tell the National Party," claimed deKlerk, "I didn't even tell my wife, Marike, what I was going to announce."[10] In fact, only a few close advisers knew, and there had been much debate over the unbanning of the SACP.

To begin with, deKlerk appeared to want to build an anti-ANC alliance with Buthelezi's IFP and other black political organizations. His idea was to take advantage of confusion in the newly unbanned ANC and allow time for Mandela's star to fade once he was released from prison and became an ordinary politician. The plan, however, backfired as negotiations went on.

DeKlerk's own image was tarnished by reports of the Goldstone Commission that revealed the gunrunning of Inkatha by security police, and police orchestration of violence in Witwatersrand. DeKlerk claimed that he knew nothing of these activities, but the black opposition perceived the measures he took against the officers involved as too mild and it criticized him for his hesitant attitude. The Boipatong massacre of 1992 also hurt deKlerk's image as blacks became convinced that he had done nothing to stop the Zulu killing. When deKlerk tried to visit the area as a gesture of reconciliation, angry demonstrators drove him out and police fired on and killed more civilians. A split, meanwhile, emerged in his cabinet between those who wanted closer relations with the ANC, and those who clung to the IFP alliance.

In the end, deKlerk gave in to the pro-ANC camp and signed the Record of Understanding. (The old guard in his cabinet accused him of sneaking it past them.) With the proposal by SACP chairman Joe Slovo of the "sunset clause" for the new constitution, deKlerk and Mandela were able to reach an agreement on power-sharing versus majority rule. The NP president originally had sought to develop a power base and constitutional system that would protect the overall position of the whites. By 1994 this strategy had been largely abandoned and deKlerk found himself part of an interim government based mainly on majority rule from which he would eventually step down and form the opposition party.

The fact that deKlerk remained, at heart, a pragmatist, is backed up by his refusal during his presidency to apologize for apartheid. To deKlerk, apartheid had begun as an "honorable vision of justice"[11] that allowed for the separate development of various groups and had to be abandoned only when it became unworkable and unjust. The historian Martin J. Murray remarked, "Without making apologies for apartheid, deKlerk wanted to pretend that it never happened,"[12] and tended to give the impression that apartheid was more a major error than a moral crime. This led to further criticism during his appearance before the Truth and Reconciliation Commission. By that time, deKlerk was prepared to apologize for apartheid and offered his apology "in a spirit of true repentence."[13] The apology was too late, however, and deKlerk's subsequent defense of his government's actions only brought criticism and indignation. In August 1997, deKlerk suddenly resigned as head of the NP and leader of the opposition, leaving his party in further disarray after the May resignation of his potential successor Roelf Meyer. Despite his waning popularity, even among his own constituents, deKlerk would still be remembered as the man who formally initiated the end of apartheid.

Chris Hani (1942–1993)
South African Communist Party General-Secretary

When Chris Hani was assassinated in 1993, the South African Communist party lost one of its most charismatic and politically shrewd leaders. Hani filled the gap necessary to accommodate the younger more radical blacks increasingly disappointed by the moderation of the ANC leadership, and in popularity he was second only to Nelson Mandela among the black population. A gifted and appealing speaker, Hani went beyond the ANC mainstream to cultivate ties with many militant populists and most likely would have propelled the SACP into a far stronger role in post-apartheid South Africa.

Hani was born on June 28, 1942, in Cofimvaba, Transkei, the son of a migrant mine worker. His mother supplemented the family income with subsistence farming, and his childhood was fairly harsh. Hani started out a devout Catholic, and his initial desire was to be a priest, but his father discouraged him from such aspirations. In 1954, during his secondary education, the apartheid government introduced bantu education. Angered by the system, Hani eventually became involved in the struggle against apartheid. In 1957, at the age of fifteen, he decided to join the ANC Youth League, and while a student at the University of Fort Hare, Hani became openly involved in the liberation movement. During this time, he was exposed to Marxist ideas and became disenchanted with the "racist capitalist system." He was at the same time fascinated by his studies in English, Latin, and Greek, and claimed later, "My studies of literature further strengthened my hatred of all forms of oppression, persecution, and obscurantism."[14] In 1961 Hani joined the SACP and was active in the Eastern and Western Cape ANC. In 1962 he joined Umkhonto we Sizwe (MK), the military wing of the ANC, and left South Africa.

As a commissar in the Luthuli Detachment, Hani took part in the joint ANC/ZAPU (Zimbabwe African People's Republic) military campaign in what was then Rhodesia in 1967. After the campaign failed disastrously, he escaped to Botswana. In 1973 he infiltrated South Africa and was then based in Lesotho. In 1982 he left Lesotho for Zambia after several attempts were made on his life. Later, right-wing critics highlighted rumors of his involvement in the execution of mutineers within Umkhonto we Sizwe in Angola, but the part he played was never clear. Hani himself claimed that he flew to Lusaka to try to get the ANC leadership to stop the executions. In 1987 he became Chief of Staff of MK. After the ANC was unbanned in 1990, Hani was installed in Transkei. He became a member of the ANC National Executive Committee, and in 1991 was elected general-secretary of the SACP. Together with Cyril Ramaphosa, general-secretary of the ANC, and Jay Naidoo, general-secretary of the Congress of South African Trade Unions (COSATU), Hani was one of the main power brokers of the ANC/SACP/COSATU alliance, and helped launch the "mass action" program following the Boipatong massacre in 1992. Although a militant critic of the capitalist apartheid system and a leader in armed resistance to apartheid, Hani had begun to soften his image in the months before his death, and had been a strong voice in the calls for peaceful resolution of conflict in the process of change.

Hani was shot down in front of his home in Boksburg by Janusz Walus, a Polish émigré, on April 10, 1993. The assassination was instigated by Clive Derby-Lewis, a CP member who had believed that he was carrying out the killing of "the Anti-Christ." There was some talk of a double conspiracy implicating the more moderate leadership of the ANC, and focusing on claims of a split between Hani and Secretary of Defense Joe Modise, but these charges were never proven. Hani's assassination led to a wave of demonstrations, and Nelson Mandela appeared on South African television to make a personal appeal to black South Africans to restrain their anger. Hani's death left a gap in the ANC's populist left wing, but it did not stop the momentum of the peace talks that led to the 1994 election.

Nelson Mandela (1918–   )
President of South Africa and ANC Leader

One of the most significant historical figures of the late twentieth century, Mandela's extraordinary life and inspiring character brought him international attention during his twenty-seven-year imprisonment, and international acclaim on his release and election as president of the government of national unity in South Africa in 1994. Born Rolihlahla Nelson Dalbhunga Mandela on June 14, 1918, the son of a Thembu chief in a small village in Transkei, Mandela was placed under the care of a relative and acting paramount chief in the capital of Thembuland at the age of nine. While at the missionary school of Healdtown, Mandela was inspired by a Xhosa poet who came to speak and predicted a day when South Africa would no longer be controlled by foreigners. In 1939 Mandela began his studies at Fort Hare University and met Oliver Tambo. The two were suspended in 1940 because of their participation in a student strike.

During this time, Mandela's tribal elders arranged a marriage for him, but Mandela could not accept the arrangement and ran off to Johannesburg where he later married Evelyn Ntoko, a nurse, and had three children. The two became estranged due to Evelyn's increased involvement with Jehovah's Witnesses and Mandela's increased involvement in politics. "I cannot remember a moment when I became politicized," wrote Mandela in his autobiography, "I had no epiphany, no singular revelation, no moment of truth, but a steady accumulation of a thousand slights, a thousand indignities, a thousand unremembered moments, produced in me an anger, a rebelliousness, a desire to fight the system that imprisoned my people."[15]

Working as a law clerk in Johannesburg in the 1940s, Mandela began a correspondence law degree at the University of Witwatersrand and joined the local ANC under the influence of Walter Sisulu. He and Oliver Tambo opened the first black law firm in Africa in 1952. After his conviction and arrest, along with Sisulu, under the Suppression of Communism Act, Mandela became disillusioned with the lack of militancy in the ANC. Together with Sisulu and Tambo, he formed the ANC Youth League, and within five years the league took over the ANC and helped write the Freedom Charter of 1955. In 1956 Mandela and Evelyn were divorced. Mandela soon met Winnie Madikezela, and admiring her courage and passion, he immediately decided she would be his wife. They were married in 1958.

After he was put on trial with other ANC activists in 1959 and finally aquitted after four years, the ANC was outlawed and Mandela and other activists set up Umkhonto we Sizwe (Spear of the Nation-MK) as the military wing of the ANC. He slipped out of the country to receive military training in Ethiopia and Algeria, then returned to South Africa to take charge of MK and launch a strategy of sabotage. With his secret orchestration of bombings of power plants, rail lines, and other government facilities, the press soon dubbed him the "Black Pimpernel." He was arrested in 1962 and eventually put on trial with seven other ANC activists, including Sisulu, where he presented a much-publicized four-hour speech in his own defense. He was sentenced to life imprisonment and sent to Robben Island, where he experienced sixteen years of hard labor, periods of solitary confinement (after speaking out for better living conditions), and strict restrictions on contact with his family. During his time in prison, Mandela continued his studies, organized his fellow prisoners to protest for better conditions, and maintained what contact he could with ANC operations within and outside South Africa. Reports of his behavior filtered out, and his reputation as a strong leader continued. In 1982 Mandela and several others were transferred to the more comfortable Pollsmoor Prison near Cape Town, and in 1988 he was hospitalized with tuberculosis. After his recovery, he was sent to Victor Verster Prison Farm.

After the Soweto uprising of 1976, Mandela began to symbolize the spirit of African resistance, a symbol that reconciled the differences between his own generation and the youth of the 1970s. With the rise of a new militant black opposition, South Africans of all different groups rallied around the slogan "Free Mandela," and the ANC activist began to be perceived as central to the future of South Africa. His imprisonment attracted international interest in the 1980s, and western powers also began calling for his release. By the 1980s, Mandela was the world's most famous political prisoner. Government officials, thus, started secret negotiations with Mandela. When Botha offered him freedom in return for a renunciation of violence by the ANC, Mandela refused. He refused again when deKlerk made the same offer in 1989. DeKlerk then agreed to Mandela's unconditional release, and the former MK leader and symbol of black liberation was freed in February 1990.

Almost from the beginning of his involvement in politics, Mandela argued for a common front of all democratic elements, and reiterated his deep-seated belief in nonracialism and pragmatism that appreciated the potential power of white, Indian, and colored allies working within the system for change. He was not only concerned with political rights, but economic and social rights, arguing from early on that racial inequality led to the breakup of African homes and families and economic deprivation. These beliefs remained consistent after Mandela's release in his roles as negotiator and president. They led to his insistence on majority rule and, as president, his Reconstruction and Development Plan for the improvement of standards of living for the majority of South Africans.

In 1992 Mandela and his wife Winnie announced their formal separation due to much controversy surrounding Winnie's behavior. In 1993 Mandela shared the Nobel Peace Prize with F. W. deKlerk. In 1994 he was elected the first president of post-apartheid South Africa, and in 1997 he resigned as ANC president, bequeathing his leadership to Deputy President Thabo Mbeki. Despite predictions that his popularity would decrease after his release from so many years in prison and that his symbolic stature would decline, Mandela's character and dignity remained intact.

Winnie Mandela (1934–   )
ANC Activist

When Nelson Mandela first met Nomzamo Winnie Madikezela in the 1950s, he was struck by "her spirit, her passion, her youth, her courage, her willfulness."[16] Winnie was sixteen years younger than Nelson and at that time a medical social worker. Her spirit and her courage sustained her and made her a hero through the years of her husband's imprisonment; her passion and her willfulness led her into trouble in the late 1980s and 1990s.

Born in Bizana, Transkei, on September 26, 1934, Winnie was the fourth of eight children. Her mother was a domestic science teacher who died when Winnie was eight. Her father later became minister of forestry and agriculture in Transkei during K. D. Matanzima's rule. Receiving a social work degree from Jan Hofmeyer School in Johannesburg and a B.A. in political science at the University of Witwatersrand, Winnie became the first black medical social worker in South Africa at Baragwanath hospital. It was at that point, she claims, that she grew increasingly politicized. In 1958 she married Nelson Mandela, and she went to work for the Child Welfare Society in 1962. Her first dentention in 1958 coincided with the mass arrests of women involved in the antipass campaign. At the same time, she became chair of the ANC Women's League. When the league was banned along with the ANC, she tried with other women leaders to continue to work through the Federation of South African Women.

While Nelson was in prison, Winnie also was jailed and detained for her outspoken defense of her husband and her continued activity on his behalf. She was banned under the Suppression of Communism Act from 1962 to 1975, was twice charged with contravening her banning order in 1967, detained under Section 6 of the Terrorism Act in 1969, and held in solitary confinement for seventeen months until she was aquitted in 1970. She continued to be banned and placed under house arrest in the 1970s, and continued to break her banning orders.

In 1977, in the wake of the 1976 Soweto riots, Winnie became too troublesome for the government to handle and was banished from Soweto to the small Orange Free State town of Brandfort. During that time her house was bombed twice. Her lively personality came to dominate the small conservative Afrikaner town, however, and she initially shocked the white townspeople by striding regally through the streets in bright colored African dresses, keeping them waiting at their own public telephone in the post office, confidently and publicly buying exotic drinks such as Cinzano and champagne, and purposely ignoring segregation signs. During that time, Winnie struck up a friendship with Piet de Waal, the lawyer who handled her legal business in Brandfort, and his wife Adele. De Waal was a close friend of Minister of Justice Kobie Coetsee and began to make diplomatic suggestions on easing the ban on Winnie and releasing Nelson Mandela. When Winnie was allowed to visit her husband in the hospital when he had an enlarged prostate gland, she ended up on the same airplane as Coetsee. Typically, after Coetsee stopped to talk to her in tourist class, she went through to first class and sat down and talked to him, convincing him to visit Mandela himself. This increased the secret negotiations between Mandela and the NP government.

Coetsee and Winnie, meanwhile, met again at his official residence. The Minister of Justice said he would permit her to return to her home in Johannesburg, but asked her not to be too extreme in her actions. It was asking too much of Mandela's wife, and she refused to give any pledges regarding her behavior. Instead, on returning to Johannesburg in 1985, Winnie began the most controversial phase of her life. She began a lengthy public campaign of challenge and embarrassment to the government and appeared periodically in the media at press conferences to describe her husband's status in prison and defiantly criticize government actions. In 1985 she received the Third World Prize and increasingly seemed to relish her role as a hero and living martyr to the black liberation movement. She also surrounded herself with a group of young aggressive men claiming to be her soccer team but actually acting as a private gang under her authority. As this group became increasingly brutal, Winnie began to lose her popularity. Things came to a head with the gang's kidnapping and beating of a group of teenage boys, one of whom, Stompie Mveketse Seipei, died at age fourteen. Jerry Richardson, the leader of the gang was sentenced to death for murder, and Winnie was sentenced to six years' imprisonment on four counts of kidnapping and accessory to assault in 1991. She appealed her sentence and it was eventually dropped, but the incident and her actions in the early 1990s put a strain on her marriage to her newly released husband. They announced their separation in 1992 and were formally divorced in 1996.

Winnie did not fade into the political background. She continued a tireless campaign among the poor in the townships and maintained her popularity among more-militant sections of the ANC. In 1993 she became president of the ANC Women's League, and in 1994 was given the post of deputy minister of arts, culture, science, and technology in the Government of National Unity. She was later dismissed from the post when the ANC leadership grew disapproving of her continued antics, and she went on to put herself forward as a candidate for deputy president at the ANC party conference in 1997. She meanwhile appeared before the Truth and Reconciliation Commission to answer questions about her role in the murder of Stompie Seipei and the doctor who treated him. Initially defiant and denying any complicity, Winnie eventually apologized for her actions and also withdrew her candidacy for ANC Deputy President. The ANC appreciated her apology and stepping aside, but she did not give up her political support for the poor; indeed, she continued to occupy a strong popular presence among the disaffected Africans in South Africa, earning the sobriquet "woman warrior."

Thabo Mbeki (1942–   )
Deputy President of South Africa

A number of people in South Africa were disappointed when Nelson Mandela picked Thabo Mbeki as his successor instead of Cyril Ramaphosa. Whereas Ramaphosa's reputation had been built up during CODESA as a tireless negotiator helping to bridge the impasses reached by the ANC and NP, Mbeki's character was more ambiguous and felt by some to be rather Machiavellian. During the early 1990s, as a member of the ANC's National Working Committee, he formed part of the "middle-of-the-road" ideology. He was a pragmatist who espoused a gradual strategy of building on tactical advantages gained during negotiations in order consistently to weaken the NP's bargaining power.

Mbeki was born on June 18, 1942, the son of the ANC activist Govan Mbeki, who was convicted with Nelson Mandela in the Rivonia trial in 1964 and sent with Mandela to Robben Island. At age fourteen, Thabo Mbeki joined the ANC Youth League and was tutored in politics by the aristocracy of the ANC, including Walter Sisulu. He was a youth organizer for the ANC from 1961 to 1962 and received a degree in economics at the University of London in 1962. In the same year, he was ordered into exile by the ANC, and earned an M.A. in economics at the University of Sussex in England in 1966. While his father began to serve life imprisonment for his political activities, Thabo began a career in ANC overseas institutions, receiving military training in the Soviet Union and becoming assistant-secretary of ANC revolutionary countries from 1971 to 1972. He was acting representative of the ANC in Swaziland and representative of the ANC in Nigeria during the 1970s, and in 1975 he was made a member of the National Executive Committee of the ANC. During the 1980s, he coordinated clandestine meetings with Afrikaner businessmen, cultural figures, and politicians in his role as director of publicity and then of international affairs.

Serving as political secretary to former ANC president Oliver Tambo, Mbeki was handpicked by Nelson Mandela in 1991 to be deputy president of the ANC. When the ANC was elected to power in 1994, Mbeki's own power increased and he used it to sideline potential rivals such as Cyril Ramaphosa and Tokyo Sexwale, who both left politics for private business. With his quiet public presence and without a core constituency in the ANC, Mbeki relied on his diplomatic skills and the loyalty of the Eastern Cape Xhosa old guard to push through the ANC's moderate economic programs. He was not a popular figure, however, with the hard left of the ANC/SACP/COSATU alliance, and he used his power to shunt this element into the background of ANC politics, not without causing resentment. Though credited with brokering the KwaZulu/Natal agreement over local elections, holding the ANC alliance together, and quietly heading the successful constitutional negotiations in 1996, Mbeki was criticized for his lack of visionary leadership. One journalist observed that his most notable achievement was "getting rid of his political opponents."[17] Mandela, however, publicly expressed his complete faith in Mbeki and gradually stepped back during his final months as ANC party leader, giving Mbeki increasing public limelight as the ANC presidential candidate in the 1999 elections.

Roelf Meyer (1947–   )
CODESA Negotiator

As deputy minister of constitutional development, Roelf Meyer became one of the chief negotiators for the NP during the CODESA talks. When the ANC walked out of CODESA in 1992, Meyer became minister of constitutional development and led the negotiating team. He acted as ANC Secretary-General Cyril Ramaphosa's opposite number, and the two developed a strict working relationship. During the months in 1992 when the NP and ANC became estranged, Meyer continued to meet with Ramaphosa until the two parties came together again to launch CODESA II.

Unlike other prominent members of the NP, Meyer offered no explanation for his transformation from apartheid politician to liberal negotiator. Born on July 16, 1947, he had had a conventional career and displayed no signs of being a rebel. He came from an ordinary farming family, and his own profile followed the standard Afrikaner rise to power: involvement in the church, member of the Afrikaner Studentebond, member of the Broederbond, and member of the NP. Meyer entered parliament at the age of thirty-two in 1979, and was referred to by one parliamentary correspondent as "klein [little] F.W."[18] Ten years apart, Meyer's and F. W. deKlerk's careers followed similar patterns. In parliament, Meyer identified with the center-right group and kept a low profile. During the Botha regime, he defended detention of political activists and was appointed chairman of Botha's Joint Management System, which coordinated security forces and service providers in order to eliminate "troublemakers" in the townships. Meyer later claimed that he was frustrated in this position.

When deKlerk came to power and launched the negotiations for a new South Africa, Meyer gravitated to the younger group of NP cabinet members concerned for their career prospects in a post-apartheid South Africa. They did not want an alliance with Buthelezi's IFP nor the stigma of the previous system to cloud their future. In 1989, when he was appointed deputy minister of constitutional development, Meyer announced publicly that he would resign if no move toward change took place within two years. Meyer, like many of his colleagues, saw an alliance with the ANC as the practical approach to a nonracial political future. This point of view gained ground after the Boipatong massacre of June 1992 caused the ANC to leave off negotiating. When the NP government and ANC rejoined to continue talks in September 1992, Meyer became a minister and the NP government's chief negotiator. He and Ramaphosa were central to the agreements that led to the election of 1994.

As chief negotiator, Meyer came into conflict with the powerful NP old guard such as Kobie Coetsee and Hernus Kriel who accused him of selling out both his party and the white population. This conflict continued after the 1994 elections as Meyer seemed much more comfortable with the ANC-led South Africa than any of his party colleagues. The hawks in the party continued to accuse him of "betrayal" and ANC "lackeyism," while his supporters defended him as a pragmatist. After his appointment by deKlerk as NP secretary-general, Meyer appeared to be the successor to the party leadership. He tried to change the nature of the NP by recognizing that the NP could not win support through a continued offensive on the ANC, and shocked his conservative party members with statements like, "There is still the perception that NP is a white party, because its leadership is white. Certainly that kind of thing will have to change."[19] When in May 1997 he began to talk of "disbanding" the NP to reconstitute it into a more acceptable party to blacks, he was ousted from the party and dropped by deKlerk, who had until then remained neutral. Meyer then left the NP to form his own political party, the New Movement Process, and to join forces with National Consultative Forum leader Bantu Holomisa who had been ejected from the ANC the previous year.

Cyril Ramaphosa (1952–)
CODESA Negotiator

Cyril Ramaphosa first became aquainted with NP member Roelf Meyer on a fishing expedition together with their families. Meyer, an inexperienced fisherman, got a hook stuck in his thumb, and Ramaphosa ended up pulling it out. The two began meeting regularly during the negotation process between the NP government and the ANC leadership from 1991 to 1994. During the stagnant months between the NP and ANC of 1992, Ramaphosa continued to meet with Meyer. When negotiations were relaunched, Ramaphosa and Meyer began to be regarded as the center of the talks. Whenever the ANC and NP reached a sticking point, the two would meet quietly in a corner to iron out difficulties. The media called their relationship "The Roelf and Cyril Show."

Ramaphosa was born in Johannesburg on November 18, 1952, attending high school in Soweto and the University of Turfloop. He became the university's SASO chair in 1974, and was imprisoned under Section 6 of the Terrorism Act for eleven months, then for six months in 1976. After his detention, Ramaphosa returned to his law studies and qualified in 1981. He was appointed legal adviser to the Council of Unions of South Africa and then became general-secretary of the National Union of Mineworkers, a post he held from 1982 to 1991. In 1990 he was made secretary-general of the ANC. He resigned to work in the private sector in 1996.

As part of the new dynamic and sophisticated younger leadership of the ANC, Ramaphosa helped his party develop a more efficient administrative machinery that could meet the demands increasingly placed on it. During the wave of strikes and street demonstrations that gathered momentum during the ANC's "mass action campaign" of 1992, Ramaphosa became a major power broker in the tripartite alliance of the ANC, SACP, and COSATU. It was his and Meyer's opening of what became known as "the Channel," that led to the September 1992 summit between Mandela and deKlerk.

The last clause of the new constitution was adopted in the early morning hours of November 18, 1993, which happened to be Ramaphosa's birthday. As part of the celebrations, Meyer presented him with a cake, and as the band started to play, the two went out onto the dance floor and swung to "In the Mood." Ramaphosa also worked on the constitution of 1996, and a number of South Africans were disappointed that he did not remain in ANC politics. He maintained a high profile in the South African business world, however, becoming involved in communications and launching the Freedom Forum African Center in Johannesburg in 1997. Many still held the belief that he would return to the political arena to challenge the ANC leadership.

Walter Sisulu (1912–)
ANC Activist

Among the dynamic motivators of the ANC Youth League of the 1950s, it was Walter Sisulu and Nelson Mandela who were the first to comprehend the harsh realities of the struggle against apartheid. Together with Oliver Tambo and Mandela, Sisulu led the political generation that rose through the ANC Youth League in the 1940s to expand and revitalize the ANC in the 1950s. He was a key figure behind the adoption of the ANC's Program of Action and was among those in the forefront of the ANC when it was banned in 1960. After his release from prison in 1989, at the age of seventy-seven,

Sisulu continued to work with other ANC leaders to broaden the antiapartheid movement and to push the government to release the remaining prisoners. The stormy politics of the early 1990s made Mandela's and Sisulu's position difficult, but both held control of the movement and worked hard to maintain their moral ascendency and popularity.

Walter Max Ulyate Sisulu was born on May 18, 1912, and brought up with his older sister in Ncgobo, Transkei, by his mother, a domestic worker, and his uncle and grandparents. The writings of Marcus Garvey were an early political influence on Sisulu as were his history lessons at the Anglican Missionary Institute in Ncgobo. Sisulu was also strongly influenced by visits from Dr. Walter Benson Rubusana, the founder of the Native Congress in the Eastern Cape. Rubusana, claimed Sisulu, had a direct political influence on him.

At age fourteen, Sisulu left school to work and from 1928 to 1940 held numerous jobs including delivery man for a dairy, miner, baker, part-time bank teller, and real-estate agent. Joining the ANC in 1940, he was a founder member of the ANC Youth League in 1943, and became its treasurer. In 1952 he was an organizer of the Defiance Campaign and was banned from attending public meetings in 1952. In 1953 he traveled to Europe, Russia, and China. He was arrested with many others in 1956, in the treason trial that ended in 1961 with comprehensive acquittals. In 1962 Sisulu was arrested for breach of house-arrest and sentenced to six years for incitement to strike. He went underground when he was freed on bail in 1963, and was arrested again on the charge of sabotage. He was sentenced with Mandela and six others to life imprisonment.

When Sisulu was released from prison in 1989, he described Robben Island and Pollsmoor Prison as providing the best kind of political education. With his fellow prisoners, he said he had learned that pressure, whether inside or outside prison or abroad, was the only way to end apartheid. Every concession that was made came after some form of pressure. Sisulu claimed, "There has never been a greater university for political education than there was in prison." Sisulu said he never felt despair during his prison years, "but there were moments when I felt very much in high spirits." He was inspired by events like the 1976 Soweto rebellion and the formation of the Congress of South African Trade Unions and the United Democratic Front.[20] Of the many political prisoners on Robben Island, Sisulu and Mandela commanded the most respect.

Sisulu's wife Albertina, whom he married in 1944, earned a reputation as a rock of stability during her husband's imprisonment. She, along with her family, continued the work Walter had begun. Among their five natural and four adopted children, one son was banned and detained, one son was jailed for resistance activities, and one son and one daughter were exiled. Albertina became a member of the ANC Women's League in 1948, and of the Federation of South African Women in 1954. She participated in the women's protest against the introduction of women's passes in 1958, and from 1964 to 1982 she was under continual banning orders, including house arrest. From 1983 to 1991, Albertina was Transvaal president of the United Democratic Front and led the UDF delegation to the United States and Britain in 1989. In 1984 she was sentenced to four years imprisonment for promoting the aims of the ANC, a charge that she successfully appealed in 1987. In 1990 she was made co-convener (with Gertrude Shape) of the ANC Women's League Task Force. When Walter was released from prison in 1989, Albertina claims she shed tears for the first time in twenty-five years and said, "I don't know how I'm going to cope with having him around the house all the time."[21]

After his release from prison, Walter Sisulu became a member of the Internal Leadership Core and was elected ANC Deputy-President at the ANC National Conference in July 1991. Ahmed Kathrada, a fellow prisoner on Robben Island described Sisulu as a father figure while in prison, and stated that, like Mandela, Sisulu never asked for exemption from work on grounds of age. "When you talk about Nelson Mandela," the prisoner claimed, you cannot leave out Walter Sisulu. They complement each other."[22]

Joe Slovo (1926–1995)
South African Communist Party Chairman

Joe Slovo was responsible for much SACP and ANC theory, and wrote numerous articles, pamphlets, and contributions to books. His famous pamphlet written in 1989 boldly faced the weaknesses of socialism and the excesses of Stalinism and challenged his party to rethink its philosophy and policies. When Slovo was questioned as chairman of the South African Communist Party on the broad agreement of the SACP and ANC and the role of the SACP, he responded, "It is the task of an independent party . . . to ensure . . . that the choices which are being debated for the future development will be made in a way that will not prejudice the working class, whom we claim to represent."[23] A loyal supporter of socialism, Slovo was not afraid to question his own party's direction after the collapse of communism in eastern Europe. He also took the lead in the black liberation movement in the 1990s in finding a solution to the stalemate between power-sharing, supported by the NP, and majority-rule, supported by the ANC. Ironically playing an increasing conciliatory role, Slovo suggested the "sunset clause" that allowed for a power-sharing interim government that would disappear after a number of years.

Slovo was born in Lithuania on May 23, 1926, and came to South Africa at a young age with his parents due to the anti-Semitism rampant in Europe at that time. His father worked as a truck driver in Johannesburg. At the Observatory Junior High School, Slovo came under the influence of his militant Irish teacher John O'Meara. Leaving school in 1941, Slovo worked as a dispatch clerk at South Africa Druggists and joined the National Union of Distributive Workers. In 1942 he joined the SACP. Influenced by tales of Red Army heroism, Slovo left South Africa to fight for the Allies in World War II and was active in the Springbok Legion. In 1949 he married Ruth First, daughter of the SACP treasurer Julius First, and in 1950 he completed his degree at the University of Witwatersrand. Both he and Ruth were listed as communists under the Suppression of Communism Act of 1954, and Ruth was later killed by a parcel bomb in 1984 believed to have been sent by the apartheid government to her office in Mozambique. (Their daughter Shawn Slovo wrote an account of her mother that was later made into the movie *A World Apart*.) Slovo later married Helen Dolny.

Joe Slovo was a founding member of the Congress of Democrats and a representative on the National Consultative Committee, which drew up the Freedom Charter in 1955. During the treason trial of 1956, Slovo was arrested and detained for two months, and in 1960 he was arrested for six months during the state of emergency declared after Sharpeville in 1960. In 1961 Slovo emerged as one of the members of the newly formed military wing of the ANC, Umkhonto we Sizwe (MK), and in 1963 he went into exile on orders from the SACP and ANC. He spent his exile years in Britain, Angola, Mozambique, and Zambia. While he was based in Mozambique in 1984, he was elected general secretary of the SACP. He also served as MK's chief of staff and became a member of the ANC National Executive Council's working committee.

After the unbanning of the SACP in 1990, Slovo returned to South Africa to participate in the negotiations between the government and the ANC. After several periods of illness, he decided not to stand again as SACP general secretary. Chris Hani was elected in his place, and Slovo became SACP chairman in 1991. For several months after the 1994 election, Slovo appeared weak, but he continued his tasks as housing minister, and before his death was attempting to build a new housing scheme to benefit South Africa's poor. He died on January 6, 1995.

Oliver Tambo (1917–1993)
ANC Leader

During his years in exile from South Africa and as president of the ANC from 1967 to 1991, Oliver Reginald Tambo emerged as the main spokesman of the ANC and became an effective representative of African interests as a whole in the international arena. His duties as president-in-exile included worldwide diplomatic representation, organizing and supplying the ANC's guerrilla force, negotiating with host governments for facilities and funds for the armed struggle, and keeping up the morale of fellow exiled South Africans thousands of miles from home. He also kept contact with the scattered internal ANC forces under constant threat from an ever-tightening government security net and solicited arms and material support, mainly from the Soviet Union. The upsurge of black action in the townships of South Africa in the 1980s gave dramatic confirmation to the strategy Tambo had spelled out at an ANC conference in 1969—the effectiveness of combining armed struggle with mass political action. With the intensified conflict of the 1980s, Tambo fully expressed the ANC's vision of South Africa's future and worked to keep up pressure on the apartheid government both within the country and from abroad until he suffered an illness in 1989, and gave up active leadership of the ANC.

Tambo was born October 27, 1917, five years after the birth of the original ANC, in Mbizana in eastern Pondoland. He went to school in the Mbizana district and studied at the University of Fort Hare, receiving his B.S. in 1941. Like many of his colleagues, Tambo first became involved in politics at Fort Hare. He led a student class boycott to demand a democratically elected Students' Representative Council. This led to his expulsion, and he was unable to complete his honors course. From 1942 to 1949, Tambo taught at St. Peter's College in Johannesburg, but he also threw himself into ANC activity. He was one of the founding members of the ANC Youth League in 1944 and was its first national secretary. In 1948 he was elected president of the Transvaal ANC Youth League and became its national vice president in 1949. He teamed up with Walter Sisulu and Nelson Mandela to bring a bolder spirit of militancy to the ANC and served on the committee that drew up the ANC's Program of Action, adopted as national policy in 1949. He then left teaching to set up a legal practice with Mandela. Strongly enthusiastic over the Freedom Charter written in 1955, he claimed that it was "the sum total of our aspirations but more: it is the road to the new life. It is the uniting creed of all the people struggling for democracy and for their rights; the mirror of the future South Africa."[24]

In 1956 Tambo was one of the 156 accused in the treason trial, and in 1958 became deputy president of the ANC. Embracing the nonracial policy of the ANC, he chastised Africanists for their isolationist strategy and determined rejection of all whites. Tambo pointed out that all democratic forces suffered oppression through the apartheid system and that it was important to build a wide base of support. In 1960, after the Sharpeville massacre, Tambo was assigned by the ANC to travel abroad, set up the ANC's international mission, and mobilize international opinion. He proceeded to work with Dr. Yusuf Dadoo to establish the South African United Front (SAUF), which helped secure the expulsion of South Africa from the British Commonwealth in 1961. (The SAUF broke up shortly after.)

Tambo initially established missions in Egypt, Ghana, Morocco, and London, and the ANC eventually acquired missions in twenty-seven countries by 1990. He presided over the joint guerrilla action of the ANC and Zimbabwe African People's Union (ZAPU) in Rhodesia from 1967 to 1968, and believed the incursion marked the beginning of a mass armed struggle. The joint action floundered, however, in the face of superior Rhodesian and South African forces. On becoming ANC president after the death of General Chief Albert J. Luthuli, Tambo's international prestige rose in the 1970s, and in 1985 he was re-elected president and also served as head of the ANC's Politico-Military Council and commander in chief of MK. In many parts of the world, he was received with the protocol usually reserved for heads of state. In 1991 Tambo returned to South Africa after over thirty years in exile and was elected national chairman of the ANC. On April 24, 1993, he died of a stroke. Tambo was hailed as a great ANC leader and one of the enduring figures of black liberation.

Eugene Terre'Blanche (1944–   )
Leader of Afrikaner Resistance Movement

The ideology of Eugene Terre'Blanche's right-wing paramilitary organization, Afrikaner Weerstandsbeweging (Afrikaner Resistance Movement–AWB), founded in 1973, was based on the belief that whites were superior to blacks and that the Afrikaner culture and nation were sacred. Terre'Blanche claimed that his organization was not racist, but racism was, in fact, central to its philosophy. Terre'Blanche at one point stated, "We will govern ourselves with our own superior white genes."[25] Born on January 31, 1944, Terre'Blanche was the grandson of a rebel in the British Cape Colony who fought on the side of the Boers, and the son of an SADF officer. Before founding the AWB, Terre'Blanche was a member of the South Africa police force, serving in Namibia, and acting as a guard for the president's and prime minister's private residences.

The AWB began its notorious reputation in 1979, when Terre'Blanche and several others physically assaulted a professor in Pretoria with tar and feathers after the professor questioned the Afrikaner interpretation of the Day of the Covenant. In 1982 Terre'Blanche and eight other AWB members were arrested for possession of arms, ammunitions, and explosives. Terre' Blanche received a suspended sentence. After the successful disruption of NP meetings in the 1980s, the membership of the AWB increased, and the growth of strength of the CP in the 1987 elections fueled the growth of the AWB. It began openly to challenge the authority of the NP government and increasingly attracted the attention of the press.

The AWB suffered a setback in 1988 when Terre'Blanche was arrested on a charge of malicious damage to property and *crimen injuria*. He was aquitted but subsequently had to contend with persistent rumors of his alleged womanizing and alcoholism. These rumors were exacerbated by reports linking him to a *Sunday Times* journalist who had had an affair with Terre' Blanche while writing his biography, but later became disillusioned, referring to her former lover as a "pig in a safari suit."[26] After this incident, the AWB's membership dropped off rapidly, and the organization became something of a laughingstock in South Africa. The AWB's reputation was not helped by Terre'Blanche's own clownish behavior; for example, he twice fell off his horse while being televised. Also, the launching of the AWB's "air force" in July 1993, which consisted of several single-engine airplanes borrowed from private owners, did not improve the AWB's or Terre'Blanche's image.

Terre'Blanche's organization also lost prestige after the failed attempt to protect the leader of Bophuthatswana in 1993. The AWB claimed responsibility for several bombings that took place on the eve of the 1994 elections, and the man who assassinated Chris Hani was later found to be a member of the AWB. After the 1994 elections, the AWB lost considerable support as several of its members became disillusioned with Terre'Blanche's failed promise to prevent the ANC from coming to power. Many were also disappointed by his failure to help wounded comrades escape after the botched invasion of Bophuthatswana and his absence from the dock when AWB militants were charged with the 1994 bombing campaign. Most of the Afrikaner population scorned Terre'Blanche as a boastful politician hopelessly out of touch with reality. The Afrikaans newspaper *Beeld* routinely depicted the AWB leader as a political anachronism, caricaturing him with a Viking's horned helmet on his head.

In June 1997 Terre'Blanche was sentenced to six years in prison for the attempted murder of one of his former farm workers, Paul Motshabi. Out on appeal, he accused the ANC of conspiring against him and maintained a blustering attitude. In November 1997 a special legal commission recommended that criminal action should be taken against Terre'Blanche and the AWB leadership for the deaths of civilians in Bophuthatswana. In December 1997 the AWB publicly apologized to the Truth and Reconciliation Commission for its activities during the apartheid era. In a four-page submission, it claimed that it regretted its acts of racism and human rights violations, particularly the deaths in Bophuthatswana. Terre'Blanche disowned the statement.

Andries Treurnicht (1921–1993)
Conservative Party Leader

From the late 1970s to the formation of the Conservative party in 1982, the majority of *verkrampte* discontent within the NP originated with Andries Treurnicht, appointed Transvaal leader of the NP in 1978. A staunch NP traditionalist, Treurnicht fought against P. W. Botha's reformist initiatives and was buoyed by the support of the right-wing movements that emerged in South Africa in the 1970s and early 1980s. Treurnicht's ideological conservatism led to his consistent criticism of what he perceived as a deviation from standard NP policy. After a series of clashes with Botha and reformists in the NP, Treurnicht and his supporters resigned from the NP cabinet and were expelled from the party. In March 1982 they formed the Conservative Party (CP) in Pretoria in front of a crowd of 8,000, including delegates from ninety-nine constituencies, and members of the AWB and other conservative groups.

Treurnicht argued that his party was not racist because racism implied "denying other people certain rights," which was not, as he claimed, part of the CP's policy of "constructive" or "positive" discrimination. Treurnicht stated, however, that he was "race conscious" and "aware of the fact that I am a white man." Even as late as 1990, CP members were suggesting that separate white and black blood banks be introduced because of the danger of AIDS, and that blacks should be "culled like seals" to control their numbers.[27]

Born in Piketberg on February 19, 1921, Treurnicht studied theology at the Universities of Cape Town and Stellenbosch. In the 1960s, he was editor of the Pretoria paper *Hoofstad*, which he used to spread the "pure message" of Afrikaner nationalism and to contradict South African Prime Minister John Vorster's foreign policy and reconciliatory attitude toward English-speaking whites. Treurnicht was elected to parliament in 1971 and made chairman of the Broederbond in 1972. After his appointment to the NP cabinet, Treurnicht became involved in a series of controversies that led to his expulsion and the formation of the CP in 1982. He criticized the speech of a fellow cabinet member who stated that apartheid was dead, and intervened on the side of the Transvaal Teaching Association when the latter decided to exclude a colored schoolboy team from the Craven Week rugby tournament in 1980. The final controversy occurred over Botha's proposal of power-sharing with Indians and coloreds and the formation of the tricameral parliament. Treurnicht held fast to the old NP policy of division of power and objected to any moves toward one system of government for all. The resulting split in the NP leading to Treurnicht's CP also divided churches, educational and cultural bodies, and the business world. The CP drew much support from small farmers and working-class whites personally threatened by the blacks' potential rise in employment status. Treurnicht also became a member of the *Afrikaner Volkswag* (AV), founded in 1984 and committed to Afrikaner unity and the coordination of right-wing cultural activities.

In 1987 the CP won twenty-three seats in the House of Assembly, overtaking the PFP as the main opposition party in South Africa and illustrating white conservative disillusionment with NP reforms. But a return to traditional NP policy became an increasingly unrealistic proposition by the end of the 1980s, and the CP began to stress partition of South African land to protect the Afrikaner population. During the deKlerk era, the CP struggled to adjust its philosophy of racial differentiation, and a rift developed within the party between hard-liners and pragmatists. Treurnicht was caught in the middle and stuck to the idea of an Afrikaner homeland. The CP leader's biggest dilemma concerned participation in negotiations. After deKlerk's February 1990 speech, Treurnicht gave warning that the NP had "awakened the tiger in the Afrikaner." When tension arose between black and white residents of the Orange Free State town of Welkom, Treurnicht blamed government reforms, stating, "People have armed themselves and they have the right to defend themselves. . . . It is not necessary for me to alert them to the need to be prepared. The government is doing this through its decisions."[28]

In December 1991 Treurnicht rejected invitations to take part in CODESA, and in 1992 the CP led the "No" campaign in deKlerk's white referendum. But the CP increasingly felt strong pressure from moderates within and conservatives outside the party to take part in negotiations. It eventually found a way with the founding of the Concerned South Africans Group (COSAG) in September 1992. As an associate of COSAG, the CP could join in negotiations.

Treurnicht died on April 22, 1993. Toward the end of his time as CP leader, he had become increasingly pragmatic and modified somewhat CP demands for an Afrikaner homeland. He was replaced by Ferdi Hartzenberg, a hard-liner with a more rigid and Verwoerdian mentality. The leadership vacuum left by Treurnicht eventually led to the first successful attempts at unity in the history of South African right-wing movements, and the founding of the *Afrikaner Volksfront* (AVF).

Archbishop Desmond Tutu (1931–   )
Archbishop of Cape Town

With the gap in organized opposition to apartheid left by the banning of the ANC, PAC, and most protest movements in the 1960s, many black church leaders emerged to protest the system. Desmond Tutu became one of the most prominent of these, and Nelson Mandela wrote of him, "Such is the character of a fighter against apartheid that he was 'public enemy number one' to the powers-that-be. And it is a tribute to his independent mind that he was not always popular."[29]

Tutu was born on February 19, 1931, in Klerksdorp, a gold mining town west of Johannesburg. He described his childhood as happy, but pointed out years later that racial discrimination resulted in a kind of brainwashing in which there was "an acquiescence in your oppression and exploitation."[30] While in the hospital with tuberculosis during his teens, Tutu made friends with Father Trevor Huddleston (later archbishop), who became one of the strongest influences on his life. In 1951 he started studying at a teacher training college but left teaching in 1958 to train for the priesthood, after the takeover of African education by the government. In 1960 he was ordained as a deacon and in 1961 became a priest. In 1962 Tutu began studying theology at King's College, London, receiving his B.A. in 1965 and his M.A. in 1966. In 1967 he returned to South Africa to teach at the Federal Theological Seminary in the Eastern Cape. After working as a lecturer in Lesotho, he became the dean of St. Mary's Cathedral in Johannesburg, the first black to hold such a high post in his church. He refused to obtain government permission to move to the deanery, which was in an exclusive white suburb, and instead lived in Soweto.

In 1976 Tutu wrote to South African Prime Minister John Vorster, warning him of the tense situation in townships and of impending violence. He issued a second warning in his speech at the funeral of Steve Biko in 1977: "Nothing, not even the most sophisticated weapon, not even the most brutally efficient police . . . will stop people once they are determined to achieve their freedom and their right to humanness."[31] In 1978 Tutu was appointed general secretary of the South African Council of Churches (SACC), and in the following year the SACC approved a resolution that advocated civil disobedience as a response to racist law. In that same year, Tutu had become deeply affected by his visits of victims of forced removals in Zweledinga in the Eastern Cape.

In the late 1970s, Tutu began calling for international economic pressure on South Africa, and continued his support of sanctions throughout the 1980s. In June 1980 Tutu met with P. W. Botha on behalf of the SACC to discuss the "rapidly deteriorating situation." Tutu based his appeal to the government on four points: a commitment to common citizenship for all South Africans, the abolition of pass laws, the end of forced relocation, and a uniform education system. The discussion did not progress very far, and future meetings collapsed due to government intransigence. Tutu, meanwhile, kept up his public criticism of apartheid. He was arrested in 1980 with several other church leaders while protesting the detention of a colleague and was jailed for one night. As part of Botha's "total strategy" to fight the supposed communist-inspired "total onslaught," the SACC was identified by the security forces as an "internal enemy." In 1981 Botha's government began a commission of inquiry into the SACC, and Tutu came forward to defend the council's activities. In 1983 Tutu became a prominent leader of the Black Consciousness National Forum Committee, which called for a stand against the government's new constitution and the tricameral parliament. He also became a patron of the United Democratic Front.

In 1984 Tutu was awarded the Nobel Peace Prize. In 1985 he was made bishop of Johannesburg, and in 1986 he became archbishop of Cape Town. During the violent uprisings of the mid-1980s, Tutu rejected the term used by the media "black-on-black" violence. He said the phrase implied a qualitative difference between blacks killing people of their own race and killing those of another. Never, said Tutu, had he seen violence in Northern Ireland described as "white-on-white." In a speech to the United National General Assembly in 1985, he made clear his complete opposition to apartheid. "Of course, apartheid cannot be reformed," he stated. "It must be dismantled. You don't reform a Frankenstein—you destroy it."[32] After U.S. President Ronald Reagan rejected sanctions against South Africa, Tutu accused him and British Prime Minister Margaret Thatcher of telling blacks that they were, in effect, "utterly dispensable." He denounced Reagan's speech on sanctions as "nauseating," and said America and the West could "go to hell." Later apologizing for his "salty" language, Tutu still defended his right to speak strongly about black suffering.[33]

In a famous meeting with Botha in 1988 to appeal the death sentence of the Sharpeville Six, Tutu lost his temper and told the president not to speak to him like a child. He was later sorry, but commented that Botha had probably never had a black person speak to him that way. After the meeting, he wrote to Botha, claiming that his apartheid policies were not only unjust and oppressive, but also unbiblical, unchristian, immoral, and evil. In the same year, Botha's government launched a campaign against Tutu. Government-backed black politicians with no apparent constituencies recruited unemployed workers for anti-Tutu protests at airports; anti-Tutu pamphlets and bumper stickers, often with crude messages, were distributed; and in August 1988, a bomb wrecked the headquarters of the SACC in Johannesburg. Tutu was undeterred, and continued to lead demonstrations and protests. When later informed that the head of the Civil Cooperation Bureau had offered an expoliceman with a criminal record R20,000 (about $7,600) to kill him, Tutu remarked that he was upset that they thought his life was worth so little.

With the lifting of restrictions on political parties in 1990, Tutu told reporters that he expected the church's role to change, and that he would personally adopt a lower profile. He denied strongly that he was a politician. Tutu, however, was continually disturbed by the violence that plagued South Africa during the negotiations process. After the Sebokeng killings in 1990, he broke down over the news of the death toll and immediately arranged a corporate pastoral visit to Sebokeng, placing himself between the crowd and an armored vehicle that arrived during the meeting. He supported the increasing claim during the 1990s that the IFP/ANC violence was fueled by a "third force," and spoke directly to deKlerk of his suspicions. (This exchange later emerged during the Truth and Reconciliation Commission hearings, as evidence that deKlerk did know of police activities in KwaZulu/Natal.) Tutu also scolded and warned blacks of the effects of violence, claiming that they had seemingly lost their sense of connectedness and compassion.

Staying out of the political arena as much as he could after the elections of 1994, Tutu continued as a strong activist for justice and became an important adviser to Nelson Mandela's cabinet. From 1996 to 1998, he was in charge of the Truth and Reconciliation Commission, putting pressure on major figures such as deKlerk and Winnie Mandela to tell the truth about their past actions and putting emphasis on the reconciliation process. Archbishop Tutu played a strong moral role in the struggle against apartheid. Nelson Mandela stated, "The negotiations process and South Africa's first democratic elections in 1994 have vindicated the struggles and sacrifices of peace-loving South Africans, among whom archbishop Tutu will remain an eminent example."[34]

NOTES

1. Steve Biko, *I Write What I Like*, ed. Aelred Stubbs (London: Heinemann, 1978), p. 49.

2. Gwendolen M. Carter, *The Politics of Inequality* (London: Thames and Hudson, 1958), p. 98.

3. Steven Debroey, *South Africa under the Curse of Apartheid* (New York: University Press of America, 1990), p. 380.

4. Colin Legum, *Vorster's Gamble for Africa* (London: R. Collings, 1976), p. 43; Johann Van Rooyen, *Hard Right: The New White Power in South Africa* (New York: I. B. Tauris Publishers, 1994), p. 118; D. and J. De Villiers, *PW* (Cape Town: Tafelberg, 1984), p. 91.

5. Allister Sparks, "The Secret Revolution," *New Yorker* 70 (April 11, 1994): 62.

6. *The Times* (London), August 17, 1989.

7. Mangosuthu Gatsha Buthelezi, *Power Is Ours* (New York: Books in Focus, 1979), pp. 26–27, 67.

8. Debroey, *South Africa under the Curse of Apartheid*, p. 502.

9. Sparks, "Secret Revolution," p. 70.

10. Ibid., 72.

11. Ibid., 69.

12. Martin J. Murray, *The Revolution Deferred* (New York: Verso, 1994), p. 3.

13. Timothy Garton Ash, "True Confessions," *The New York Review of Books* 44 (July 17, 1997): 33–38.

14. Chris Hani, "My Life," at http://www.sacp.org.za/biographies.

15. Nelson Mandela, *Long Walk to Freedom* (Boston: Little, Brown and Company, 1994), p. 83.

16. Kathlyn Gay and Martin Gay, *Heroes of Conscience* (Santa Barbara, CA: ABC-CLIO, 1996), p. 244.

17. *Electronic Mail and Guardian* (Johannesburg), December 31, 1996.

18. *Electronic Mail and Guardian*, February 9, 1996.

19. Ibid.

20. Sheridan Johns and R. Hunt Davis, Jr., eds., *Mandela, Tambo, and the African National Congress* (New York: Oxford University Press, 1991), p. 162.

21. Sparks, "Secret Revolution," p. 72.

22. *Alongside Nelson Mandela: Reminiscences of a Former Political Prisoner under Apartheid*, Interview by Harry Kreisler, Institute of International Studies, University of California at Berkeley, November 8, 1996, at http://globetrotter.berkeley.edu/conversations/Kathrada/kathrada07.html.

23. Ian Liebenberg, et al., *The Long March* (Cape Town: HAUM, 1994), p. 40.

24. Debroey, *South Africa under the Curse of Apartheid*, p. 276.

25. Graham Leach, *The Afrikaners: Their Last Great Trek* (Johannesburg: Southern Book Publishers, 1989), p. 100.

26. Van Rooyen, *Hard Right: The New White Power in South Africa*, pp. 93–94.

27. Ibid., pp. 53, 49.

28. *The Argus* (Johannesburg), February 6, 1990, April 26, 1990.

29. Desmond Tutu, *The Rainbow People of God* (New York: Doubleday, 1994), p. xi.

30. Shirley Du Boulay, *Tutu: Voice of the Voiceless* (Grand Rapids, MI: William E. Eerdmans, 1988), p. 399.

31. Ibid., p. 20.

32. Ibid., p. 99.

33. Gay & Gay, *Heroes of Conscience*, p. 401.

34. Tutu, *The Rainbow People of God*, p. xi.

Primary Documents of the End of Apartheid in South Africa

OPPOSITION TO APARTHEID

When the National Party came to power in South Africa in 1948, it began to introduce legislation that made apartheid a legal fact. Among the laws passed that clearly separated Africans, Indians, coloreds, and whites, the Group Areas Act (Document 1), which implemented geographical separation, became, in the words of Prime Minister Magnus Malan, the essence of apartheid policy. The document also illustrates the complications of defining races that dogged apartheid legislation.

In 1955 the ANC formed a coalition called the Congress of the People that stretched across the boundaries of South African society. The objective was mass mobilization of blacks and international attention to and sympathy for opposition to apartheid. On June 26, 1955, at Kliptown near Johannesburg, the Congress adopted the Freedom Charter (Document 2), a document written by a committee of blacks and whites that would become the foundation of ANC policy. In 1960 Mandela and fellow ANC leaders decided to adopt a military strategy for ANC opposition to apartheid. The decision to press harder in opposition was illustrated in Mandela's 1961 letter from the underground (Document 3), in which he urged further mass resistance to government policy and apartheid institutions.

Document 1
GROUP AREAS ACT, NO. 41, 1950 (Excerpts)

2. (1) For the purposes of this Act, there shall be the following groups:

(a) a white group, in which shall be included any person who in appearance, obviously is, or who is generally accepted as a white person, other than a person who although in appearance obviously a white person, is generally accepted as a coloured person, or who is in terms of sub-paragraph (ii) of paragraphs (b) and (c) or of the said sub-paragraphs read with paragraph (d) of this sub-section and paragraph (a) of sub-section (2), a member of any other group;

(b) a native group, in which shall be included:

(i) any person who in fact is, or is generally accepted as a member of an aboriginal race or tribe of Africa, other than a person who is, in terms of sub-paragraph (ii) of paragraph (c), a member of the coloured group; and

(ii) any woman to whichever race, tribe or class she may belong, between whom and a person who is, in terms of sub-paragraph (1), a member of a native group, there exists a marriage or who cohabits with such a person;

(c) a colored group, in which shall be included:

(i) any person who is not a member of the white group or of the native group; and

(ii) any woman, to whichever race, tribe or class she may belong, between whom and a person who is, in terms of sub-paragraph (1), a member of the coloured group, there exists a marriage, or who cohabits with such a person; and

(d) any group of persons which is under sub-section (2) declared to be a group.

3. (1) The Governor-General may, whenever it is deemed expedient, by proclamation in the *Gazette*:

(a) declare that as from a date specified in the proclamation, which shall be a date not less than one year after the date of the publication thereof, the area defined in the proclamation shall be an area for occupation by members of the group specified therein; or

(b) declare that, as from a date specified in the proclamation, the area defined in the proclamation shall be an area for ownership by members of the group specified therein.

4. (1) As from the date specified in the relevant proclamation under paragraph (a) of sub-section (1) of section *three*, and notwithstanding anything contained in any special or other statutory provision relating to the occupation of land or premises, no disqualified person shall occupy and no person shall allow any disqualified person to occupy any land or premises in any group area to which the proclamation relates, except under the authority of a permit.

(2) The provisions of sub-section (1) shall not render it unlawful for any disqualified person to occupy land or premises in any group area:

(a) as a *bona fide* servant or employee of the State, or a statutory body or as a domestic servant of any person lawfully occupying the land or premises;

(b) as a *bona fide* visitor for a total of not more than ninety days in any calendar year of any person lawfully residing on the land or premises or as a *bona fide* guest in an hotel;

(c) as a *bona fide* patient in a hospital, asylum or similar institution controlled by the State or a statutory body or in any such institution in existence at the commencement of the Act, which is aided by the State, or as an inmate of a prison, work colony, inebriate home or similar institution so controlled; or

(d) as the *bona fide* employee (other than a domestic servant) of any person or as the husband, wife, minor child or dependant of any person (including a domestic servant or employee) who is lawfully occupying such land or premises: Provided that the provisions of this paragraph shall apply in respect of any group area or any part of any group area only if the Governor-General has by proclamation in the *Gazette*, declared them to apply in respect of that group area, or that part thereof, and only to the extent and subject to the conditions (if any) which may be specified in the proclamation.

(3) Any provision in the title deed of any immovable property situated in any group area referred to in sub-section (1) prohibiting or restricting the occupation or use of such property by persons who are members of the group for which that area has been established shall lapse as from the date referred to in the said sub-section, and no such provision shall thereafter be inserted in the title deed of any immovable property in such group area.

Source: Edgar H. Brookes, *Apartheid: A Documentary Study of Modern South Africa* (New York: Barnes and Noble, Inc., 1968), pp. 131–36.

Document 2
FREEDOM CHARTER

PREAMBLE

We, the people of South Africa, declare for all our country and the world to know

That South Africa belongs to all who live in it, black and white, and that no government can justly claim authority unless it is based on the will of the people; That our people have been robbed of their birthright to land, liberty, and peace by a form of government founded on injustice and inequality; That our country will never be prosperous or free until all our people live in brotherhood, enjoying equal rights and opportunities; That only a democratic state, based on the will of the people, can secure to all their birthright without distinction of colour, race, sex, or belief;

And therefore, we, the people of South Africa, black and white, together—equals, countrymen, and brothers—adopt this Freedom Charter. And we pledge ourselves to strive together, sparing nothing of our strength and courage, until the democratic changes here set out have been won.

THE PEOPLE SHALL GOVERN!

Every man and woman shall have the right to vote for and stand as a candidate for all bodies which make laws.

All the people shall be entitled to take part in the administration of the country.

The rights of the people shall be the same regardless of race, colour, or sex.

All bodies of minority rule, advisory boards, councils, and authorities shall be replaced by democratic organs of self-government.

ALL NATIONAL GROUPS SHALL HAVE EQUAL RIGHTS!

There shall be equal status in the bodies of state, in the courts, and in the schools for all national groups and races; All national groups shall be protected by law against insults to their race and national pride; All people shall have equal rights to use their own language and to develop their own folk culture and customs; The preaching and practice of national, race, or colour discrimination and contempt shall be a punishable crime; All apartheid laws and practices shall be set aside.

THE PEOPLE SHALL SHARE IN THE COUNTRY'S WEALTH!

The national wealth of our country, the heritage of all South Africans, shall be restored to the people; The mineral wealth beneath the soil, the banks, and monopoly industry shall be transferred to the ownership of the people as a whole; All other industries and trades shall be controlled to assist the well-being of the people; All people shall have equal rights to trade where they choose, to manufacture, and to enter all trades, crafts, and professions.

THE LAND SHALL BE SHARED AMONG THOSE WHO WORK IT!

Restriction of land ownership on a racial basis shall be ended, and all the land redivided amongst those who work it, to banish famine and land hunger; The state shall help the peasants with implements, seed, tractors, and dams to save the soil and assist the tillers; Freedom of movement shall be guaranteed to all who work on the land; All shall have the right to occupy land wherever they choose; People shall not be robbed of their cattle, and forced labour and farm prisons shall be abolished.

ALL SHALL BE EQUAL BEFORE THE LAW!

No one shall be imprisoned, deported, or restricted without a fair trial; No one shall be condemned by the order of any government official; The courts shall be representative of all the people; Imprisonment shall be only for serious crimes against the people and shall aim at reeducation, not vengeance; The police force and army shall be open to all on an equal basis and shall be the helpers and protectors of the people; All laws which discriminate on grounds of race, colour, or belief shall be repealed.

ALL SHALL ENJOY EQUAL HUMAN RIGHTS!

The law shall guarantee to all their right to speak, to organise, to meet together, to publish, to preach, to worship, and to educate their children; The privacy of the house from police raids shall be protected by law; All shall be free to travel without restriction from countryside to town, from province to province, and from South Africa abroad; Pass laws, permits, and all other laws restricting these freedoms shall be abolished.

THERE SHALL BE WORK AND SECURITY!

All who work shall be free to form trade unions, to elect their officers and to make wage agreements with their employers; The state shall recognise the right and duty of all to work and to draw full unemployment benefits; Men and women of all races shall receive equal pay for equal work; There shall be a forty-hour working week, a national minimum wage, paid annual leave, and sick leave for all workers, and maternity leave on full pay for all working mothers; Miners, domestic workers, farm workers, and civil servants shall have the same rights as all others who work; Child labour, compound labour, the tot system, and contract labour shall be abolished.

THE DOORS OF LEARNING AND OF CULTURE SHALL BE OPENED!

The government shall discover, develop, and encourage national talent for the enhancement of our cultural life; All the cultural treasures of mankind shall be open to all, by free exchange of books, ideas, and contact with other lands; The aim of education shall be to teach the youth to love their people and their culture, to honour human brotherhood, liberty, and peace; Education shall be free, compulsory, universal, and equal for all children; Higher education and technical training shall be opened to all by means of state allowances and scholarships awarded on the basis of merit; Adult illiteracy shall be ended by a mass state education plan; Teachers shall have all the rights of other citizens; The colour bar in cultural life, in sport, and in education shall be abolished.

THERE SHALL BE HOUSES, SECURITY AND COMFORT!

All people shall have the right to live where they choose, to be decently housed, and to bring up their families in comfort and security; Unused housing space is to be made available to the people; Rent and prices shall be lowered, food plentiful, and no one shall go hungry; A preventive health scheme shall be run by the state; Free medical care and hospitalisation shall be provided for all, with special care for mothers and young children; Slums shall be demolished, and new suburbs built where all have transport, roads, lighting, playing fields, crèches, and social centres; The aged, the orphans, the disabled, and the sick shall be cared for by the state; Rest, leisure, and recreation shall be the right of all; Fenced locations and ghettos shall be abolished, and laws which break up families shall be repealed.

THERE SHALL BE PEACE AND FRIENDSHIP!

South Africa shall be a fully independent state, which respects the rights and sovereignty of all nations; South Africa shall strive to maintain world peace and the settlement of all international disputes by negotiation—not war; Peace and friendship amongst all our people shall be secured by upholding the equal rights, opportunities, and status of all; The people of the protectorates—Basutoland, Bechuanaland, and Swaziland—shall be free to decide for themselves their own future; The right of all the peoples of Africa to independence and self-government shall be recognised and shall be the basis of close cooperation.

Let all who love their people and their country now say, as we say here: "THESE FREEDOMS WE WILL FIGHT FOR, SIDE BY SIDE, THROUGHOUT OUR LIVES, UNTIL WE HAVE WON OUR LIBERTY."

Source: Sheridan Johns and R. Hunt Davis, Jr., eds., *Mandela, Tambo, and the African National Congress: The Struggle against Apartheid, 1948–1990, A Documentary Survey* (New York: Oxford University Press, 1991), pp. 81–85.

Document 3
OUTLAW IN MY OWN LAND: LETTER BY NELSON MANDELA, RELEASED JUNE 26, 1961, FROM UNDERGROUND HEADQUARTERS

The magnificent response to the call of the National Action council for a three-day strike and the wonderful work done by our organizers and field workers throughout the country proves once again that no power on earth can stop an oppressed people determined to win freedom. Today is 26 June, a day known throughout the length and breadth of our country as Freedom Day. It is fit and proper that on this historic day I should speak to you and announce fresh plans for the opening of the second phase in the fight against the Verwoerd Republic, and for a National Convention.

NON-COLLABORATION IS OUR WEAPON

You will remember that the Pietermaritzburg resolutions warned that if the Government did not call a National Convention before the end of May 1961, Africans, Coloureds, Indians, and European democrats would be asked not to collaborate with the Republic or any Government based on force. On several occasions since then the National Action Council explained that the last strike marked the beginning of a relentless mass struggle for the defeat of the Nationalist Government, and for a sovereign multiracial convention. We stressed that the strike would be followed by other forms of mass pressure to force the race maniacs who govern our beloved country to make way for a democratic government of the people, and for the people.

A full-scale and country-wide campaign of non-cooperation with the Government will be launched immediately. The precise form of the contemplated actions, its scope and dimensions and duration, will be announced to you at the appropriate time.

At the present moment it is sufficient to say that we plan to make government impossible. Those who are voteless cannot be expected to continue paying taxes to a Government which is not responsible to them. People who live in poverty and starvation cannot be expected to pay exorbitant house rents to the Government and industry. We produce the work of the gold mines, the diamonds and the coal, of the farms and industry, in return for miserable wages.

Why should we continue enriching those who steal the products of our sweat and blood? Those who side with the government when we stage peaceful demonstrations to assert our claims and aspirations? How can Africans serve on school boards and committees which are part of "Bantu Education," a sinister scheme of the Nationalist government to deprive the African people of real education in return for tribal education? Can Africans be expected to be content with serving on advisory boards and Bantu Authorities when the demand all over the continent of Africa is for national independence and self-government? Is it not an affront to the African people that the Government should now seek to extend Bantu Authorities to the cities, when people in the rural areas have refused to accept the same system and fought against it tooth and nail? Which African does not burn with indignation when thousands of our people are sent to gaol [jail] every month under cruel pass laws? Why should we continue carrying badges of slavery?

Non-collaboration is a dynamic weapon. We must refuse. We must use this weapon to send this Government to the grave. It must be used vigorously and without delay. The entire resources of the black people must be mobilized to withdraw all cooperation with the Nationalist Government.

Various forms of industrial and economic action will be employed to undermine the already tottering economy of the country. We will call upon the international bodies to expel South Africa and upon nations of the world to sever economic and diplomatic relations with the country.

THE STRUGGLE IS MY LIFE

I am informed that a warrant for my arrest has been issued, and that the police are looking for me. The National Action Council has given full and serious consideration to this question, and has sought advice of many trusted friends and bodies and they have advised me not to surrender myself. I have accepted this advice and will not give myself up to a Government I do not recognize. Any serious politician will realize that, under the present-day conditions in this country to seek for cheap martyrdom by handing myself to the police is naive and criminal. We have an important programme before us and it is important to carry it out very seriously and without delay.

I have chosen this latter course which is more difficult and which entails more risk and hardship than sitting in gaol. I have had to separate myself from my dear wife and children, from my mother and sisters, to live as an outlaw in my own land. I have had to close my business, to abandon my profession, and to live in poverty and misery, as many of my people are doing. I will continue to act as the spokesman of the National Action Council during the phase that is unfolding and in the tough struggles that lie ahead.

I shall fight the Government side by side with you, inch by inch, and mile by mile, until victory is won.

What are you going to do? Will you come along with us, or are you going to cooperate with the Government in its efforts to suppress the claims and aspirations of your own people? Or are you going to remain silent and neutral in a matter of life and death to my people, to our people?

For my part I have made the choice, I will not leave South Africa, nor will I surrender. Only through hardship, sacrifice and militant action can freedom be won. The struggle is my life.

I will continue fighting for freedom until the end of my days.

Source: Freedom, Justice and Dignity for All in South Africa: Statements and Articles by Mr. Nelson Mandela (New York: Centre against Apartheid, United Nations Department of Political and Security Council Affairs, 1978), pp. 6–8.

NEGOTIATING THE END OF APARTHEID

After F. W. deKlerk became president, he made clear his intentions to introduce reform and to go further than his predecessor P. W. Botha in addressing the inherent problems of the system of apartheid. Few were prepared, however, for the sweeping changes he announced in his address to parliament on February 2, 1990 (Document 4). These included lifting the ban on the ANC and other organizations, the repeal of the Separate Amenities Act, and the unconditional release of Nelson Mandela. When Nelson Mandela made his first public speech in over twenty-seven years (Document 5), however, he made it clear that his release from prison did not mark the end of the struggle against apartheid, but merely a step toward the end. He called on the government, his supporters, and the international community to continue pressing for final eradication of all aspects of apartheid. The ANC and the NP government immediately began serious negotiating, starting with talks in Pretoria in August 1990 (Document 6). The ANC suspended its armed struggle, the government agreed to release all political prisoners, and both groups began addressing the problem of violence. After his speech of 1990 announcing the end of apartheid, deKlerk in the following year declared the dismantling of the remaining pillars of apartheid (Document 7), particularly the Group Areas Act, which had helped create the strict geographical and population separation in South Africa. DeKlerk also stressed the protection of property rights, as he was increasingly aware of the fears of his white constituents on that issue.

Because of continued township violence in South Africa, the leadership of the ANC, NP government, and Inkatha signed the National Peace Accord (Document 8) in September 1991. Not entirely successful at defusing grass roots violence, it did set up administrative mechanisms for local mediation and formed a Peace Monitoring Force, which proved to be successful in certain cases. The National Peace Accord allowed for no clandestine operations (indicating alleged NP government fueling of Inkatha/ANC clashes), and called for discouragement of members of all parties from carrying dangerous weapons at demonstrations and mass meetings.

Document 4
"NORMALIZING THE POLITICAL PROCESS": ADDRESS BY PRESIDENT F. W. DEKLERK TO THE SECOND SESSION OF THE NINTH PARLIAMENT OF THE REPUBLIC OF SOUTH AFRICA

Mr. Speaker, Members of Parliament. The general election on September the 6th, 1989, placed our country irrevocably on the road of drastic change. Underlying this is the growing realisation by an increasing number of South Africans that only a negotiated understanding among the representative leaders of the entire population is able to ensure lasting peace.

On its part, the Government will accord the process of negotiation the highest priority. The aim is a totally new and just constitutional dispensation in which every inhabitant will enjoy equal rights, treatment and opportunity in every sphere of endeavour—constitutional, social and economic.

The countries of Southern Africa are faced with a particular challenge: Southern Africa now has an historical opportunity to set aside its conflicts and ideological differences and draw up a joint programme of reconstruction.

The Government is prepared to enter into discussions with other Southern African countries with the aim of formulating a realistic development plan. The Government believes that the obstacles in the way of a conference of Southern African states have now been removed sufficiently.

Hostile postures have to be replaced by cooperative ones; confrontation by contact; disengagement by engagement; slogans by deliberate debate.

The season of violence is over. The time for reconstruction and reconciliation has arrived.

The government accepts the principle of the recognition and protection of the fundamental individual rights which form the constitutional basis of most Western democracies. We acknowledge, too, that the most practical way of protecting those rights is vested in a declaration of rights justifiable by an independent judiciary. However, it is clear that a system for the protection of the rights of individuals, minorities and national entities has to form a well-rounded and balanced whole. South Africa has its own national composition and our constitutional dispensation has to take this into account. The formal recognition of individual rights does not mean that the problems of a heterogeneous population will simply disappear. Any new constitution which disregards this reality will be inappropriate and even harmful.

Naturally, the protection of collective, minority and national rights may not bring about an imbalance in respect of individual rights. It is neither the Government's policy nor its intention that any group—in whichever way it may be defined—shall be favoured above or in relation to any of the others.

A changed dispensation implies far more than political and constitutional issues. It cannot be pursued successfully in isolation from problems in other spheres of life which demand practical solutions. Poverty, unemployment, housing shortages, inadequate education and training, illiteracy, health needs and numerous other problems still stand in the way of progress and prosperity and an improved quality of life.

One matter about which it is possible to make a concrete announcement, is the Separate Amenities Act, 1953. Pursuant to my speech before the President's Council late last year, I announce that this Act will be repealed during this Session of Parliament.

In conclusion, I wish to focus the spotlight on the process of negotiation and related issues. At this stage I am refraining deliberately from discussing the merits of numerous political questions which undoubtedly will be debated during the next few weeks. The focus, now, has to fall on negotiation.

Against this background I committed the Government during my inauguration to giving active attention to the most important obstacles in the way of negotiation. Today I am able to announce far-reaching decisions in this connection.

I believe that these decisions will shape a new phase in which there will be a movement away from measures which have been seized upon as a justification for confrontation and violence. The emphasis has to move, and will move, now, to a debate and discussion of political economic points of view as part of the process of negotiation.

The steps that have been decided are the following:

—The prohibition of the African National Congress, the Pan Africanist Congress, the South African Communist Party and a number of subsidiary organisations is being rescinded.

—People serving prison sentences merely because they were members of one of these organisatons or because they committed another offence which was merely an offence because a prohibition on one of the organisations was in force, will be identified and released. Prisoners who have been sentenced for other offences such as murder, terrorism or arson are not affected by this.

—The media emergency regulations as well as the education emergency regulations are being abolished in their entirety.

—The security emergency regulations will be amended to still make provision for effective control over visual material pertaining to scenes of unrest.

—The restrictions in terms of the emergency regulations on 33 organisations are being rescinded. The organisations included the following: National Education Crisis Committee, South African National Students Congress, United Democratic Front, Cosaty, De Blande Bevrydingsbeweging van Suid-Afrika.

—The conditions imposed in terms of the security emergency regulations on 374 people on their release, are being rescinded and regulations which provide for such conditions are being abolished.

—The period of dentention in terms of the security emergency regulations will be limited henceforth to six months. Detainees also acquire the right to legal representation and a medical practitioner of their own choosing. . . .

Implementation will be immediate and, where necessary, notices will appear in the Government Gazette from tomorrow. . . .

On the state of emergency I have been advised that an emergency situation, which justifies these special measures which have been retained, still exists. There is still conflict which is manifesting itself mainly in Natal, but as a consequence of the country wide political power struggle. In addition, there are indications that radicals are still trying to disrupt the possibilities of negotiation by means of mass violence.

It is my intention to terminate the state of emergency completely as soon as circumstances justify it, and I request the cooperation of everybody towards this end.

The agenda is open and the overall aims to which we are aspiring should be acceptable to all reasonable South Africans.

Among other things, those aims include a new, democratic constitution; universal franchise; no domination; equality before an independent judiciary; the protection of minorities as well as of individual rights; freedom of religion; a sound economy based on proven economic principles and private enterprise; dynamic programmes directed at better education, health services, housing and social conditions for all.

In this connection Mr. Nelson Mandela could play an important part. The Government has noted that he has declared himself to be willing to make a constructive contribution to the peaceful political process in South Africa.

I wish to put it plainly that the Government has taken a firm decision to release Mr. Mandela unconditionally. I am serious about bringing this matter to finality without delay. The Government will make a decision soon on the date of his release. Unfortunately, a further short passage of time is unavoidable.

Today's announcements, in particular, go to the heart of what Black leaders—also Mr. Mandela—have been advancing over the years as their reason for having resorted to violence. The allegation has been that the Government did not wish to talk to them and that they were deprived of their right to normal political activity by the prohibition of their organisations.

Without conceding that violence has ever been justified, I wish to say today to those who argued in this manner:

—The unconditional lifting of the prohibition on the said organisations places everybody in a position to pursue politics freely.

—The justification for violence which was always advanced, no longer exists.

These facts place everybody in South Africa before a fait accompli. On the basis of numerous previous statements there is no longer any reasonable excuse for the continuation of violence. The time for talking has arrived and whoever still makes excuses does not really wish to talk.

I ask of Parliament to assist me on the road ahead. There is much to be done.

I call on the international community to re-evaluate its position and to adopt a positive attitude towards the dynamic evolution which is taking place in South Africa.

Mr. Speaker, Members of Parliament, I now declare this Second Session of the Ninth Parliament of the Republic of South Africa to be duly opened.

Source: Vital Speeches of the Day, vol 56 (Mount Pleasant, SC: City News Publishing Company, 1991), pp. 290–95.

Document 5
SPEECH BY NELSON MANDELA IN CAPE TOWN FOLLOWING HIS RELEASE FROM PRISON, FEBRUARY 11, 1990

AMANDLA! (Power!) [*The crowd responds: "Ngawethu!" (It is ours!)*] *i-Africa!* [*The crowd responds: "Mayibuye!" (Let it come back!)*]

Friends, comrades, and fellow South Africans:

I greet you all in the name of peace, democracy, and freedom for all. I stand here before you not as a prophet but as humble servant of you, the people. Your tireless and heroic sacrifices have made it possible for me to be here today. I therefore place the remaining years of my life in your hands.

On this day of my release, I extend my sincere and warmest gratitude to the millions of my compatriots and those in every corner of the globe who have campaigned tirelessly for my release.

Before I go any further, I wish to make the point that I intend making only a few preliminary comments at this stage. I will make a more complete statement only after I have had the opportunity to consult with my comrades.

Today the majority of South Africans, black and white, recognize apartheid has no future. It has to be ended by our own decisive mass action in order to build peace and security. The mass campaigns of defiance and other actions of our organization and people can only culminate in the establishment of democracy.

The apartheid destruction on our subcontinent is incalculable. The fabric of family life of millions of my people has been shattered. Millions are homeless and unemployed. Our economy lies in ruins and our people are embroiled in political strife.

Our resort to the armed struggle in 1960 with the formation of the military wing of the ANC, Umkhonto we Sizwe, was a purely defensive action against the violence of apartheid.

The factors which necessitated the armed struggle still exist today. We have no option but to continue. We express the hope that climate conducive to a negotiated settlement will be created soon so that there may no longer be the need for the armed struggle.

I am a loyal and disciplined member of the African National Congress. I am therefore in full agreement with all of its objectives, strategies, and tactics.

The need to unite the people of our country is as important a task now as it always has been. No individual leader is able to take on this enormous task on his own. It is our task as leaders to place our views before our organization and to allow the democratic structures to decide on the way forward.

On the question of democratic practice, I feel duty-bound to make the point that a leader of the movement is a person who has been democratically elected at a national conference. This is a principle which must be upheld without any exceptions.

Today, I wish to report to you that my talks with the government have been aimed at normalizing the political situation in the country. We have not as yet begun discussing the basic demands of the struggle. I wish to stress that I myself had at no time entered into negotiations about the future of our country, except to insist on a meeting between the ANC and the government.

Mr. deKlerk has gone further than any other Nationalist president in taking real steps to normalize the situation. However, there are further steps as outlined in the Harare Declaration that have to be met before negotiations on the basic demands of our people can begin.

I reiterate our call for, inter alia, the immediate ending of the state of emergency and the freeing of all, and not only some, political prisoners.

Only such a normalized situation which allows for free political activity can allow us to consult our people in order to obtain a mandate. The people need to be consulted on who will negotiate and on the content of such negotiations.

Negotiations cannot take place above the heads or behind the backs of our people. It is our belief that the future of our country can only be determined by a body which is democratically elected on a nonracial basis.

Negotiations on the dismantling of apartheid will have to address the overwhelming demand of our people for a democratic, nonracial, and unitary South Africa. There must be an end to white monopoly on political power and a fundamental restructuring of our political and economic systems to ensure that the inequalities of apartheid are addressed and our society thoroughly democratized.

It must be added that Mr. deKlerk himself is a man of integrity who is acutely aware of the dangers of a public figure not honoring his undertakings. But as an organization, we base our policy and strategy on the harsh reality we are faced with, and this reality is that we are still suffering under the policy of the Nationalist government.

Our struggle has reached a decisive moment. We call on our people to seize this moment to insure that the process towards democracy is rapid and uninterrupted. We have waited too long for our freedom. We can no longer wait. Now is the time to intensify the struggle on all fronts.

To relax our efforts now would be a mistake which generations to come will not be able to forgive. The sight of freedom looming on the horizon should encourage us to redouble our efforts. It is only through disciplined mass action that our victory can be assured.

We call on our white compatriots to join us in the shaping of a new South Africa. The freedom movement is the political home for you too.

We call on the international community to continue the campaign to isolate the apartheid regime. To lift sanctions now would be to run the risk of aborting the process towards the complete eradication of apartheid.

Our march to freedom is irreversible. We must not allow fear to stand in our way.

Universal suffrage on a common voters' roll in a united, democratic, and nonracial South Africa is the only way to peace and racial harmony.

In conclusion, I wish to go to my own words during my trial in 1964. They are as true today as they were then. I quote:

"I have fought against white domination, and I have fought against black domination. I have cherished the idea of a democratic and free society in which all persons live together in harmony and with equal opportunities. It is an ideal which I hope to live for and to achieve. But if needs be, it is an ideal for which I am prepared to die."

I hope you will disperse with discipline, and not a single one of you should do anything which will make other people say that we can't control our people.

Source: Greg McCartan, *Nelson Mandela: Speeches 1990* (New York: Pathfinder Press, 1990), pp. 19–24.

Document 6
AGREEMENT REACHED BY THE GOVERNMENT OF SOUTH AFRICA AND THE AFRICAN NATIONAL CONGRESS OF SOUTH AFRICA AT THE CONCLUSION OF TALKS HELD AT PRETORIA ON 6 AUGUST 1990

The Government and the African National Congress of South Africa (ANC) have held discussions at the Presidency, Pretoria, today, 6 August 1990.

1. The Government and ANC have again committed themselves to the Groote Schuur Minute.

2. The final report of the Working Group on political offences, dated 21 May 1990, as amended, was accepted by both parties. The guidelines to be formulated in terms of the report will be applied in a phased manner. The report makes provision for the formulation of guidelines that will be applied in dealing with members of all organizations, groupings or institutions, governmental or otherwise, who committed offences on the assumption that a particular cause was being served or opposed. The meeting has instructed the Working Group to draw up a plan for the release of ANC-related prisoners and the granting of indemnity to people in a phased manner and to report before the end of August 1990. . . . This programme will be implemented on the basis of the report of the Working Group.

3. In the interest of moving as speedily as possible towards a negotiated peaceful political settlement and in the context of the agreements reached, ANC announced that it was now suspending all armed actions with immediate effect. As a result of this, no further armed actions and related activities by ANC and its military wing *Umkhonto We Sizwe* will take place. It was agreed that a working group would be established to resolve all outstanding questions arising out of this decision, to report by 15 September 1990. Both sides once more committed themselves to do everything in their power to bring about a peaceful solution as quickly as possible.

4. Both delegations expressed serious concern about the general level of violence, intimidation and unrest in the country, especially in Natal. They agreed that in the context of the common search for peace and stability, it was vital that understanding should grow among all sections of the South African population that problems can and should be solved through negotiations. Both parties committed themselves to undertake steps and measures to promote and expedite the normalization and stabilization of the situation in line with the spirit of mutual trust obtaining among the leaders involved.

Source: United Nations Centre against Apartheid: Notes and Documents (New York: United Nations, 1990), pp. 1–3.

Document 7
PRESIDENT DEKLERK ANNOUNCES IN PARLIAMENT FURTHER MEASURES TO REPEAL MAIN PILLARS OF APARTHEID LEGISLATION FEBRUARY 1991

REMOVAL OF STATUTORY DISCRIMINATION

The elimination of racial discrimination goes hand in hand with the constitution process. The Government has expressed its intention repeatedly to remove discriminatory laws and practices. Many of them have been abolished already. Those remaining could not be repealed out of hand, because their complex nature required in-depth investigation.

These investigations have now been completed to the extent that I am able to make certain announcements today.

Legislation is to be tabled shortly for the repeal of the Land Acts of 1913 and 1936, the Group Areas Act of 1966 and the Development of Black Communities Act of 1984, as well as all other stipulations that determine rights concerning land according to membership of population groups.

The Government will also table a White Paper in which it will fully state its approach to the future treatment of land and land questions. Both the White Paper and the relevant legislation will be at the disposal of members shortly.

No one dares underestimate the emotions and even the conflict potential relating to land rights.

Everybody has a natural need for access to land and its utilization as living space and source of livelihood. Therefore, much more is necessary than the mere repeal of discriminatory legislation. At the same time, provision will have to be made for the protection of rights and of making land ownership accessible.

On the one hand, there is a need for the protection of private property rights and security of title and tenure with due consideration for common and indigenous law. On the other hand, land ownership and financing for it have to be accessible to all in a non-discriminatory manner.

These points of departure will be contained in the envisaged White Paper.

The Population Registration Act of 1950 has been subjected to scrutiny as well.

On the part of the Government, the view was held that the Population Registration Act would have to be repealed eventually, but that this could not be done immediately because the Act was technically necessary for the maintenance of the present constitutional dispensation. Therefore, it would be implemented. Following investigation, it would, in fact, appear possible to repeal this Act, provided that this is accompanied by the adoption of temporary transitional measures towards the acceptance of a new constitution. Consequently, I announce that legislation to this effect will be tabled during this session of Parliament.

Should Parliament adopt the Government's proposals, the South African statute book will be devoid, within months, of the remnants of racially discriminatory legislation which have become known as the cornerstones of apartheid.

Source: United Nations Centre against Apartheid: Notes and Documents (New York: United Nations, 1991), p. 7.

Document 8
THE NATIONAL PEACE ACCORD, JOHANNESBURG, SEPTEMBER 14, 1991

PREAMBLE

This Accord is intended to promote peace and prosperity in violence-stricken communities. The right of all people to live in peace and harmony will be promoted by the implementation of this Accord. . . .

CHAPTER 2: CODE OF CONDUCT FOR POLITICAL PARTIES AND ORGANIZATIONS

. . . 2. All political parties and organizations shall actively contribute to the creation of a climate of democratic tolerance by:

(a) Publicly and repeatedly condemning political violence and encouraging among their followers an understanding of the importance of democratic pluralism and culture of political tolerance;

(b) Acting positively, also *vis-à-vis* all public authorities, including local and traditional authorities, to support the right of all political parties and organizations to have reasonable freedom of access to their members, supporters and other persons in rural and urban areas, whether they be housed on public or private property.

3. No political party or organization or any official or representative of any such party, shall:

(a) Kill, injure, apply violence to, intimidate or threaten any other person in connection with that person's political beliefs, words, writings or actions;

(b) Remove, disfigure, destroy, plagiarize or otherwise misrepresent any symbol or other material of any other political party or organizations;

(c) Interfere with, obstruct or threaten, any other person or group travelling to or from or intending to attend any gathering for political purposes;

(d) Seek to compel, by force or threat of force, any person to join any party or organization, attend any meeting, make any contribution, resign from any post or office, boycott any occasion or commercial activity or withhold his or her labour or fail to perform a lawful obligation;

(e) Obstruct or interfere with any official or representative of any other political party or organization's message to contact or address any group of people.

4. All political parties and organizations shall respect and give effect to the obligation to refrain from incitement to violence or hatred.

5. All political parties and organizations shall provide full assistance and cooperation to the police in the investigation of violence and the apprehension of individuals involved. The signatories to this Accord specifically undertake not to protect or harbor their members and supporters to prevent them from being subjected to the processes of justice.

CHAPTER 3: SECURITY FORCES: GENERAL PROVISIONS

1. General principles and requirements

(a) The police shall endeavour to protect the people of South Africa from all criminal acts and shall do so in a rigorously non-partisan fashion, regardless of the political belief and affiliation, race, religion, gender or ethnic origin of the perpetrators or victims of such acts.

(b) The police shall endeavour to prevent crimes and shall attempt to arrest and investigate all those reasonably suspected of committing crimes and shall take the necessary steps to facilitate the judicial process. . . .

(d) The police, as law enforcement officers, shall expect a higher standard of conduct from its members in the execution of their duties than they expect from others, and in pursuance hereof, support prompt and efficient investigation and prosecution of its own members alleged to have acted unlawfully and shall commit itself to continue the proper training and retraining of its members in line with the objectives of professional policing and the principles set out in this Accord.

(e) The police shall exercise restraint in the pursuance of their duties and shall use the minimum force that is appropriate in the circumstances. . . .

3. Clandestine or covert operations

(a) No public funds shall be used to promote the interests of any political party or political organization and to political party no political organization shall accept any public funds to promote its interests which shall have the effect of interfering negatively in the political process.

(b) The government shall not allow any operation by the security forces with the intention to undermine, promote or influence any political party or political organization at the expense of another by means of any acts, or by means of disinformation.

Source: United Nations Centre against Apartheid: Notes and Documents (New York: United Nations, 1991).

POST-APARTHEID DOCUMENTS

The Truth and Reconciliation Commission put penetrating questions to both the NP and ANC in its examination of the apartheid years (Documents 9 and 11). The ANC's submissions ran from 216 to 261 pages, the NP's submissions were only 18 and 42 pages. Both second submissions (Documents 10 and 12) took more accusatory positions toward each other as the commission queried them on violent acts committed during apartheid for political or security reasons. The NP's submission, written by deKlerk, became particularly defensive and contained language more suited to an opposition party than the self-examination of a former government. The ANC's submission blamed the NP government for its violent actions. The final constitution for South Africa was meanwhile drafted in May 1996 and signed into law December 1996. The constitution's bill of rights (Document 13) reflected the goals of the Freedom Charter of 1955 (see Document 2). It included many rights found in the U.S. Constitution such as freedom of religion, freedom of assembly, and the rights associated with arrest and detainment. It also expressed more progressive guarantees such as reproductive rights, the right to adequate housing, labor rights, environmental rights, and children's rights.

Document 9
TRUTH AND RECONCILIATION COMMISSION
QUESTIONS PUT TO NP AFTER ITS SUBMISSION OF
AUGUST 1996

QUESTIONS ON MOTIVES, CONTEXT AND PERSPECTIVE

1. The Promotion of National Unity and Reconciliation Act, No. 34, 1995, requires that we give expression in our Final Report to "the motives and perspectives" of persons involved. Our request is that you kindly make available to us a two to three-page statement on your views, motivations and perspectives on the nature of the South African conflict.

2. The submission states that "we defended South Africa against those who planned to seize power by violent and unconstitutional means." How does one achieve power constitutionally if one is disenfranchised and denied many of one's most basic constitutional rights? Later you refer to the government as "legally constituted and internationally recognised." Apartheid

has been condemned as a crime against humanity, by the United Nations General Assembly and by the Security Council as well as in international instruments. This has been generally accepted as customary international law. Furthermore the government was internationally isolated on the diplomatic, economic, cultural, sporting and academic fronts. Is it not important to concede that it was Apartheid that was in fact unconstitutional, illegal by international standards and internationally condemned? Do you in retrospect agree that apartheid is morally indefensible? Can one legitimately equate the struggle against apartheid with the struggle to defend it?

QUESTIONS OF A GENERAL KIND AND THOSE ARISING FROM THE NATIONAL PARTY SUBMISSION

5. How does one explain the alleged ignorance of the former State President and his predecessors of gross human rights violations committed by the security forces and others? Why were the accusations of the state's critics, the media and former agents of the state not adequately investigated?

14. The notion of "moral responsibility," as used in relation to the State, implies that leaders of the State need to take responsibility for acts committed by their agents who acted in compliance with their orders of general policy. It further means that where agents acted without specific orders—while their behavior remained unpunished by the State—it is the officers the State who are obliged to accept moral culpability.

Does the National Party accept responsibility for the gross human rights violations committed by its agents in the name of upholding the regime? As the government of the day, does the National Party accept that irrespective of whether individual leaders directly participated or collaborated in gross human rights violations or not, that the government is morally obliged to accept responsibility for what happened? Does the government and former State President in particular, consider that enough was done to put an end to gross human rights violations being perpetrated by the security arms of the state?

Document 10
SECOND SUBMISSION OF THE NATIONAL PARTY TO THE TRUTH AND RECONCILIATION COMMISSION, MARCH 1997

INTRODUCTION

The purpose of this submission is to comment on the Truth and Reconciliation process thus far; to respond to the submission of the ANC; and to reply to the questions that the Commission submitted to the National Party on 12 December 1996.

GENERAL COMMENTS

We would like, at the outset to wish the Chairman a complete and speedy recovery after his recent illness.

We would also like to congratulate him and the commission on the role that they played in securing the extension of the cut-off date for amnesty to 27 April 1994.

Apart from this we are deeply concerned about the manner in which the truth and reconciliation process is developing.

Most seriously, it has become evident that the Commission is losing its credibility among some of our communities and parties, including a large majority of members of the National Party. The reasons for this loss of credibility include the following:

- Despite the often praiseworthy efforts of the Chairman, the Commission is not perceived to be impartial. Its composition is seen to be overwhelmingly representative of only one side in the former conflict. An analysis of the statements and speeches of some leading members of the Commission indicates that they tend to view the conflict of the past from the broad perspective of the ANC and its allies.

- The Commission's actions and hearings are beginning to create a skewed perception of the conflict, based as they are on the highly emotive testimony of victims who represent predominantly only one side of the conflict. These perceptions are being fanned and magnified by the SABC [South African Broadcast Company], which uses every opportunity to cast a pall of collective guilt over anyone associated with the former Government or with our party. . . . The overwhelming majority of the members of our Party have been horrified by the revelations of abuses that have come to light as a result of the activities of the Commission and other investigations that preceded it.

- The Commission is becoming increasingly involved in the party political process. Some of the Commission's actions and statements, such as its press conference on 16 January 1997, have created the impression that it has adopted a partisan stance against our Party and its leaders.

We have recently seen an example of this: a leading member of the ANC, himself an applicant for amnesty, has on the basis of testimony brought before the TRC, accused me as Leader of our Party of having known about political assassinations, apparently committed by the security forces during my presidency. This led a leading newspaper to publish a headline proclaiming "deKlerk's death farms"—as though this were a matter of proven fact. All this occurred despite the lack of any supporting evidence whatsoever and categorical denials from me that I had ever been aware of such developments.

The absence of any significant representation from the side of the former government on the Commission will inevitably raise questions regarding the

TRC's impartiality. The fact that most of the Commission's hearings are in public and that testimony before it is subject to proper examination, opens the possibility for abuse, for the stirring up of divisive emotions and for trial by media.

In raising these points, the National Party wishes to emphasize that it has no problem with bona fide efforts to establish the truth regarding the conflict of the past. It will also enthusiastically support any genuine effort to promote national reconciliation. It believes, however, that the Commission's present approach is seriously flawed and that unless it can take rapid and effective steps to convince all parties of its impartiality it will not succeed with its historic task. One-sided "truth" is no truth at all. Facts taken out of perspective can be as misleading as lies.

THE SUBMISSION OF THE ANC

Whereas I avoided playing politics in my criticism of the ANC in my submission and tried to understand the historic framework within which the ANC had operated, no such effort was made by the ANC in its submission. Instead, the ANC has clung to its own rigid and doctrinaire interpretation of the conflict. It has made no effort to seek the common ground that is so essential for reconciliation and has reverted to the hackneyed polemics and diatribes of the past.

GROSS VIOLATIONS OF HUMAN RIGHTS PERPETRATED BY THE ANC AND ITS ALLIES

The ANC's submission deals only in the most superficial manner with its own involvement in the gross violations of human rights.

Necklace Murders

The ANC and its allies cannot absolve themselves of responsibility for necklacing which caused the deaths of more than 500 people in the most horrible circumstances imaginable. Neither can they shift the blame for these atrocities onto the security forces as they are trying to do.

The point that we wished to make in our first submission was that—although one might understand the motivation of those who embarked on a policy of armed insurrection—there is a very real question as to whether this was an effective or correct option. Undoubtedly, it contributed to the spiral of violence and to the intensity of the conflict.

THE LEGALITY OF THE SOUTH AFRICAN GOVERNMENT AND ITS INTERNATIONAL ISOLATION

It is a matter of fact that South Africa was "legally constituted and internationally recognized" throughout this period—even though the "legitimacy" of this Government was increasingly questioned. Throughout this period South Africa remained a member of the United Nations and its ambassadors were accepted by the UN Secretary-General and regularly participated in the deliberations of the UN Security Council. The South African Government was also recognised as a sovereign government by the governments of most of the leading countries of the world.

WAS APARTHEID MORALLY DEFENSIBLE?

You ask whether, in retrospect, we agree that apartheid is morally defensible. Once again, you do not appear to have read our submission. We have not argued that apartheid is morally defensible. However, it is surely morally defensible for a people to struggle to maintain their right to national self-determination, but not at the expense of the human rights of others—and this is what apartheid came to signify. Although—as I stated on page 7 of my submission, there was originally a strong element of idealism in separate development and although many positive developments occurred—the policy was a dismal failure. On pages 9–10, we state quite clearly that

"Instead of providing a just and workable solution, it led to hardship, suffering and humiliation—to institutionalized discrimination on the basis of race and ethnicity. Instead of promoting peaceful inter-group relations, it precipitated a cycle of widespread resistance and repression in which unacceptable actions were committed by all sides. Instead of providing a solution, it had led to injustice, growing international isolation and to the escalation of the conflict that had been smouldering since the early sixties."

As I have pointed out above, those who fought on the government side were motivated by a number of factors, including their determination to maintain their right to national self-determination to maintain their right to resist the expansion of global communism; and their duty to defend individuals and the state and to uphold law and order. All these factors are, in my opinion, legitimate and had nothing to do with racism and apartheid per se.

Document 11
TRUTH AND RECONCILIATION COMMISSION: REQUESTS FOR CLARIFICATION OF MATTERS RAISED IN THE ANC SUBMISSION

1. ANC ACTIVITIES

Definition of Justified Targets

A further clarification of the definition of a justified target is needed. The ANC quotes a pamphlet identifying justified targets (page 52) as "the racist army, police, death squads, agents and stooges in our midst." Can this definition possibly be used to legitimise the killing of policemen, alleged informers, community councillors, and co-opted parliamentarians? Is there any other documentation or recorded instructions to further specify legitimate targets? Can the ANC elaborate what is meant by "stooges in our midst"?

MK Activities within the Policy of the ANC

- The ANC submission does not give details about MK missions within the framework of the just war. For our research purposes we request information on scope and scale of legitimate MK operations. The information should contain type of action, time, damage caused, death or injuries to civilians and/or state agents, and chain of command. The victims classified as legitimate targets need to be specified (e.g. SAP, kitskonstables, SADF, community councillors).

MK Activities not in Accordance with ANC Policy

- It is suggested that the ANC fought a relatively "clean war." According to the ANC submission, attacks not in accordance with ANC policy became a trend in the late 80s (page 53). Some examples of such acts were illustrated in the submission.

- Can the ANC give a full indication of the scope of such attacks, with particular attention to time and place, intended target, loss of lives and injuries, type of victims and chain of command?

- Can the ANC elaborate and substantiate efforts made to avoid such attacks on civilian targets? What steps were taken, after the incidents, to investigate them? Were ANC cadres disciplined for their involvement in such activities?

- To what extent did militant rhetoric and ambiguous statements possibly lead to misinterpretations of ANC policy on soft targets? . . .

4. FURTHER QUESTIONS WHICH ARRIVED LATE

The Conflict in KwaZulu Natal

- 1. What was the ANC's military policy towards the IFP in the years before its unbanning from the beginning of violent conflict in 1984 until 1990? Were IFP personnel perceived to be legitimate military targets? Did MK play any role in the violent conflict between the UDF and the IFP in KwaZulu or Natal?

Document 12

SECOND SUBMISSION OF THE ANC TO THE TRUTH
AND RECONCILIATION COMMISSION, MAY 1997

A full list of all MK camps, a list of rehabilitation centres, and the names of the commanders, is provided in Appendix 2.

The TRC has asked how these various sectors interacted, and which formal and informal channels of communication were in place. These questions, we believe, will be answered in the context of the detailed operational reports. . . .

2. ANC POLICIES

Defining Targets, 1961–the Early 1980s

In our main submission, we referred to this subject on a number of occasions. The draft document *Operation Mayibuye* (see p. 48) defined targets as "strategic road, railways and other communications; power stations; police stations, camps, and military forces; and irredeemable government stooges."

In 1978, after the Politico-Military Strategy Commission, a report was produced in which it was stated that the role of armed activity at that time was to "concentrate on armed propaganda actions whose immediate purpose is to support and stimulate political activity and organisation, rather than to hit at the enemy."

In November 1980 the ANC declared its adherence to the Geneva Conventions.

In 1983, the document *Planning for People's War* noted that there should be "more concentration on destroying enemy personnel," universally understood within the ANC to mean members of the SAP, SADF, other security structures, and their collaborators.

In the light of these quotations illustrating the ANC's definition of justified targets, it is clear that action against the machinery of repression—SAP and SADF members and informers—was considered legitimate. These people had chosen to act in the front-line of repression in defence of the apartheid regime.

In most cases those who were attacked by MK were notorious members of the Security Branch, or those involving themselves in a particularly direct manner in acts of violence against communities. There were also many petrol-bomb attacks on the homes of members of the SAP which were carried out by local activists. A survey of ANC statements will show that we consistently called on members of the SAP and SADF to turn their arms on the oppressor, and come over to the side of the liberation struggle.

Informers were essential tools of the security forces; without them, the apartheid regime would have been seriously hampered in their attempts to crush resistance. Many informers and "turned" cadres were directly responsible for the imprisonment, detention and deaths of literally thousands of activists and ANC leaders.

Defining Targets in the Context of People's War

There have been recent attempts to portray the 1983 constitutional changes—against which the UDF mobilised millions of South Africans—as evidence of progress towards a more equitable society, a process in which the ANC should have participated, rather than intensifying the armed struggle.

We feel it necessary to review this period briefly in order to ensure that our understanding of the context in which the general uprisings of 1984 onwards took place, and in which the ANC called for the intensification of the struggle on all fronts, is conveyed to the Commission.

In the late 1970's the NP had begun to realise that it needed to extend the base for military conscription; the SADF was in favour of extending the call-up to "coloured" and Indian communities. However, it was generally recognised that it would be difficult to conscript people who did not have the vote.

The majority of South Africans—those not classified "white," "coloured" or "Indian"—were *explicitly barred* from the new racist "tricameral" parliamentary system, which unashamedly sought to further entrench apartheid by drawing allies into the laager [conservative camp] to assist in preventing democratic change.

These moves were combined with the three Koornhof Bills, which also aimed to further entrench—not dismantle—existing apartheid institutions. . . .

The ANC called on people to mobilise against and destroy the structures created in terms of these laws, as did many community-based organizations within the country which rallied under the banner of the United Democratic Front. There were mass boycotts of elections of these puppet structures. Many councillors were elected on pathetically low polls, and there was intense pressure from communities on councillors and MPs to resign from these structures. In many cases councillors resigned and were welcomed back into their communities.

The TRC has asked us to define what we meant by "stooges in our midst." These could be described as those among the oppressed who chose to directly assist in apartheid oppression and repression. Councillors and those who chose to serve in the tricameral parliament and participate in repression, certainly fell into this group of collaborators with apartheid.

A critical point which must be made is that a *guarantee for conflict at local level was built into this new legislation:* the new community councils had to be self-financing.

A survey of available information shows that the overwhelming majority of attacks on the homes of town councillors (or members of the tricameral legislature) were carried out by local activists, and were often in the context of explosive anger on the ground in response to initiatives by councils or brutalities by the security forces. The number of deaths and injuries which resulted from these attacks were extremely limited when compared with the deaths and injuries inflicted on members of anti-apartheid organisations. Whilst the ANC (and UDF) leadership did not order such attacks, and took no pleasure in any loss of life resulting from such actions, it certainly did not condemn them in principle. Although the ANC leadership did not at all times approve of the methods adopted by people, actions of this nature were in essence the result of state repression, and they were in line with the ANC's stated policy to mobilise people against institutions designed to yet further entrench apartheid.

The SAIRR [South African Institute of Race Relations]'s statistics for 1985 show that twenty-six members of the security forces were killed by residents of townships, while one was killed by "guerrillas." In the same period, 441 township residents had been killed by members of the security forces. These statistics do not include a breakdown of the large numbers of deaths and serious injuries caused by state-sponsored "vigilante" groups which intensified suddenly in the latter half of 1985. MK units were encouraged to support communities in ridding the country of these violent collaborators with apartheid.

The Phenomenon of "Necklacing"

As the mass-based resistance against apartheid took root in the mideighties, the ANC leadership strongly disapproved of some of the methods chosen by people to kill informers and other collaborators, particularly the "necklace," and stated this on more than one occasion. UDF leaders also condemned the use of the "necklace" on several occasions. But the ANC leadership refused, and will always refuse to condemn those who believed they were part of the struggle for liberation led by the ANC and the UDF, and were making their contribution by ridding communities of informers and those amongst them who directly collaborated in apartheid violence (please refer to our first submission, pp. 77–78).

The extent to which the NP has consistently tried to use the phenomenon of "necklacing" to damage the ANC and divert attention from their own atrocities has always raised the suspicion that they were involved in some of these incidents. It was certainly their agent Joe Mamasela, who was centrally involved in creating the conditions under which the first recorded "necklacing" took place, which was conveniently filmed in horrific detail, immediately sent out world-wide, and portrayed as evidence of the "savagery" of the ANC.

Targets in the Context of Violence in KwaZulu in the 1980s

The TRC has asked what was the ANC's "military policy" towards Inkatha, and whether the ANC leadership considered members of Inkatha to be "legitimate military targets." The ANC had no "military policy" with regard to Inkatha. The ANC has never considered Inkatha members or officials as targets simply because they aligned themselves with Inkatha.

The predominant feature of the violence in KwaZulu-Natal in the 1980s was attacks on whole communities. "Warlords" played a pivotal role in this violence, assisted by elements within the SAP who either refused to intervene or actively supported the aggressors.

Source for Documents 9–12: Truth and Reconciliation Commission Written Submissions, at
    http://www.truth.org.za/submit/index.htm.

Document 13
CONSTITUTION FOR THE REPUBLIC OF SOUTH AFRICA, ADOPTED BY THE CONSTITUTIONAL ASSEMBLY MAY 8, 1996, AND AMENDED OCTOBER 11, 1996

CHAPTER 2: BILL OF RIGHTS

Rights

7. (1) This Bill of Rights is a cornerstone of democracy in South Africa. It enshrines the rights of all people in our country and affirms the democratic values of human dignity, equality and freedom.

(2) The state must respect, protect, promote, and fulfill the rights in the Bill of Rights. . . .

Equality

9. (1) Everyone is equal before the law and has the right to equal protection and benefit of the law.

(2) Equality includes the full and equal enjoyment of all rights and freedoms. To promote the achievement of equality, legislative and other meas-

ures designed to protect or advance persons, or categories of persons, disadvantaged by unfair discrimination may be taken.

(3) The state may not unfairly discriminate directly or indirectly against anyone on one or more grounds, including race, gender, sec, pregnancy, marital status, ethnic or social origin, colour, sexual orientation, age, disability, religion, conscience, belief, culture, language, and birth. . . .

Human Dignity

10. Everyone has inherent dignity and the right to have their dignity respected and protected.

Life

11. Everyone has the right to life.

Freedom and Security of the Person

12. (1) Everyone has the right to freedom and security of the person, which includes the right—(a) not to be deprived of freedom arbitrarily or without just cause; (b) not to be detained without trial; (c) to be free from all forms of violence from both public and private sources; (d) not to be tortured in any way; and (e) not to be treated or punished in a cruel, inhuman or degrading way.

(2) Everyone has the right to bodily and psychological integrity, which includes the right—(a) to make decisions concerning reproduction; (b) to security in and control over their body; and (c) not to be subjected to medical or scientific experiments without their informed consent. . . .

Freedom of Expression

16. (1) Everyone has the right to freedom of expression, which includes—(a) freedom of the press and other media; (b) freedom to receive and impart information and ideas; (c) freedom of artistic creativity; and (d) academic freedom and freedom of scientific research.

(2) The right in subsection (1) does not extend to—(a) propaganda for war; (b) incitement of imminent violence; or (c) advocacy of hatred that is based on race, ethnicity, gender or religion, and that constitutes incitement to cause harm. . . .

Labour Relations

23. (1) Everyone has the right to fair labour practices.

(2) Every worker has the right—(a) to form and join a trade union; (b) to participate in the activities and programmes of a trade union; and (c) to strike.

(3) Every employer has the right—(a) to form and join an employers' organisation; and (b) to participate in the activities and programmes of an employers' organisation.

(4) Every trade union and every employers' organisation has the right—(a) to determine its own administration, programmes and activities; (b) to organise; (c) to bargain collectively; and (d) to form and join a federation.

(5) The provisions of the Bill of Rights do not prevent legislation recognising union security arrangements contained in collective agreements.

Environment

24. Everyone has the right—(a) to an environment that is not harmful to their health or well-being; and (b) to have the environment protected, for the benefit of present and future generations, through reasonable legislative and other measures that—(i) prevent pollution and ecological degradation; (ii) promote conservation; and (iii) secure ecologically sustainable development and use of natural resources while promoting justifiable economic and social development.

Property

25. (1) No one may be deprived of property except in terms of law of general application, and no law may permit arbitrary deprivation of property. . . .

(6) A person or community whose tenure of land is legally insecure as a result of past racially discriminatory laws or practices is entitled, to the extent provided by an Act of Parliament, either to tenure which is legally secure, or to comparable redress.

(7) A person or community dispossessed of property after 19 June 1913 as a result of past racially discriminatory laws or practices is entitled, to the extent provided by an Act of Parliament, either to restitution of that property, or to equitable redress.

Housing

26. (1) Everyone has the right to have access to adequate housing.

(2) The state must take reasonable legislative and other measure, within its available resources, to achieve the progressive realisation of this right.

(3) No one may be evicted from their home, or have their home demolished, without an order of court made after considering all the relevant circumstances. No legislation may permit arbitrary evictions.

Health Care, Food, Water, and Social Security

27. (1) Everyone has the right to have access to—(a) health care services, including reproductive health care; (b) sufficient food and water; and (c) so-

cial security, including, if they are unable to support themselves and their dependants, appropriate social assistance.

(2) The state must take reasonable legislative and other measures, within its available resources, to achieve the progressive realisation of each of these rights.

(3) No one may be refused emergency medical treatment.

Children

28. (1) Every child has the right—(a) to a name and a nationality from birth; (b) to family care, parental care, or appropriate alternative care when removed from the family environment; (c) to basic nutrition, shelter, basic health care services, and social services; (d) to be protected from maltreatment, neglect, abuse, or degradation; (e) to be protected from exploitative labor practices; (f) not to be required or permitted or perform work or provide services that—(i) are inappropriate for a person of that child's age; or (ii) place at risk the child's well-being, education, physical or mental health, or spiritual, moral or social development. . . .

(2) A child's best interest is of paramount importance in every matter concerning the child.

(3) In this section, "child" means a person under the age of 18 years.

Education

29. (1) Everyone has the right—(a) to a basic education, including adult basic education; and (b) to further education, which the state must take reasonable measures to make progressively available and accessible.

(2) Everyone has the right to receive education in the official language or languages of their choice in public educational institutions where that education is reasonably practicable. . . .

Cultural, Religious and Linguistic Communities

31. (1) Persons belonging to a cultural, religious or linguistic community may not be denied the right, with other members of their community, to—(a) enjoy their culture, practise their religion and use their language; and (b) form, join and maintain cultural, religious and linguistic associations and other organs of civil society.

(2) This right may not be exercised in a manner inconsistent with any provision of the Bill of Rights. . . .

Arrested, Detained and Accused Persons

35. (2) Everyone who is detained, including every sentenced prisoner, has the right . . . (e) to conditions of detention that are consistent with human dig-

nity, including at least exercise and the provision, at state expense, of adequate accommodation, nutrition, reading material, and medical treatment; and (f) to communicate with, and be visited by, that person's (i) spouse or partner; (ii) next of kin; (iii) chosen religious counsellor; and (iv) chosen medical practitioner.

Source: Public Affairs Office, South African Embassy, Washington, D.C.

Glossary of Selected Terms

African National Congress (ANC): Party founded in 1912 to oppose racial discrimination in South Africa. It was reconstituted in the 1950s under the leadership of Nelson Mandela and Walter Sisulu, adopted a military strategy in 1960, and became the leading opposition to apartheid from the 1960s to the 1990s.

Afrikaans: Language and identity of descendants of Dutch settlers (Boers) in South Africa.

Afrikaner Volksfront (AVF): Party formed by General Constand Viljoen in 1993 combining many right-wing groups in South Africa.

Afrikaner Weerstandsbeweging (AWB): Right-wing paramilitary organization formed in South Africa in 1973 and led by Eugene Terre'Blanche.

Azanian People's Liberation Army (APLA): Military wing of the Pan-Africanist Congress.

Azanian People's Organization (AZAPO): Political foundation of the Black Consciousness movement formed in South Africa in the 1970s; marked by ideological purity and a noncompromising philosophy.

Bantu: Linguistically related Africans of central and southern Africa; became white term for Africans in South Africa during apartheid.

Bantu Authorities Act (1951): Apartheid law that created a system of local and regional government in African reserves, restructuring the old councils and elevating the chiefs.

Bantu Education Act (1953): Apartheid law that removed education for Africans from missions and provincial authorities and put it under the control of the Secretary of Native Affairs. Vernacular languages replaced English as the medium of instruction up to the eighth year of schooling, and emphasis was put on technical training.

Black Consciousness Movement (BC): Opposition movement launched in South Africa by black intellectuals in the 1970s stressing that black people take pride in their own identity.

Broederbond: Secret society of Afrikaners founded in 1918 to promote Afrikaner nationalism and culture; influenced early Nationalist party policy but later became source of strategy for change away from apartheid.

Coloreds: South African people descended in various degrees from the Khoisan, whites, and imported slaves from Asia, Malagasy, and tropical Africa.

Conference for a Democratic South Africa (CODESA): Forum for negotiations among parties in South Africa established in 1991 that led to the election of 1994.

Congress of South African Trade Unions (COSATU): Union movement formed in 1985 and allied with the ANC and SACP.

Conservative Party (CP): South African right-wing party, led by Andries Treurnicht, that broke away from the NP in 1982 in opposition to P. W. Botha's reforms.

Contralesa: Congress of Traditional Leaders of South Africa, formed as apartheid ended to protect the position of tribal chiefs in the homelands.

Disinvestment: Policy of withdrawal of capital from South African companies carried out by the United States and other countries during the 1980s as part of the international protest against apartheid.

Dutch Reformed Church: Predominant Protestant church of Afrikaner population; of Calvinist origin, it was supported by the government before and during apartheid.

Eminent Persons Group: Formed in 1986 and made up of seven senior British Commonwealth politicans led by former Prime Minister of Australia Malcolm Fraser. The EPG visited South Africa to meet with the NP government and black opposition groups, and to draw up a plan for the reform of apartheid.

Freedom Alliance: Party alliance that consisted of the AVF, the CP, IFP, and homeland leaders of Ciskei, KwaZulu, and Bophuthatswana. It pressed demands for a federal system of government.

"The Great Trek": Mass migration of Boers of the South African colony north and west between 1836 and 1854 in protest of British encroachment and policies; symbol of Afrikaner nationalism.

Group Areas Act (1950): Forced relocation by apartheid government of Indian, colored, and African populations away from urban centers.

Growth, Employment, and Redistribution: Postapartheid government's economic plan for South Africa published in 1996.

Homelands: Reserves created by the apartheid government from 1959 to 1976 to separate Africans geographically from whites. Africans were forced to return to their supposed region of origin and later to accept a false independence (for example, Transkei, Ciskei, Bophuthatswana).

Inkatha Freedom Party (IFP): Party formed in 1990 as the political representative of Inkatha, a Zulu cultural movement dating back to 1928 and led since the 1970s by Chief Mangosuthu Buthelezi.

Mfecane: Series of Zulu wars (1817–1828) that led to the transformation of the farming societies of southeastern Africa, and the development of African groups in what later became Malawi, Zambia, Tanzania, Swaziland, and South Africa.

National Party (NP): White South African party that arose in the 1940s and came to power in 1948. It catered to the principle of white supremacy, established the apartheid system, and remained in power in South Africa until 1994.

Natives Land Act (1913): South African law that prohibited Africans from buying or leasing land outside the reserves from non-Africans.

"Necklacing": Form of violent attack in the townships of South Africa in the 1980s. A tire would be placed around a victims's neck and set on fire.

Pan-Africanist Party (PAC): African nationalist party that broke from the ANC in 1959 in opposition to its socialist and multiracial approach.

Population Registration Act (1950): Apartheid law calling for compulsory racial classification on a national register.

Progressive Federal Party: Party of white progressives in South Africa dating back to 1959 and represented primarily by Helen Suzman. Committed to reform of apartheid, the party merged with the Democratic party in 1989 and joined the ANC in 1992.

Rand: South African currency.

Reconstruction and Development Plan (RDP): Ambitious welfare plan of the postapartheid government that started projects aimed at raising the standard of living among the majority of South Africans.

Record of Understanding: Agreement drawn up between the ANC and NP in September 1992 to revive the constitutional talks that had broken down in June 1992.

Rivonia Trial (1963–1964): Celebrated trial by the apartheid government of Nelson Mandela and other ANC activists, including Govan Mbeki and Walter Sisulu, for sabotage. Mandela, Mbeki, Sisulu, and five others received life sentences.

Robben Island: Island fourteen miles off the coast of Cape Town that became a maximum security prison for "nonwhite" males in 1959. Nelson Mandela was imprisoned on Robben Island from 1964 to 1982 and was then transferred to Pollsmoor Prison.

Sestiger Movement: Movement of South African writers, beginning in the 1960s, whose essays, poetry, and novels questioned and challenged the system of apartheid.

Sharpeville (1960): African location south of Johannesburg where a peaceful demonstration by ANC and PAC protesters ended in the killing of sixty-nine demonstrators by South African police; significant event in the history of apartheid and symbol of further protest.

South African Communist Party (SACP): Party formed in South Africa in 1953 and led by Joe Slovo until 1995; allied with the ANC and COSATU.

South African Defense Forces (SADF): Government army in South Africa during the era of apartheid.

Soweto: In the late 1940s, approximately 70,000 squatters settled outside Johannesburg, mainly beyond the city's southwestern borders in an area that became known as Southwestern Township (Soweto). It became the center of black protest in the 1970s.

"Total Strategy": Policy adopted by the government under P. W. Botha in the 1980s; combined reform of apartheid with increased repression by the South African Defense Force.

Tricameral Parliament: Parliament established by NP government in 1983 that allowed representation for Indians and coloreds, but not for Africans.

Truth and Reconciliation Commission (TRC): Commission formed in South Africa in 1996 under the leadership of Archbishop Desmond Tutu to investigate the political crimes of the apartheid era and grant amnesty to confessors.

Ubuntu: Concept linked with African tradition in South Africa that is claimed to encompass compassion, reconciliation, humanity, and the recognition of human dignity.

Umkhonto we Sizwe (MK): Military wing of the ANC formed in 1960.

United Democratic Front (UDF): Broad-based resistance movement formed in South Africa in 1983 to fill the gap left by the banning of the ANC, PAC, and other parties. It disbanded in 1990.

Verkrampte: "Unenlightened" (conservative) members of NP during the party's split in the 1960s.

Verligte: "Enlightened" (liberal) members of the NP during the party's split in the 1960s.

Warlordism: Postapartheid development in the homelands, most notably Kwa-Zulu/Natal, whereby former traditional leaders commandeered power through force and intimidation.

Xhosa: Language and identity of Africans of eastern Cape of South Africa.

Zulu: Language and identity of Africans primarily occupying northeastern Natal in South Africa.

Annotated Bibliography

Africa Report, vols. 36–39, 1991–1994. Contains articles by journalists in South Africa that give information on the negotiations process and particular aspects of the overall process of change.

Alden, Chris. *Apartheid's Last Stand*. New York: St. Martin's Press, 1996. Carefully analyzes the NP government's strategy of reform and repression from the 1970s through the 1980s, concluding that the continued racist policies of the government fueled internal disruption and international censure.

Beinart, William. *Twentieth-Century South Africa*. New York: Oxford University Press, 1994. Valuable overview of the rise of racial division in South Africa, including rural resistance, black urban and white culture, industrialization, and the black struggle against apartheid.

Biko, Stephen. *I Write What I Like*. London: Heinemann, 1978. Collection of Biko's essays and autobiography of Biko. Gives insight into Black Consciousness thought and the origins of the BC movement.

Cock, Jacklyn, and Laurie Nathan, eds. *War and Society: The Militarization of South Africa*. New York: St. Martin's Press, 1989. Gives a detailed picture of the internal struggles of South Africa in the 1980s, and argues, through twenty-four essays from different contributors, that South Africa during that time was a society engaged in military conflict.

Davis, Stephen M. *Apartheid's Rebels: Inside South Africa's Hidden War*. New Haven, CT: Yale University Press, 1987. Gives a sense of the ANC in exile and explores its strategies in the 1980s.

Edgar, Robert E., ed. *Sanctioning Apartheid*. Trenton, NJ: Africa World Press, 1990. Essays examining the sanctions question and the effect of international pressure on South Africa, including black reaction and feelings about the United States.

Electronic Mail and Guardian. http://www.mg.co.za/mg/za/news.html. Weekly South African newspaper based in Johannesburg providing significant information and liberal interpretations of the South African situation.

James, Wilmot, Daria Caliguire, and Kerry Cullinan. *Now That We Are Free: Coloured Communities in a Democratic South Africa*. Boulder, CO: Lynne Rienner, 1996. Papers presented at conference sponsored by the Institute for Democracy in South Africa in 1995 that focused on the Western Cape. Provides insight into the coloreds' search for identity and tensions with the African community in South Africa.

Johns, Sheridan, and R. Hunt Davis, Jr., eds. *Mandela, Tambo, and the African National Congress*. New York: Oxford University Press, 1991. Collection of sixty-three documents, mainly speeches, relating to the ANC from 1948 to 1990, and six essays giving historical background. Illustrates consistency and determination of ANC.

Johnson, Richard William, and Laurence Schlemmer. *Launching Democracy in South Africa: The First Open Election, April 1994*. New Haven, CT: Yale University Press, 1996. Contains major surveys of attitudes in South Africa during the elections and includes observations on all groups, political analysis, and full elections results. Examines the problems of a lack of tradition of full participation in South African politics.

Juckes, Tim J. *Opposition in South Africa: The Leadership of Z. K. Matthews, Nelson Mandela, and Stephen Biko*. Westport, CT: Praeger, 1995. Detailed research tracing the political development of three prominent black leaders in South Africa, and explaining why Mandela's generation turned to a more militant response to the violence of apartheid.

Kitchen, Helen, ed. *South Africa: In Transition to What?* Westport, CT: Praeger, 1988. Collection of papers exploring the direction of South Africa by the end of the 1980s. Gives overview of political movements during that time.

Kitchen, Helen, and J. Coleman Kitchen, eds. *South Africa: Twelve Perspectives on the Transition*. Westport, CT: Praeger, 1994. Published with the Centre for Strategic and International Studies; African specialists examine internal and external aspects of change in South Africa.

Lemon, Anthony, ed. *The Geography of Change in South Africa*. New York: John Wiley and Sons, 1995. Analyses of geographical restructuring of South Africa in transition.

Liebenberg, Ian, et al. *The Long March*. Cape Town: HAUM, 1994. Historical narrative from popular perspective of South Africa's development from apartheid to post-apartheid state. Focuses on liberation movements with contributions from Joe Slovo and Alex Boraine of the Truth and Reconciliation Commission.

Mandela, Nelson. *Long Walk to Freedom*. Boston: Little, Brown and Company, 1994. Description of Mandela's life from childhood to election as president of South Africa. Explains the development of his understanding of white oppression of blacks in South Africa, the ANC decision to turn to guerrilla strategy, Mandela's continued political struggle in prison, and the nature of leadership.

Mandy, Nigel. *A City Divided: Johannesburg and Soweto*. New York: St. Martin's Press, 1984. Gives insight into aspects of township life that led to the struggles of the 1980s and describes and analyzes the problems of Johannesburg in the midst of P. W. Botha's "total strategy."

Maré, Gerhard, and Georgina Hamilton. *An Appetite for Power: Buthelezi's Inkatha and South Africa*. Johannesburg: Ravan, 1987. Detailed account of Inkatha and Buthelezi. Argues that Inkatha is mainly a reactionary organization.

Marx, Anthony W. *Lessons of the Struggle: South African Internal Opposition 1960–1990*. Oxford: Oxford University Press, 1991. Gives detailed information on major political activists in the 1980s; examines the interplay of actions and ideology in movements such as the UDF and BC.

Mermelstein, David. *The Anti-Apartheid Reader*. New York: Grove Press, 1987. Gives useful and extensive information on the various parties and movements in South Africa.

Murray, Martin J. *The Revolution Deferred: The Painful Birth of Post-Apartheid South Africa*. London: Verso, 1994. Analyzes events in South Africa from the 1980s through the ending of apartheid in the 1990s and argues that much of the old white system remains in post-apartheid South Africa.

———. *South Africa: Time of Agony, Time of Destiny*. London: Verso, 1987. Explains in detail the uprisings in South Africa of the 1980s, resistance to apartheid, effects on the struggle of social deprivation, and the determined suppressive attitude of the NP government under P. W. Botha.

Pampallis, John. *Foundations of the New South Africa*. Cape Town: Maskew, Miller, Longman, 1991. ANC interpretation of South African history.

Price, Robert M. *The Apartheid State in Crisis: Political Transformation in South Africa 1975–1990*. Oxford: Oxford University Press, 1991. Analyzes the social and economic conditions in South Africa from the 1970s to 1990 that caused the interaction of black protest, government strategy, and international pressure. Focuses on the nationalist struggle between Africans and Afrikaners as an important influence on South African politics.

Race Relations Survey. Johannesburg: South African Institute of Race Relations, 1930– . Annual report begun in 1930 providing statistics and information on racial interraction in South Africa. Reports of the 1980s are particularly useful.

Reynolds, Andrew. *Election '94 South Africa*. New York: St. Martin's Press, 1994. Observations by mostly South African academics on the 1994 elections, including party campaigns and the role of the media.

Sethi, S. Prakash, ed. *The South African Quagmire: In Search of a Peaceful Path to Democratic Pluralism*. Cambridge, MA: Ballinger Publishing Co., 1987. Thirty-seven papers exploring the question of disinvestment and sanctions against South Africa. Provides insight into the debate over sanctions in the 1980s.

Shepherd, George W., Jr., ed. *Effective Sanctions on South Africa*. Westport, CT: Greenwood Press, 1991. Exploration of argument for sanctions against South Africa. Contends that United States resistance to sanctions was not justified and that the costs to the U.S. were exaggerated by opponents of economic pressure on South Africa.

Slovo, Joe. *Slovo: The Unfinished Autobiography*. London: Hodder and Stoughton, 1995. Traces Slovo's revolutionary career from early activist years to contribution and adaption to post-apartheid ANC policy. Reveals complexity of SACP's commitment to liberation and relations with communist countries.

Sparks, Allister. *The Mind of South Africa*. New York: Knopf, 1990. Journalistic explanation of the psychology of apartheid. Explores Afrikaner and African nationalism and the rise of black radicalism in response to the oppressive manifestations of apartheid.

———. *Tomorrow Is Another Country*. New York: Hill and Wang, 1995. Detailed account of personalities involved in the negotiations process, and violent periods after Mandela's release and just before the 1994 elections. Argues that South Africa will survive and not slip into chaos.

Thompson, Leonard. *A History of South Africa*. New Haven, CT: Yale University Press, 1990. Valuable interpretive overview of South African history beginning with early African settlement and tracing race relations and politics through the apartheid era.

Truth and Reconciliation Commission Web site at http://www.truth.org.za. Complete texts of submissions to, and questions and hearings of the commission. Provides insight into the brutality of the apartheid regime and NP and ANC strategy, and illustrates personal suffering of individuals in particular cases.

Tutu, Desmond. *The Rainbow People of God*. New York: Doubleday, 1994. Collection of speeches, letters, and essays of Archbishop Desmond Tutu from 1976 to 1994, with historical background. Expresses liberation theory and Tutu's support for sanctions.

Van Rooyen, Johann. *Hard Right: The New White Power in South Africa*. New York: I. B. Tauris, Publishers, 1994. Detailed study of white right-wing in South Africa. Argues that potential danger of white extremists is still threatening South Africa.

Worden, Nigel. *The Making of Modern South Africa*. Cambridge, MA: Blackwell, 1994. Explores the modern political history of South Africa and examines the reasons for the country's transformation. Breaks from standard views on how apartheid came about and the sources of nationalism in South Africa.

FILMS AND VIDEOS

Cry Freedom, 1987, directed by Richard Attenborough. Adapted from former editor of the *East London Daily Dispatch* Donald Woods's *Biko*, and *Asking for Trouble*; gives an account of Woods's friendship with Stephen Biko. The first half of the film provides a sense of the work and struggle of Biko in the Black Consciousness movement. The second half of the film, in focusing mainly on Woods and his family, has been criticized for flattering the sympathies of white audiences.

A Dry White Season, 1989, directed by Euzhan Palcy. Tells the story of a white man's pursuit of justice for his African gardener during the Soweto uprisings of 1976. Based on a novel by André Brink and directed by a black woman, the film shows more of black experience in South Africa than other popular films dealing with apartheid.

Human Rights Television, *RIGHTS AND WRONGS: Show #304–SOUTH AFRICA*. New York: Global Communications Foundation, Inc., 1995. Hosted by Charlayne Hunter-Gault; reports on the 1994 election, reconstruction and transformation in South Africa, and a reunion at Robben Island, using excerpts from other documentaries; appearances by Nelson Mandela, Allister Sparks, Eugene Terre'Blanche, Dr. Makazewe Mandela (Nelson Mandela's daughter), and human rights advocates in South Africa.

A World Apart, 1988, directed by Chris Menges. Film based on the memoirs of Shawn Slovo, daughter of Joe Slovo and Ruth First; tells the story of a teenage girl's conflict with her mother in the latter's struggle against apartheid. The film gives a sense of Ruth First's intimidation by South African authorities, and of white society in South Africa in the 1960s.

Index

About the Author

LINDSAY MICHIE EADES lectured in history at the University of Transkei in South Africa from 1989 to 1991. She has also taught at Kelly College, Devon, England, and from 1992 to 1997, was a history professor at Chowan College, East Carolina University and Greensboro College in North Carolina. She is author of *A Case Study of an Appeaser: Robert Hadow in the Foreign Office, 1931–1939* (Praeger, 1996).